SIMON SPURRIER × MATÍAS BERGARA

CODA ™

VOLUME THREE

BOOM!
STUDIOS

CODA Volume Three, October 2019.
Published by BOOM! Studios, a division of
Boom Entertainment, Inc. Coda is ™ &
© 2019 Simon Spurrier, Ltd. & Matías
Bergara. Originally published in single
magazine form as CODA No. 9-12. ™ &
© 2019 Simon Spurrier, Ltd. & Matías Bergara. All rights reserved. BOOM!
Studios™ and the BOOM! Studios logo are trademarks of Boom Entertainment,
Inc., registered in various countries and categories. All characters, events, and
institutions depicted herein are fictional. Any similarity between any of the
names, characters, persons, events, and/or institutions in this publication to
actual names, characters, and persons, whether living or dead, events, and/
or institutions is unintended and purely coincidental. BOOM! Studios does not
read or accept unsolicited submissions of ideas, stories, or artwork.

BOOM! Studios, 5670 Wilshire Boulevard, Suite 400, Los Angeles, CA 90036-
5679. Printed in China. First Printing.

ISBN: 978-1-68415-429-6, eISBN: 978-1-64144-546-7

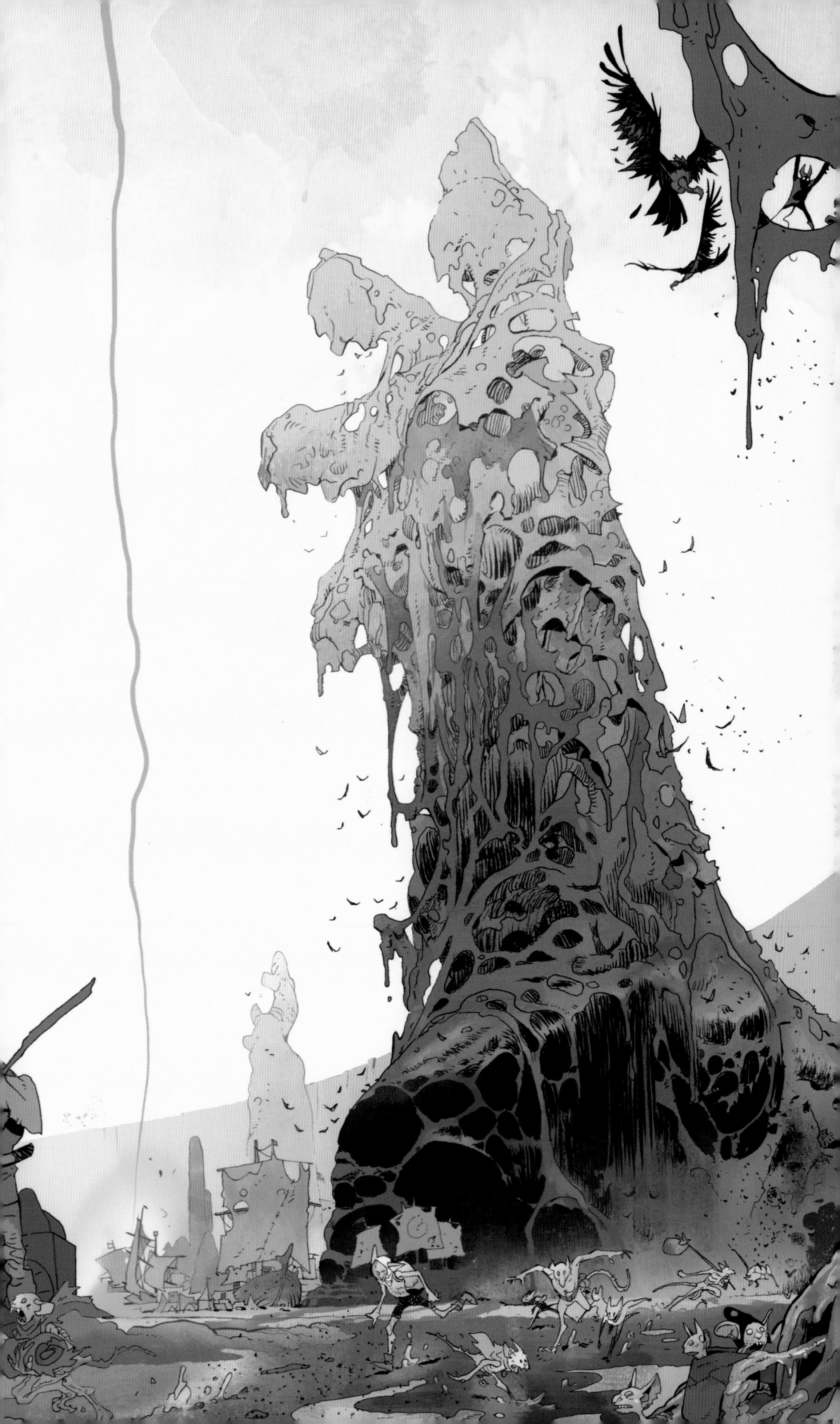

CODA™

CREATED BY **SIMON SPURRIER & MATÍAS BERGARA**

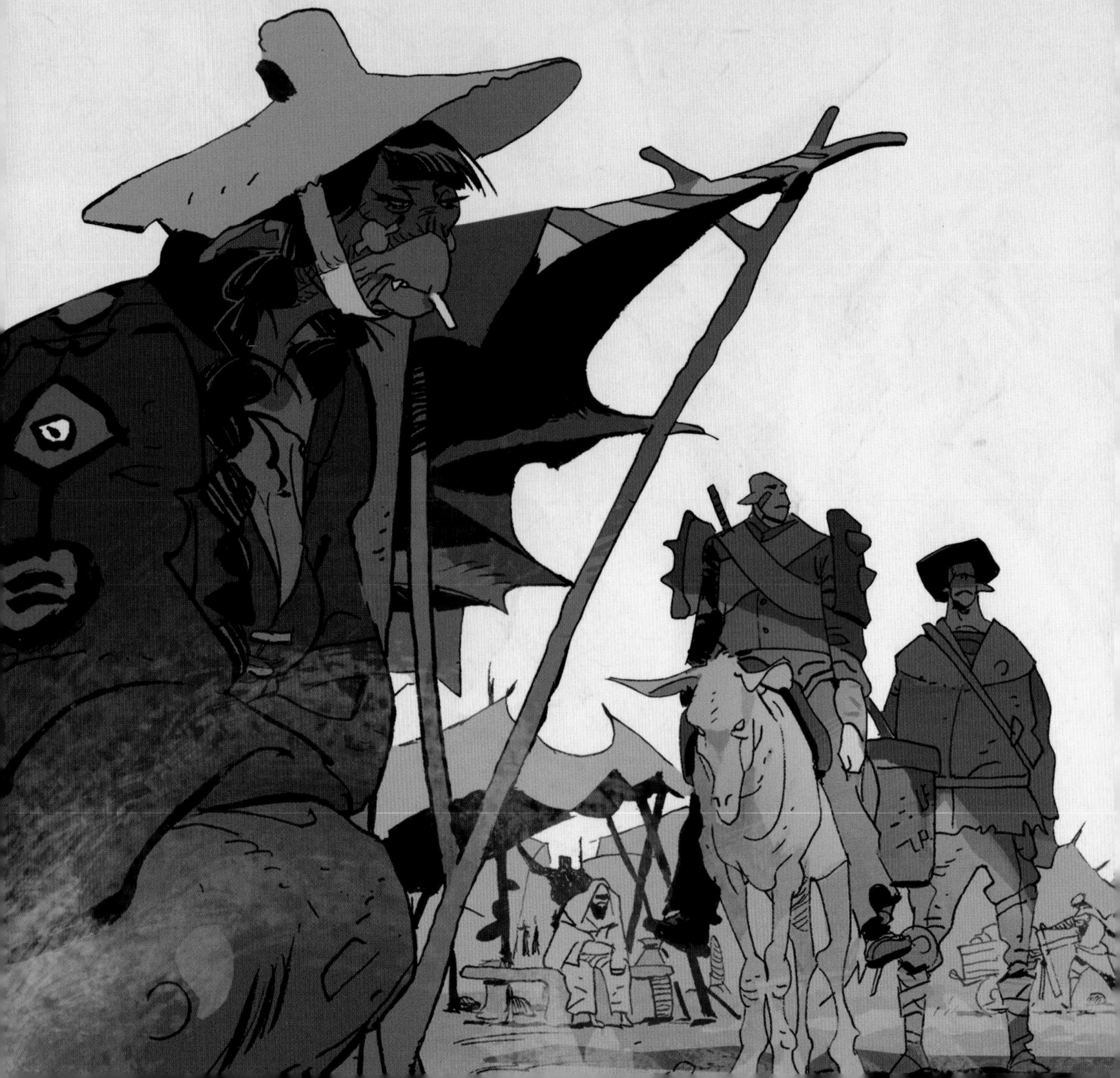

WRITTEN BY **SIMON SPURRIER**

ILLUSTRATED BY **MATÍAS BERGARA**

WITH COLOR ASSISTS BY **MICHAEL DOIG**

LETTERED BY **JIM CAMPBELL**

COVER BY **MATÍAS BERGARA**

SERIES DESIGNER **MARIE KRUPINA**

COLLECTION DESIGNER **CHELSEA ROBERTS**

ASSISTANT EDITOR **GAVIN GRONENTHAL**

EDITOR **ERIC HARBURN**

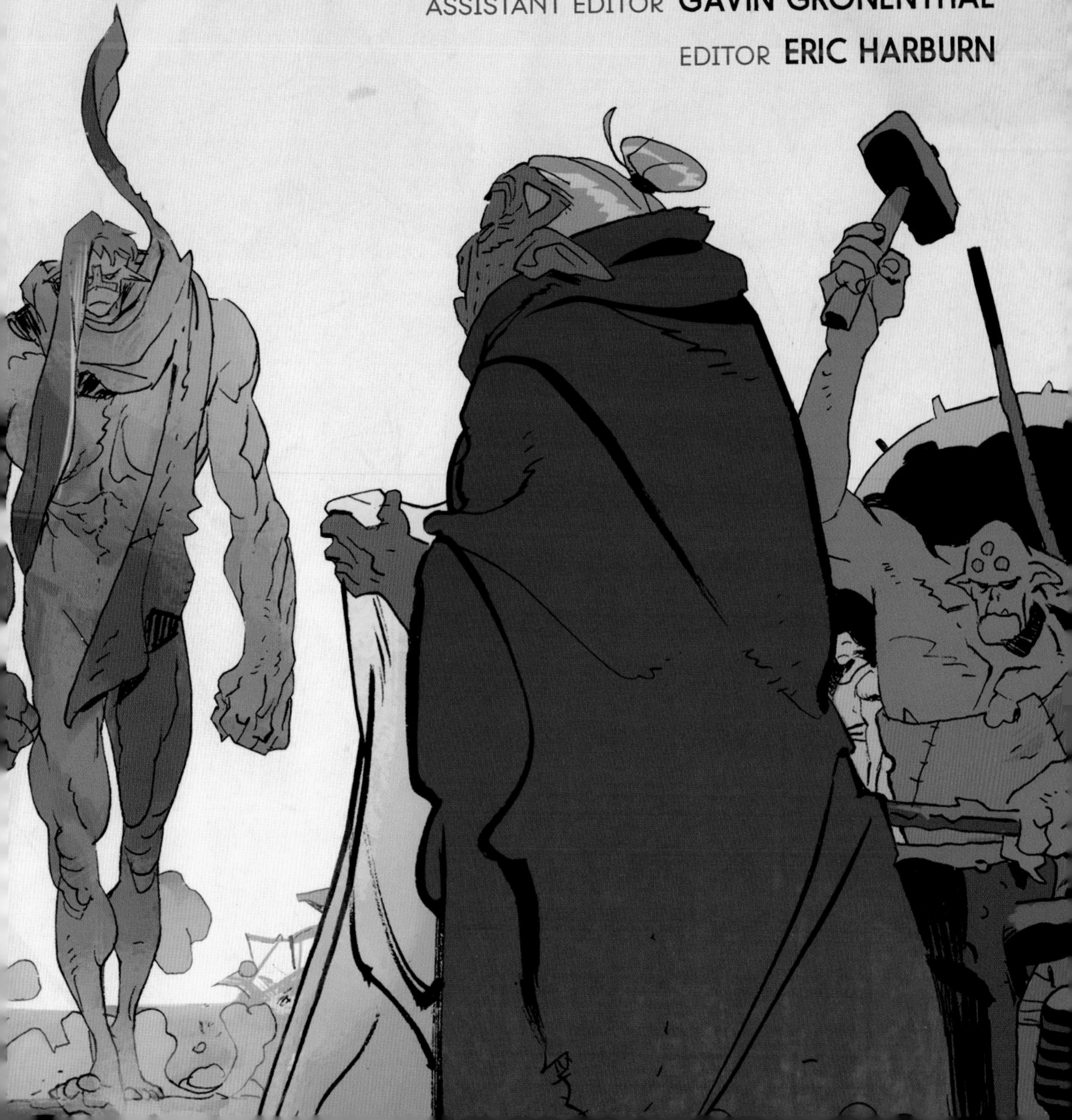

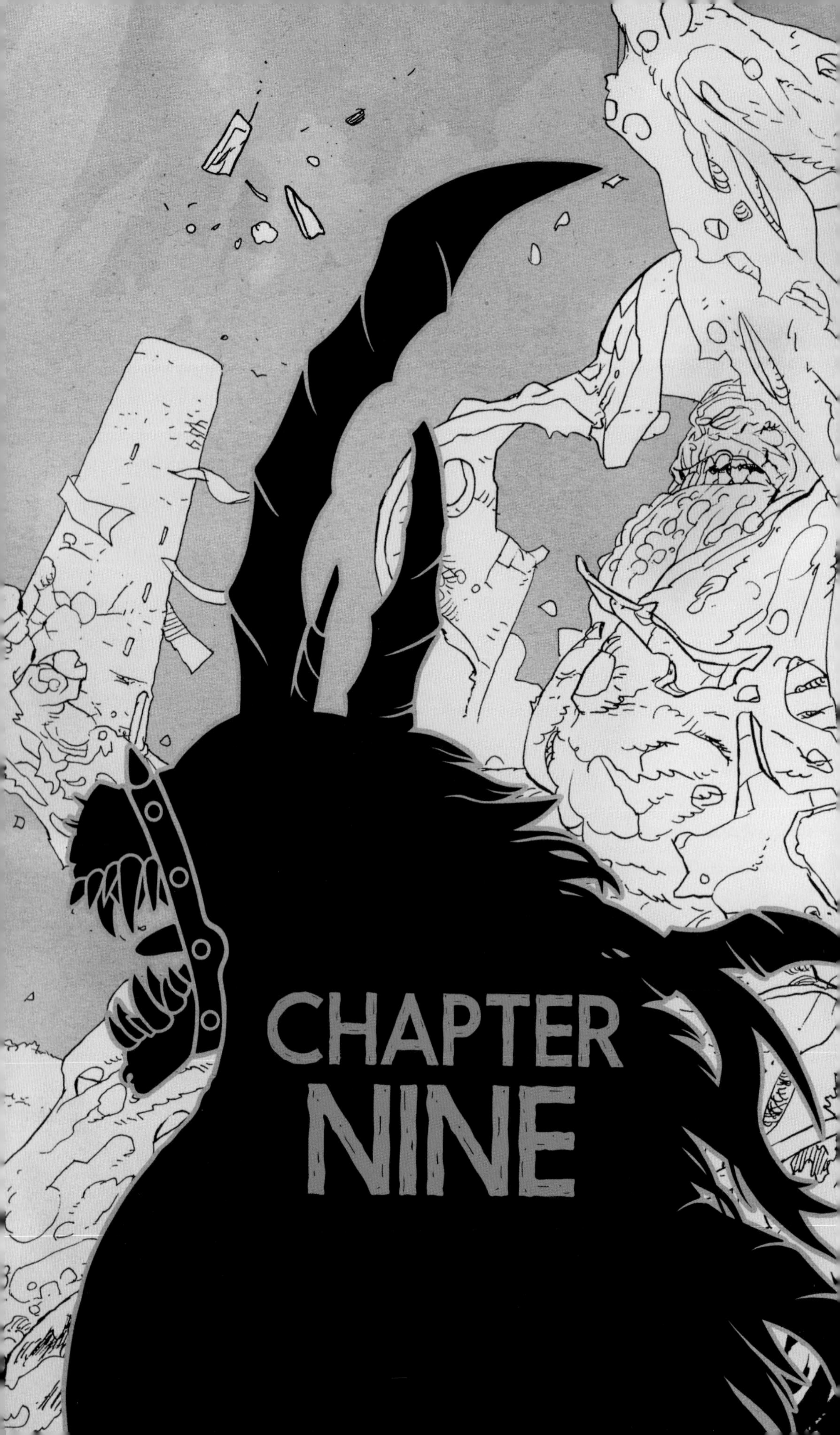
CHAPTER
NINE

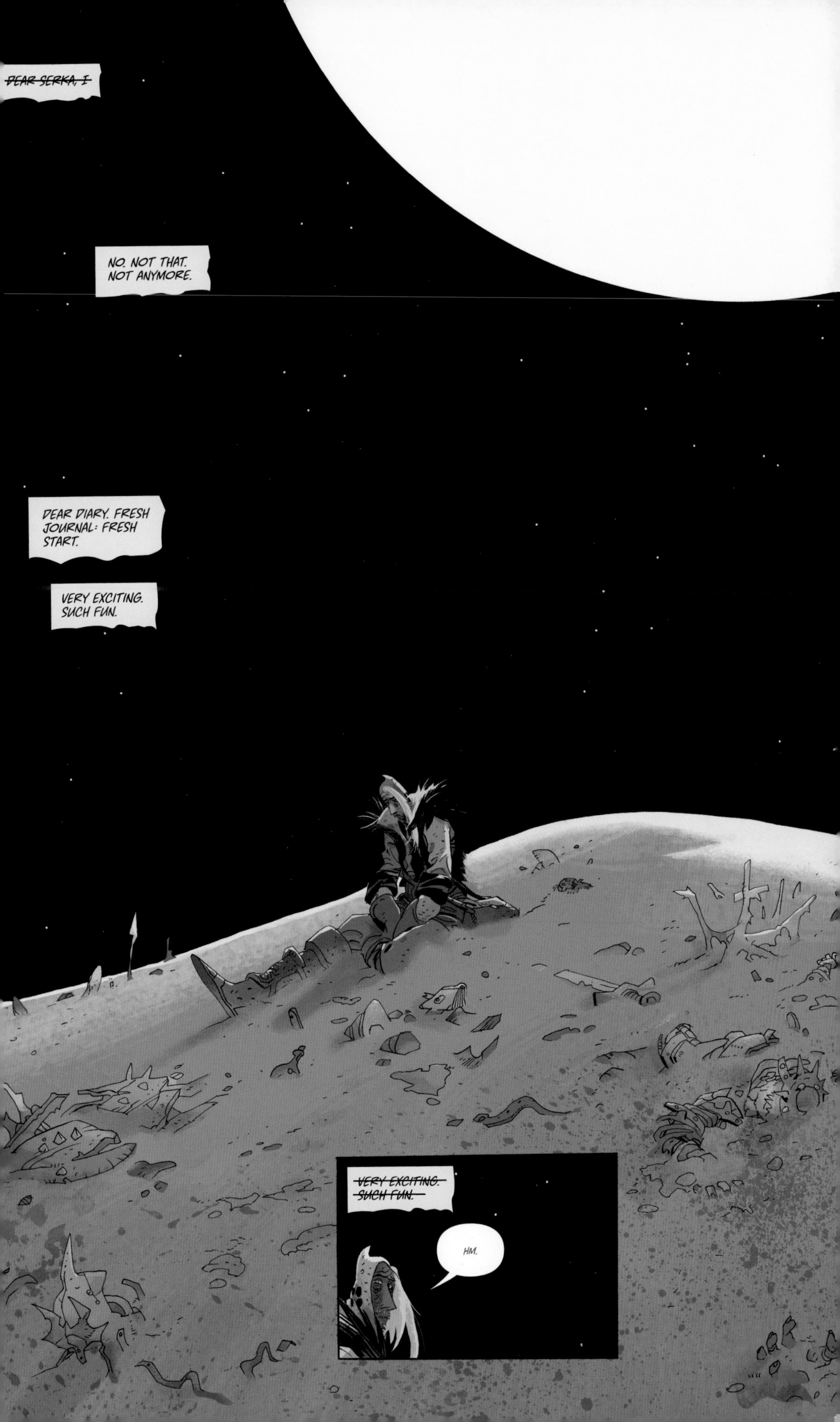
DEAR SERKA, I
NO. NOT THAT. NOT ANYMORE.
DEAR DIARY. FRESH JOURNAL: FRESH START.
VERY EXCITING. SUCH FUN.
VERY EXCITING. SUCH FUN.
HM.

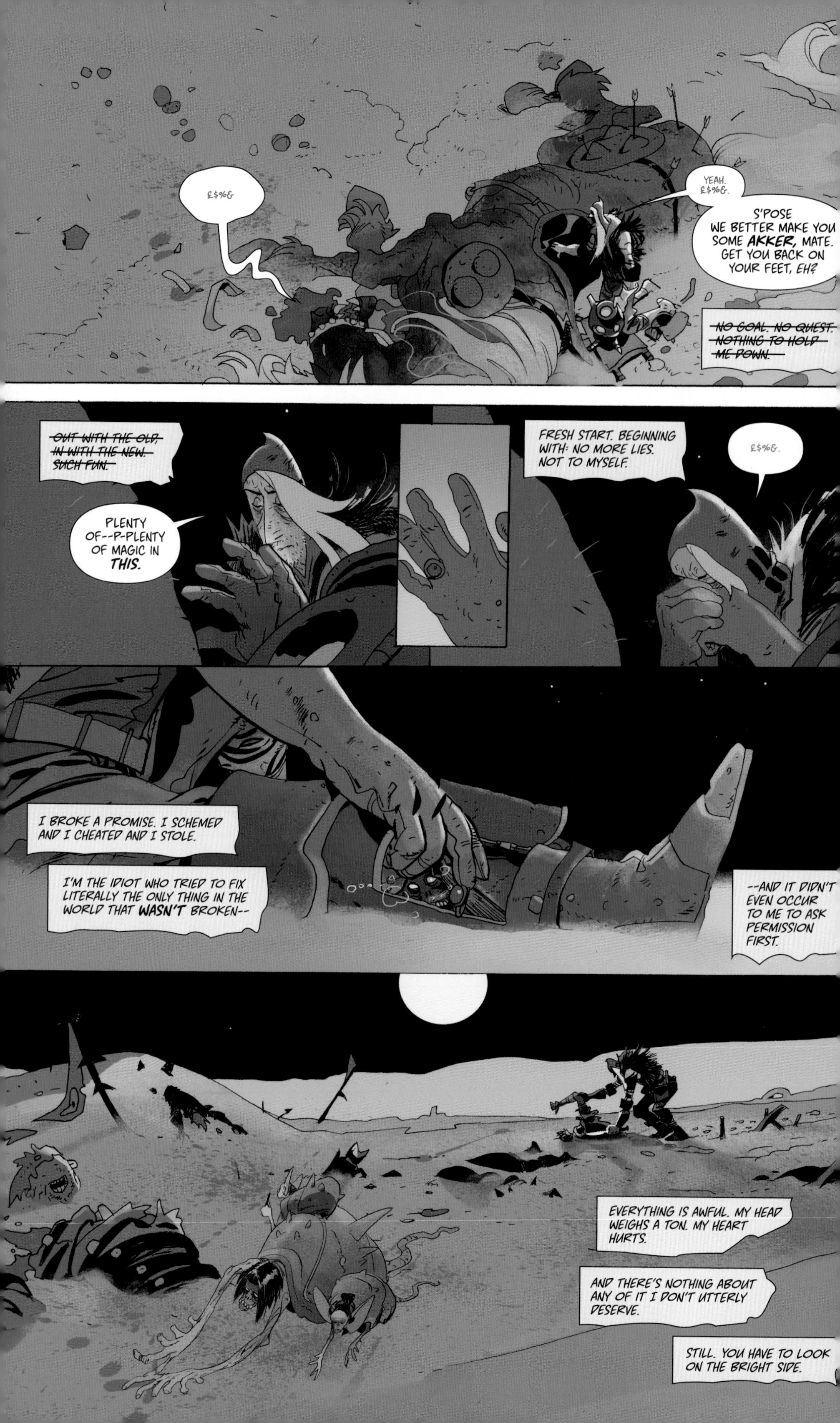
£$%&
YEAH. £$%&.
S'POSE WE BETTER MAKE YOU SOME AKKER, MATE. GET YOU BACK ON YOUR FEET, EH?
~~NO GOAL. NO QUEST. NOTHING TO HOLD ME DOWN.~~
~~OUT WITH THE OLD, IN WITH THE NEW. SUCH FUN.~~
PLENTY OF--P-PLENTY OF MAGIC IN THIS.
FRESH START. BEGINNING WITH: NO MORE LIES. NOT TO MYSELF.
£$%&.
I BROKE A PROMISE. I SCHEMED AND I CHEATED AND I STOLE.
I'M THE IDIOT WHO TRIED TO FIX LITERALLY THE ONLY THING IN THE WORLD THAT WASN'T BROKEN--
--AND IT DIDN'T EVEN OCCUR TO ME TO ASK PERMISSION FIRST.
EVERYTHING IS AWFUL. MY HEAD WEIGHS A TON. MY HEART HURTS.
AND THERE'S NOTHING ABOUT ANY OF IT I DON'T UTTERLY DESERVE.
STILL. YOU HAVE TO LOOK ON THE BRIGHT SIDE.

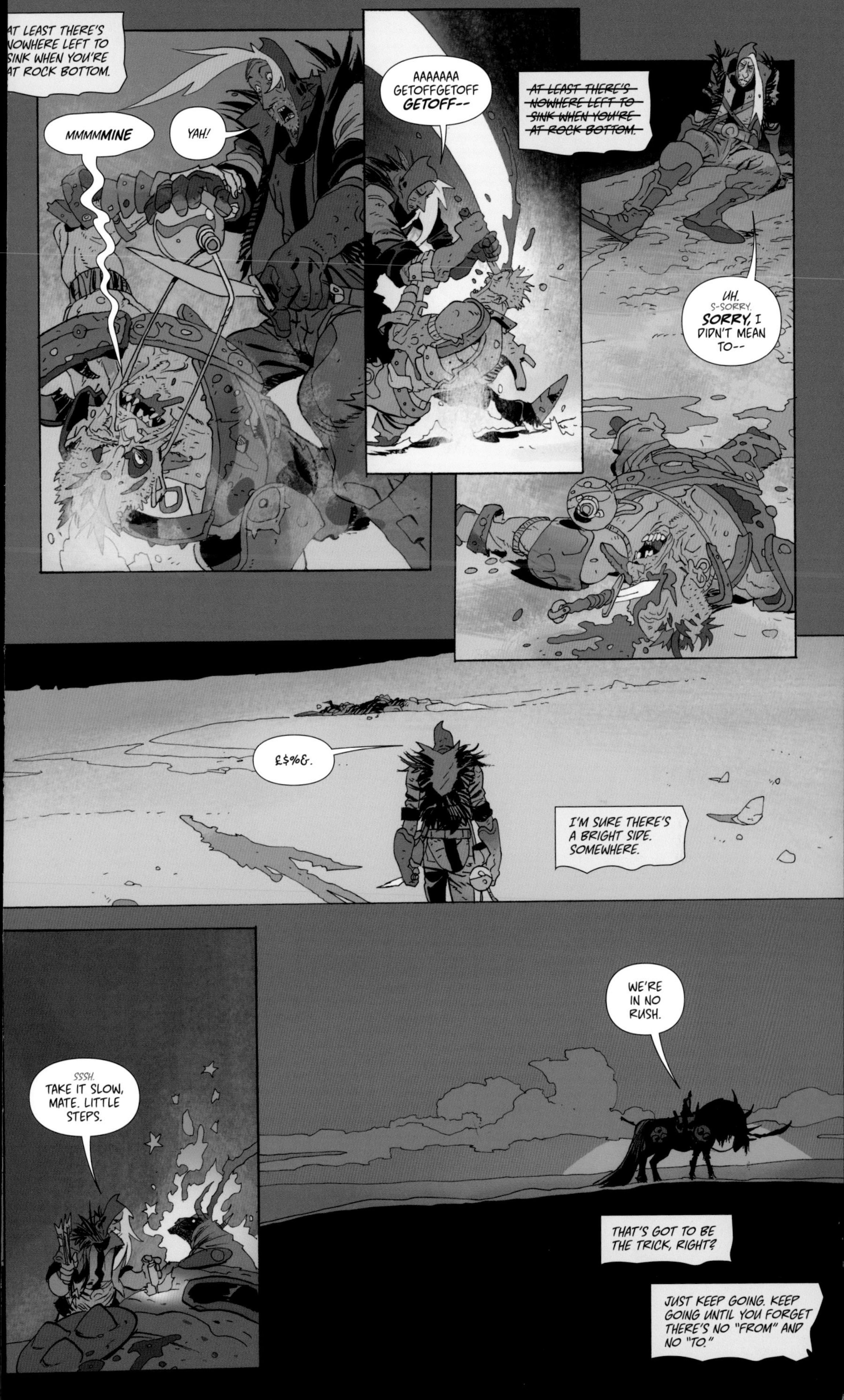
AT LEAST THERE'S NOWHERE LEFT TO SINK WHEN YOU'RE AT ROCK BOTTOM.
MMMMMINE
YAH!
AAAAAAA GETOFFGETOFF GETOFF--
~~AT LEAST THERE'S NOWHERE LEFT TO SINK WHEN YOU'RE AT ROCK BOTTOM.~~
UH. S-SORRY. SORRY, I DIDN'T MEAN TO--
£$%&.
I'M SURE THERE'S A BRIGHT SIDE. SOMEWHERE.
SSSH. TAKE IT SLOW, MATE. LITTLE STEPS.
WE'RE IN NO RUSH.
THAT'S GOT TO BE THE TRICK, RIGHT?
JUST KEEP GOING. KEEP GOING UNTIL YOU FORGET THERE'S NO "FROM" AND NO "TO."

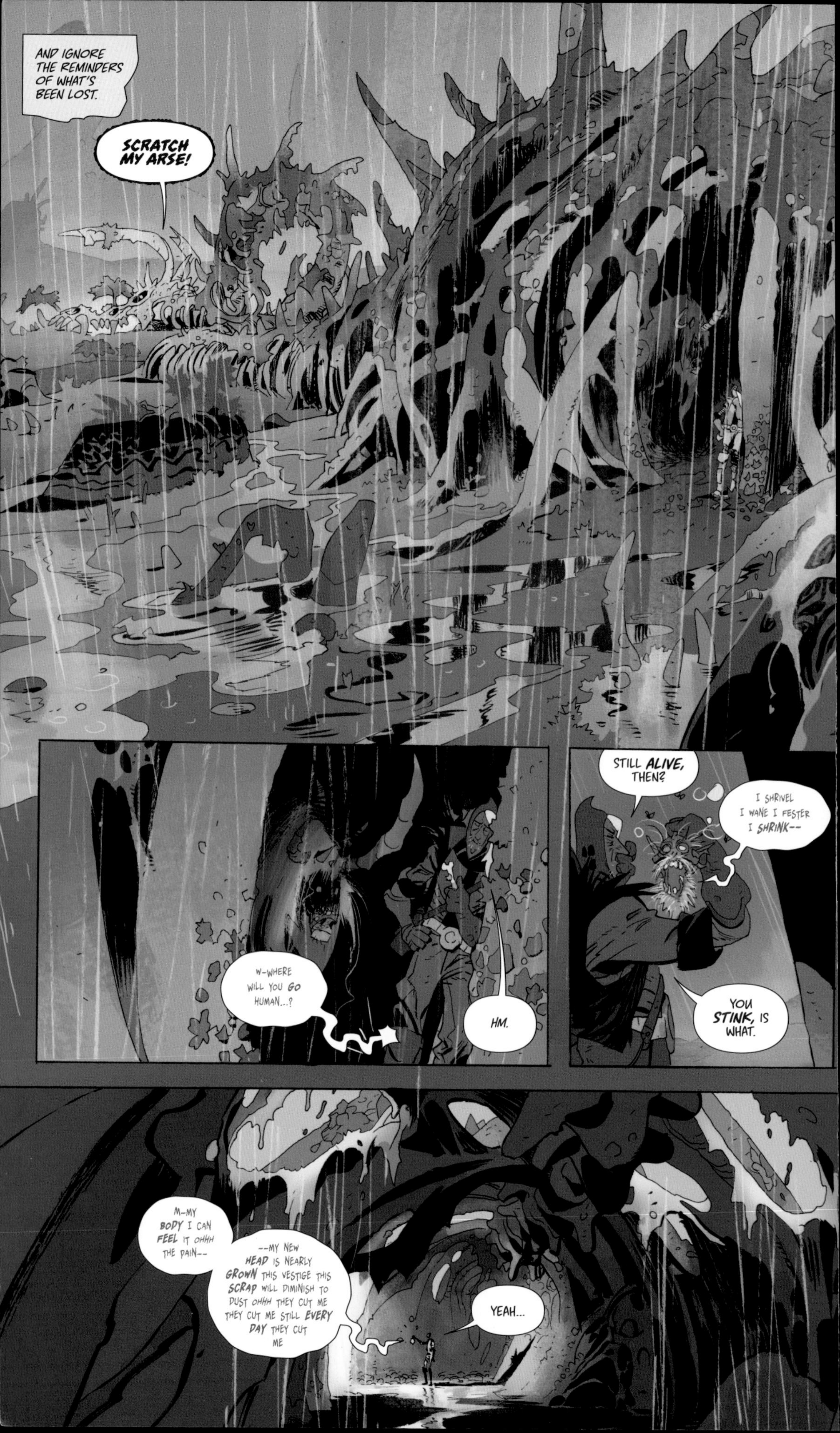
AND IGNORE THE REMINDERS OF WHAT'S BEEN LOST.
SCRATCH MY ARSE!
W-WHERE WILL YOU GO HUMAN...?
HM.
STILL ALIVE, THEN?
I SHRIVEL I WANE I FESTER I SHRINK--
YOU STINK, IS WHAT.
M-MY BODY I CAN FEEL IT OHHH THE PAIN--
--MY NEW HEAD IS NEARLY GROWN THIS VESTIGE THIS SCRAP WILL DIMINISH TO DUST OHHH THEY CUT ME THEY CUT ME STILL EVERY DAY THEY CUT ME
YEAH...

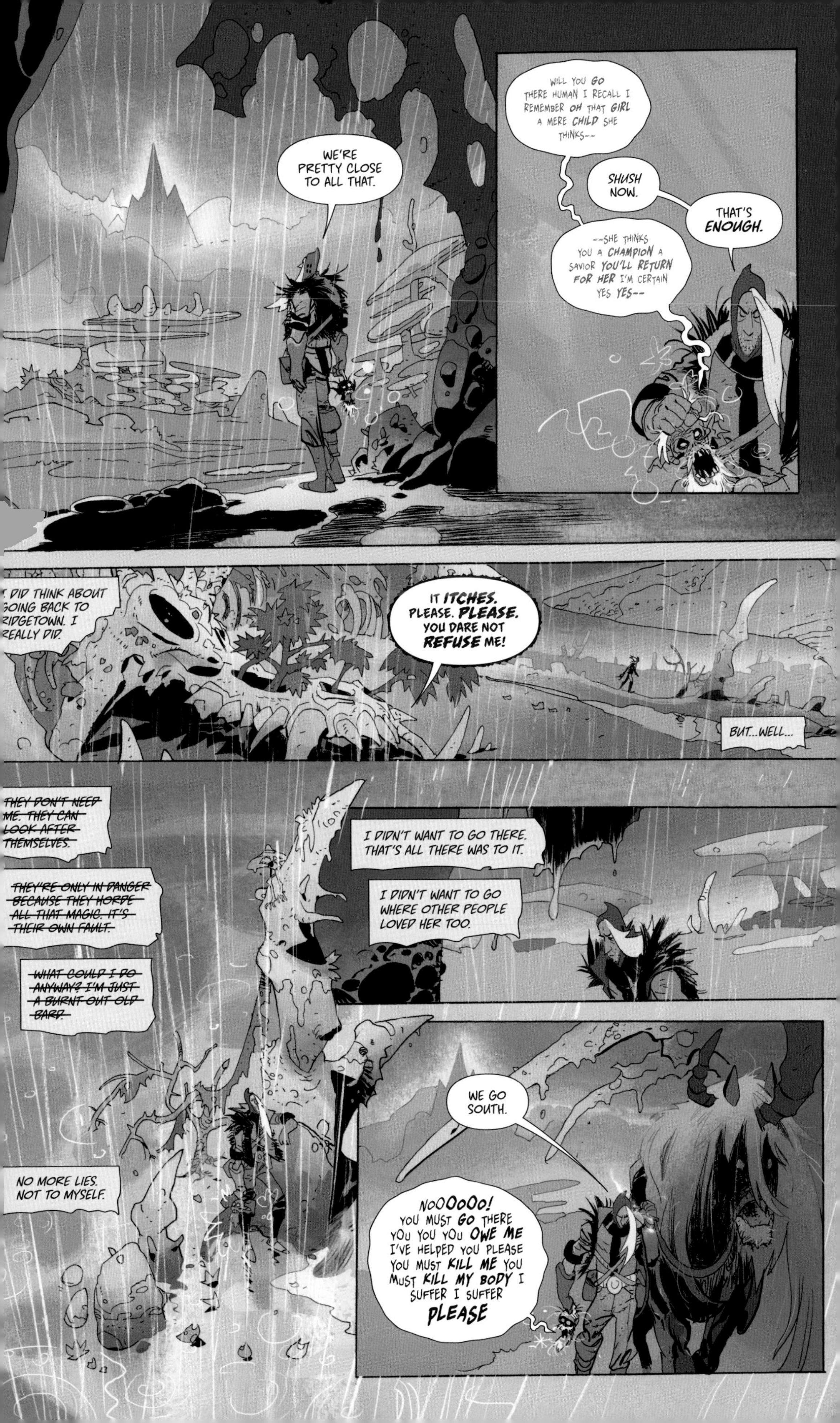
WE'RE PRETTY CLOSE TO ALL THAT.
WILL YOU GO THERE HUMAN I RECALL I REMEMBER OH THAT GIRL A MERE CHILD SHE THINKS--
SHUSH NOW.
--SHE THINKS YOU A CHAMPION A SAVIOR YOU'LL RETURN FOR HER I'M CERTAIN YES YES--
THAT'S ENOUGH.
I DID THINK ABOUT GOING BACK TO RIDGETOWN. I REALLY DID.
IT ITCHES. PLEASE. PLEASE. YOU DARE NOT REFUSE ME!
BUT...WELL...
THEY DON'T NEED ME. THEY CAN LOOK AFTER THEMSELVES.
THEY'RE ONLY IN DANGER BECAUSE THEY HORDE ALL THAT MAGIC. IT'S THEIR OWN FAULT.
WHAT COULD I DO ANYWAY? I'M JUST A BURNT OUT OLD BARD.
I DIDN'T WANT TO GO THERE. THAT'S ALL THERE WAS TO IT.
I DIDN'T WANT TO GO WHERE OTHER PEOPLE LOVED HER TOO.
NO MORE LIES. NOT TO MYSELF.
WE GO SOUTH.
NOOOOOO! YOU MUST GO THERE YOU YOU YOU OWE ME I'VE HELPED YOU PLEASE YOU MUST KILL ME YOU MUST KILL MY BODY I SUFFER I SUFFER PLEASE

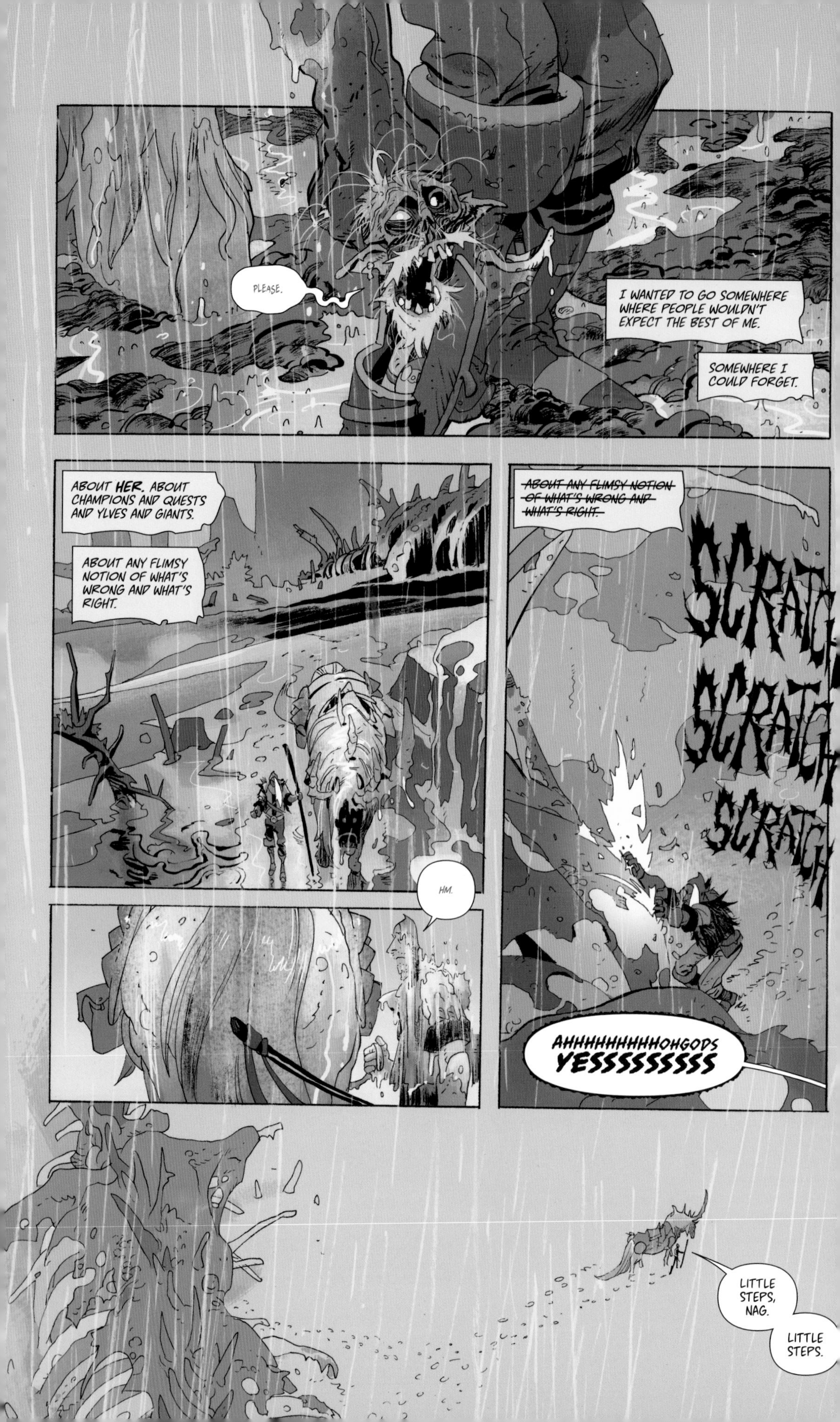
PLEASE.
I WANTED TO GO SOMEWHERE WHERE PEOPLE WOULDN'T EXPECT THE BEST OF ME.
SOMEWHERE I COULD FORGET.
ABOUT HER. ABOUT CHAMPIONS AND QUESTS AND YLVES AND GIANTS.
ABOUT ANY FLIMSY NOTION OF WHAT'S WRONG AND WHAT'S RIGHT.
~~ABOUT ANY FLIMSY NOTION OF WHAT'S WRONG AND WHAT'S RIGHT.~~
SCRATCH
SCRATCH
SCRATCH
HM.
AHHHHHHHHHOHGODS YESSSSSSSSS
LITTLE STEPS, NAG.
LITTLE STEPS.

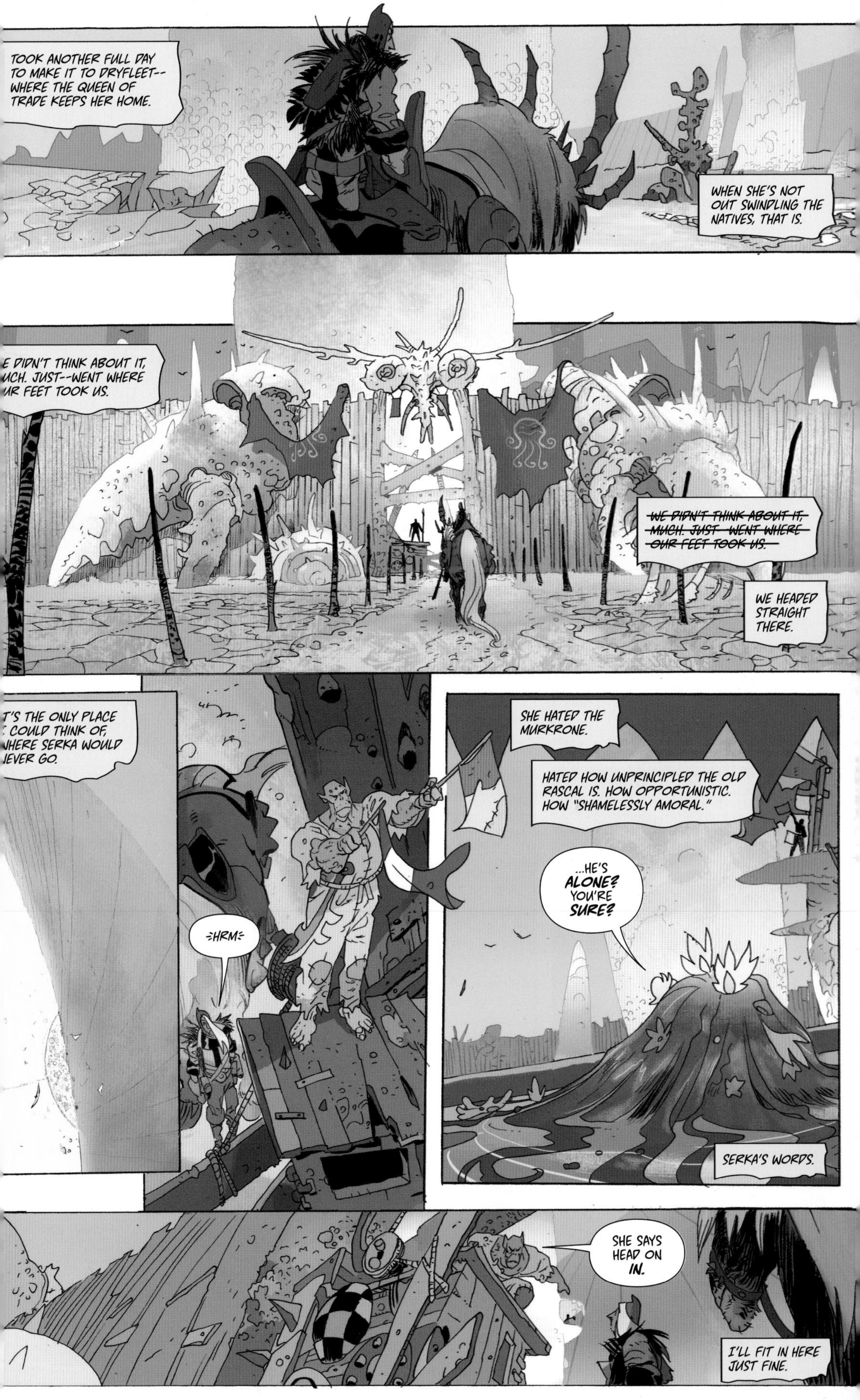
TOOK ANOTHER FULL DAY TO MAKE IT TO DRYFLEET--WHERE THE QUEEN OF TRADE KEEPS HER HOME.
WHEN SHE'S NOT OUT SWINDLING THE NATIVES, THAT IS.
E DIDN'T THINK ABOUT IT, UCH. JUST--WENT WHERE UR FEET TOOK US.
~~WE DIDN'T THINK ABOUT IT, MUCH. JUST--WENT WHERE OUR FEET TOOK US.~~
WE HEADED STRAIGHT THERE.
T'S THE ONLY PLACE COULD THINK OF, WHERE SERKA WOULD NEVER GO.
SHE HATED THE MURKRONE.
HATED HOW UNPRINCIPLED THE OLD RASCAL IS. HOW OPPORTUNISTIC. HOW "SHAMELESSLY AMORAL."
...HE'S **ALONE?** YOU'RE **SURE?**
HRM
SERKA'S WORDS.
SHE SAYS HEAD ON **IN.**
I'LL FIT IN HERE JUST FINE.

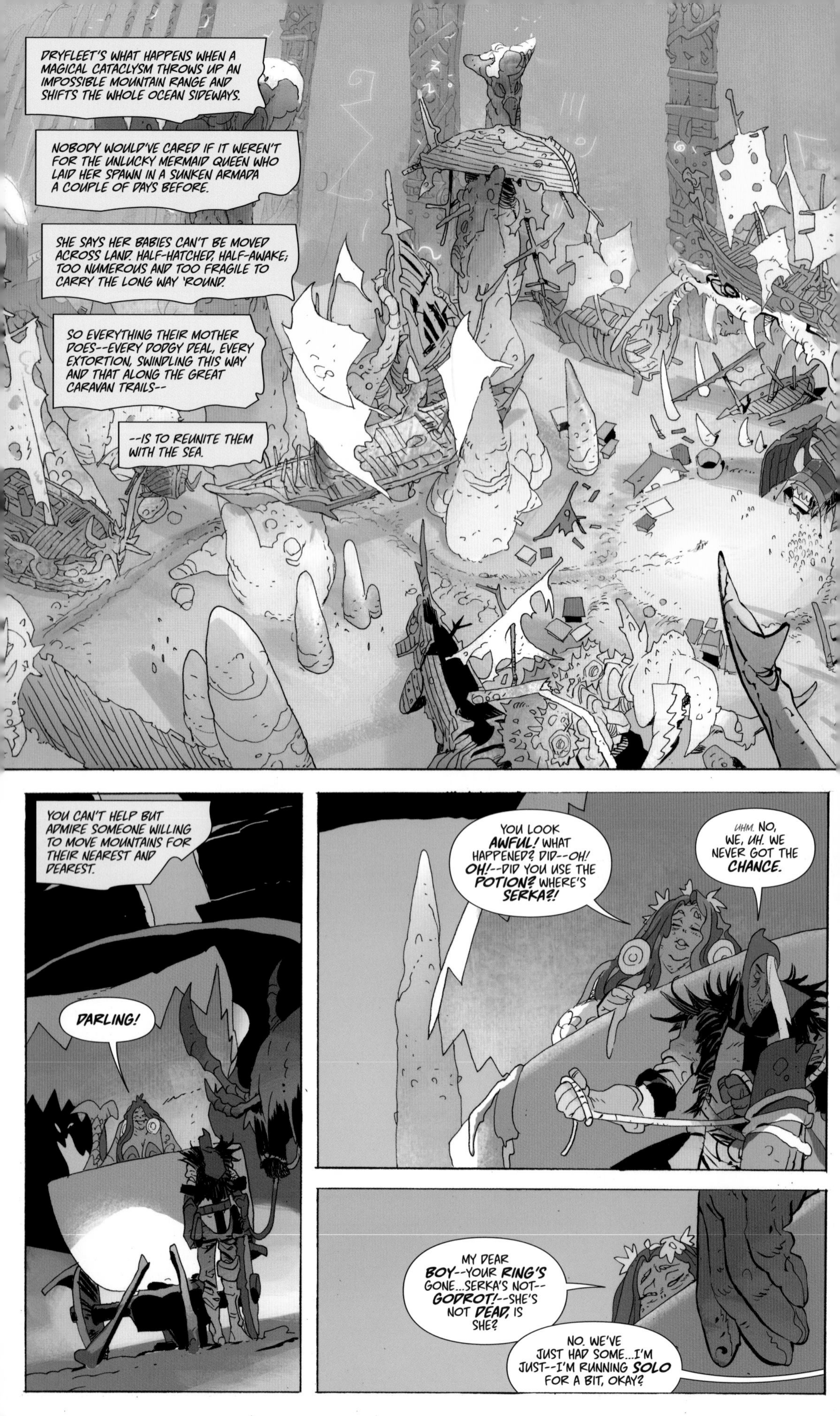
DRYFLEET'S WHAT HAPPENS WHEN A MAGICAL CATACLYSM THROWS UP AN IMPOSSIBLE MOUNTAIN RANGE AND SHIFTS THE WHOLE OCEAN SIDEWAYS.
NOBODY WOULD'VE CARED IF IT WEREN'T FOR THE UNLUCKY MERMAID QUEEN WHO LAID HER SPAWN IN A SUNKEN ARMADA A COUPLE OF DAYS BEFORE.
SHE SAYS HER BABIES CAN'T BE MOVED ACROSS LAND. HALF-HATCHED, HALF-AWAKE; TOO NUMEROUS AND TOO FRAGILE TO CARRY THE LONG WAY 'ROUND.
SO EVERYTHING THEIR MOTHER DOES--EVERY DODGY DEAL, EVERY EXTORTION, SWINDLING THIS WAY AND THAT ALONG THE GREAT CARAVAN TRAILS--
--IS TO REUNITE THEM WITH THE SEA.
YOU CAN'T HELP BUT ADMIRE SOMEONE WILLING TO MOVE MOUNTAINS FOR THEIR NEAREST AND DEAREST.
DARLING!
YOU LOOK AWFUL! WHAT HAPPENED? DID--OH! OH!--DID YOU USE THE POTION? WHERE'S SERKA?!
UHM. NO, WE, UH. WE NEVER GOT THE CHANCE.
MY DEAR BOY--YOUR RING'S GONE...SERKA'S NOT--GODROT!--SHE'S NOT DEAD, IS SHE?
NO. WE'VE JUST HAD SOME...I'M JUST--I'M RUNNING SOLO FOR A BIT, OKAY?

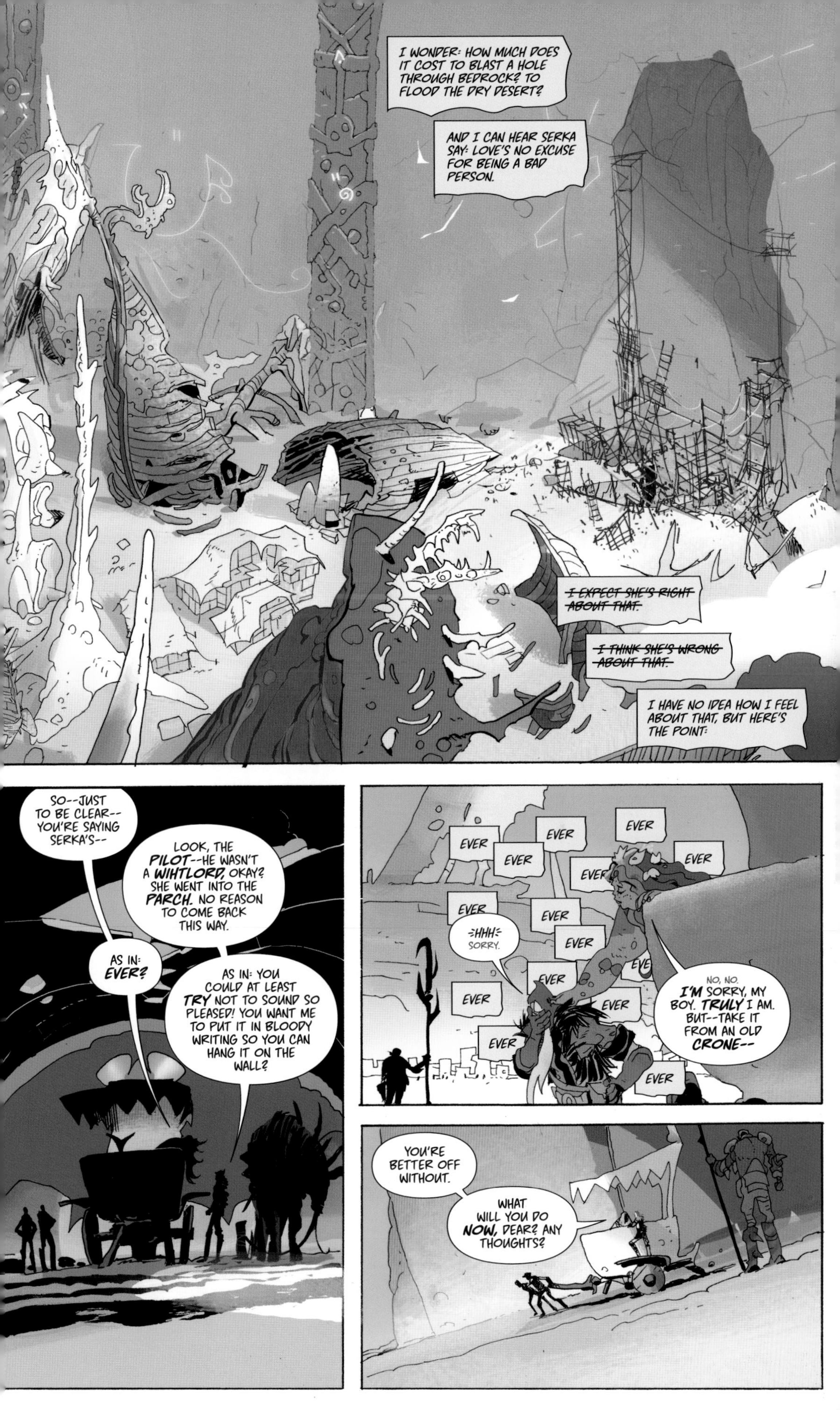
I WONDER: HOW MUCH DOES IT COST TO BLAST A HOLE THROUGH BEDROCK? TO FLOOD THE DRY DESERT?
AND I CAN HEAR SERKA SAY: LOVE'S NO EXCUSE FOR BEING A BAD PERSON.
~~I EXPECT SHE'S RIGHT ABOUT THAT.~~
~~I THINK SHE'S WRONG ABOUT THAT.~~
I HAVE NO IDEA HOW I FEEL ABOUT THAT, BUT HERE'S THE POINT:
SO--JUST TO BE CLEAR--YOU'RE SAYING SERKA'S--
LOOK, THE PILOT--HE WASN'T A WIHTLORD, OKAY? SHE WENT INTO THE PARCH. NO REASON TO COME BACK THIS WAY.
AS IN: EVER?
AS IN: YOU COULD AT LEAST TRY NOT TO SOUND SO PLEASED! YOU WANT ME TO PUT IT IN BLOODY WRITING SO YOU CAN HANG IT ON THE WALL?
EVER
EVER
EVER
EVER
EVER
EVER
EVER
EVER
EVER
EVER
EVER
EVER
EVER
EVER
EVER
EVER
=HHH= SORRY.
NO, NO. I'M SORRY, MY BOY. TRULY I AM. BUT--TAKE IT FROM AN OLD CRONE--
YOU'RE BETTER OFF WITHOUT.
WHAT WILL YOU DO NOW, DEAR? ANY THOUGHTS?

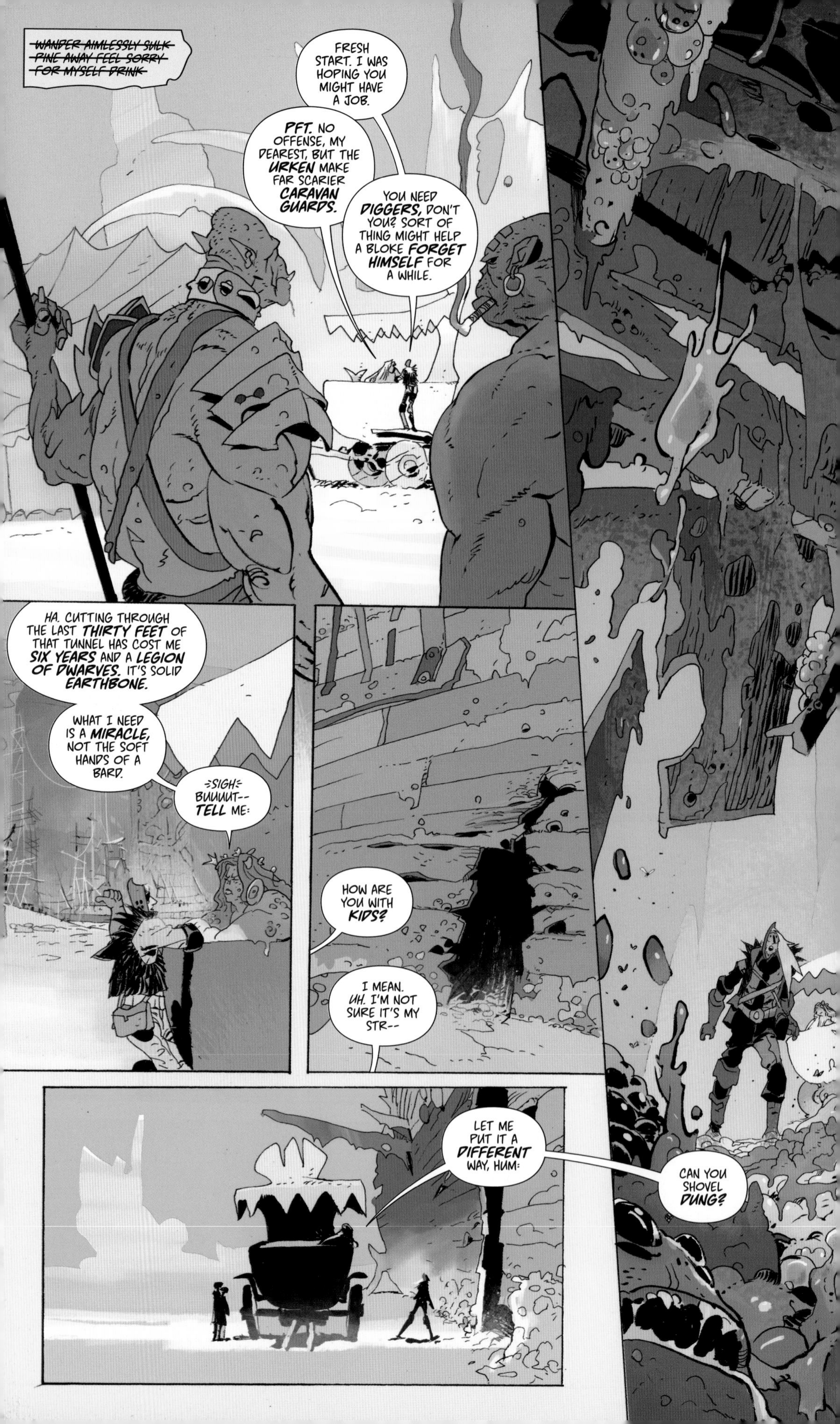
WANDER AIMLESSLY SULK PINE AWAY FEEL SORRY FOR MYSELF DRINK
FRESH START. I WAS HOPING YOU MIGHT HAVE A JOB.
PFT. NO OFFENSE, MY DEAREST, BUT THE URKEN MAKE FAR SCARIER CARAVAN GUARDS.
YOU NEED DIGGERS, DON'T YOU? SORT OF THING MIGHT HELP A BLOKE FORGET HIMSELF FOR A WHILE.
HA. CUTTING THROUGH THE LAST THIRTY FEET OF THAT TUNNEL HAS COST ME SIX YEARS AND A LEGION OF DWARVES. IT'S SOLID EARTHBONE.
WHAT I NEED IS A MIRACLE, NOT THE SOFT HANDS OF A BARD.
=SIGH= BUUUUT-- TELL ME:
HOW ARE YOU WITH KIDS?
I MEAN. UH. I'M NOT SURE IT'S MY STR--
LET ME PUT IT A DIFFERENT WAY, HUM:
CAN YOU SHOVEL DUNG?

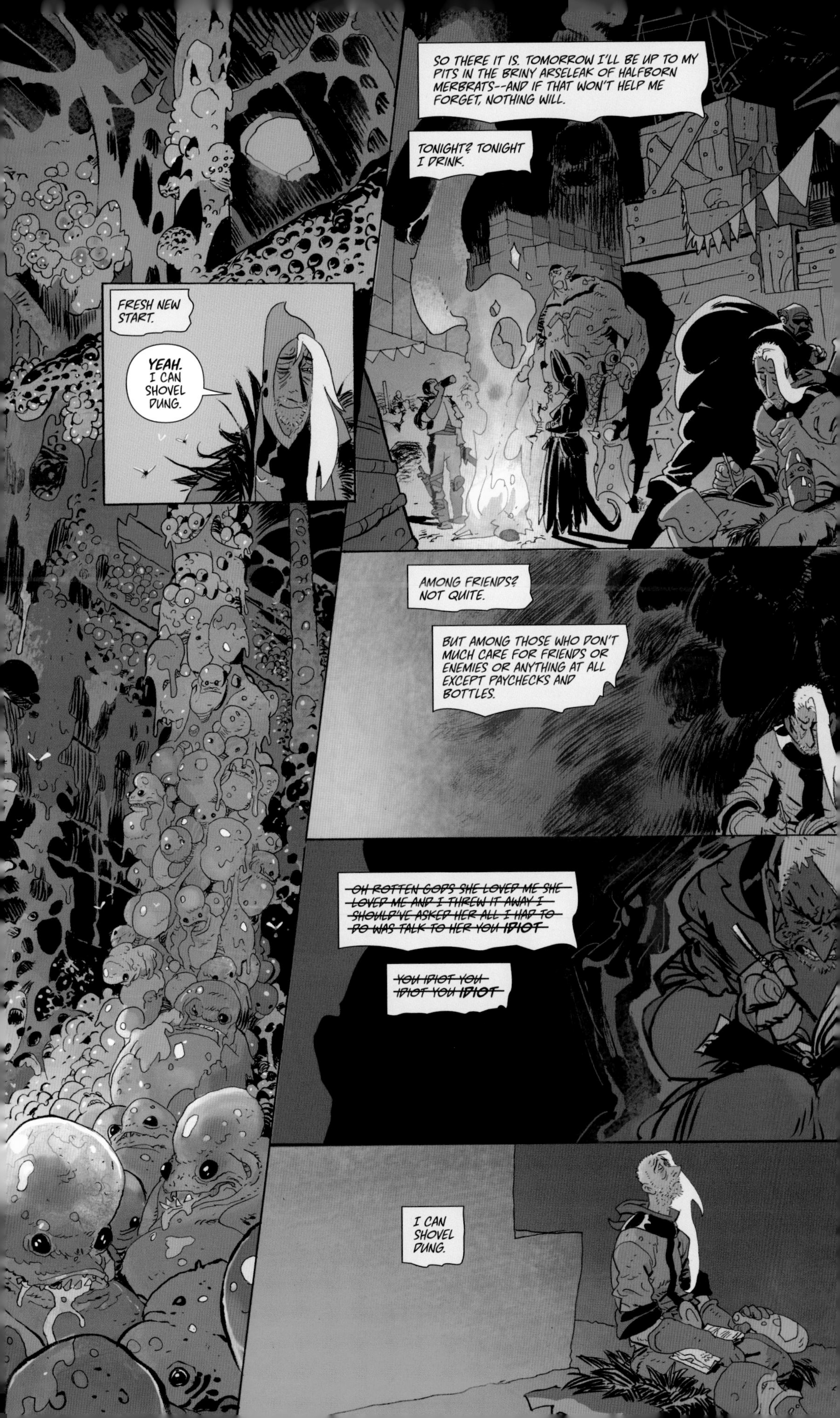
FRESH NEW START.
YEAH. I CAN SHOVEL DUNG.
SO THERE IT IS. TOMORROW I'LL BE UP TO MY PITS IN THE BRINY ARSELEAK OF HALFBORN MERBRATS--AND IF THAT WON'T HELP ME FORGET, NOTHING WILL.
TONIGHT? TONIGHT I DRINK.
AMONG FRIENDS? NOT QUITE.
BUT AMONG THOSE WHO DON'T MUCH CARE FOR FRIENDS OR ENEMIES OR ANYTHING AT ALL EXCEPT PAYCHECKS AND BOTTLES.
~~OH ROTTEN GODS SHE LOVED ME SHE LOVED ME AND I THREW IT AWAY I SHOULD'VE ASKED HER ALL I HAD TO DO WAS TALK TO HER YOU IDIOT~~
~~YOU IDIOT YOU IDIOT YOU IDIOT~~
I CAN SHOVEL DUNG.

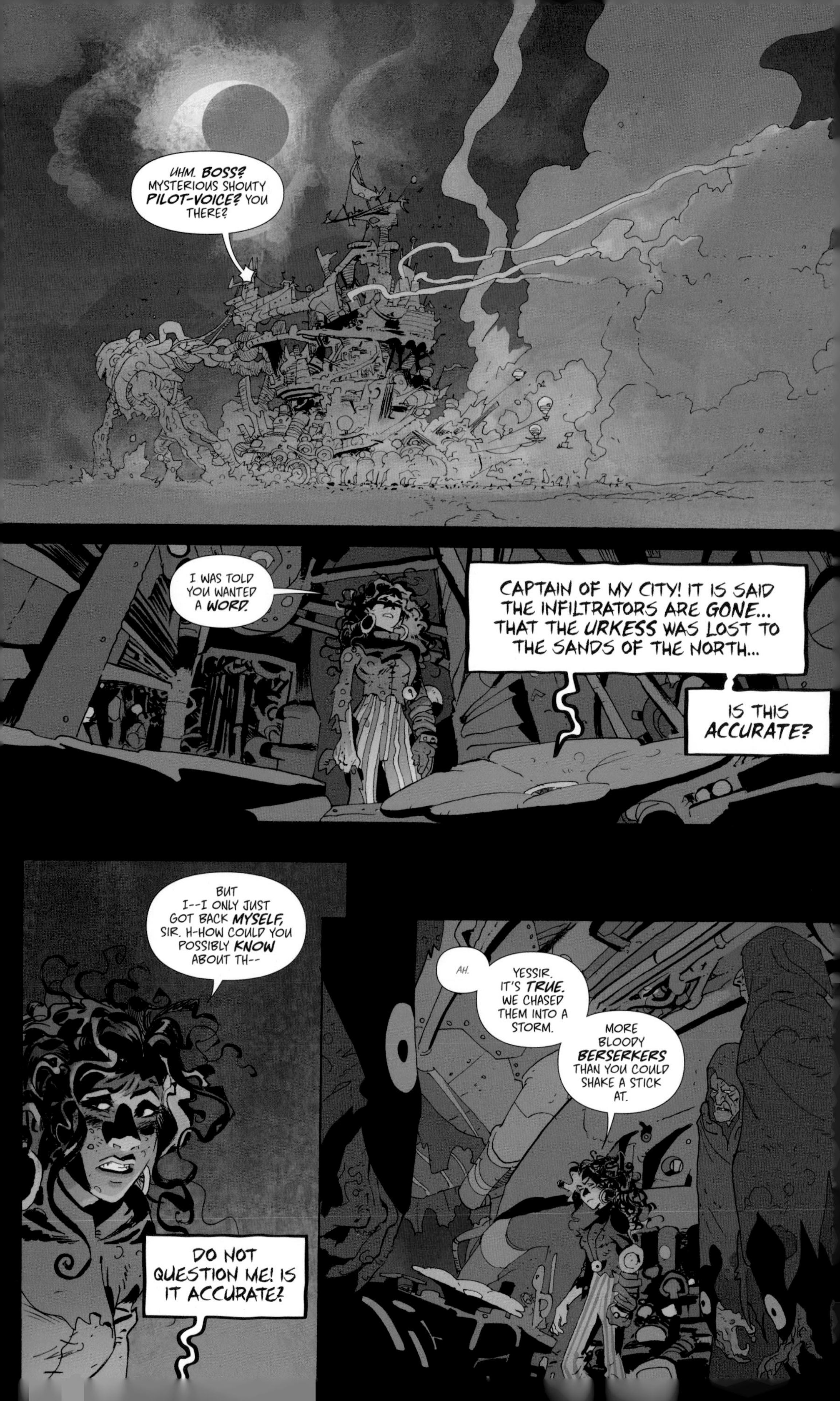
UHM. BOSS? MYSTERIOUS SHOUTY PILOT-VOICE? YOU THERE?
I WAS TOLD YOU WANTED A WORD.
CAPTAIN OF MY CITY! IT IS SAID THE INFILTRATORS ARE GONE... THAT THE URKESS WAS LOST TO THE SANDS OF THE NORTH...
IS THIS ACCURATE?
BUT I--I ONLY JUST GOT BACK MYSELF, SIR. H-HOW COULD YOU POSSIBLY KNOW ABOUT TH--
DO NOT QUESTION ME! IS IT ACCURATE?
AH.
YESSIR. IT'S TRUE. WE CHASED THEM INTO A STORM.
MORE BLOODY BERSERKERS THAN YOU COULD SHAKE A STICK AT.

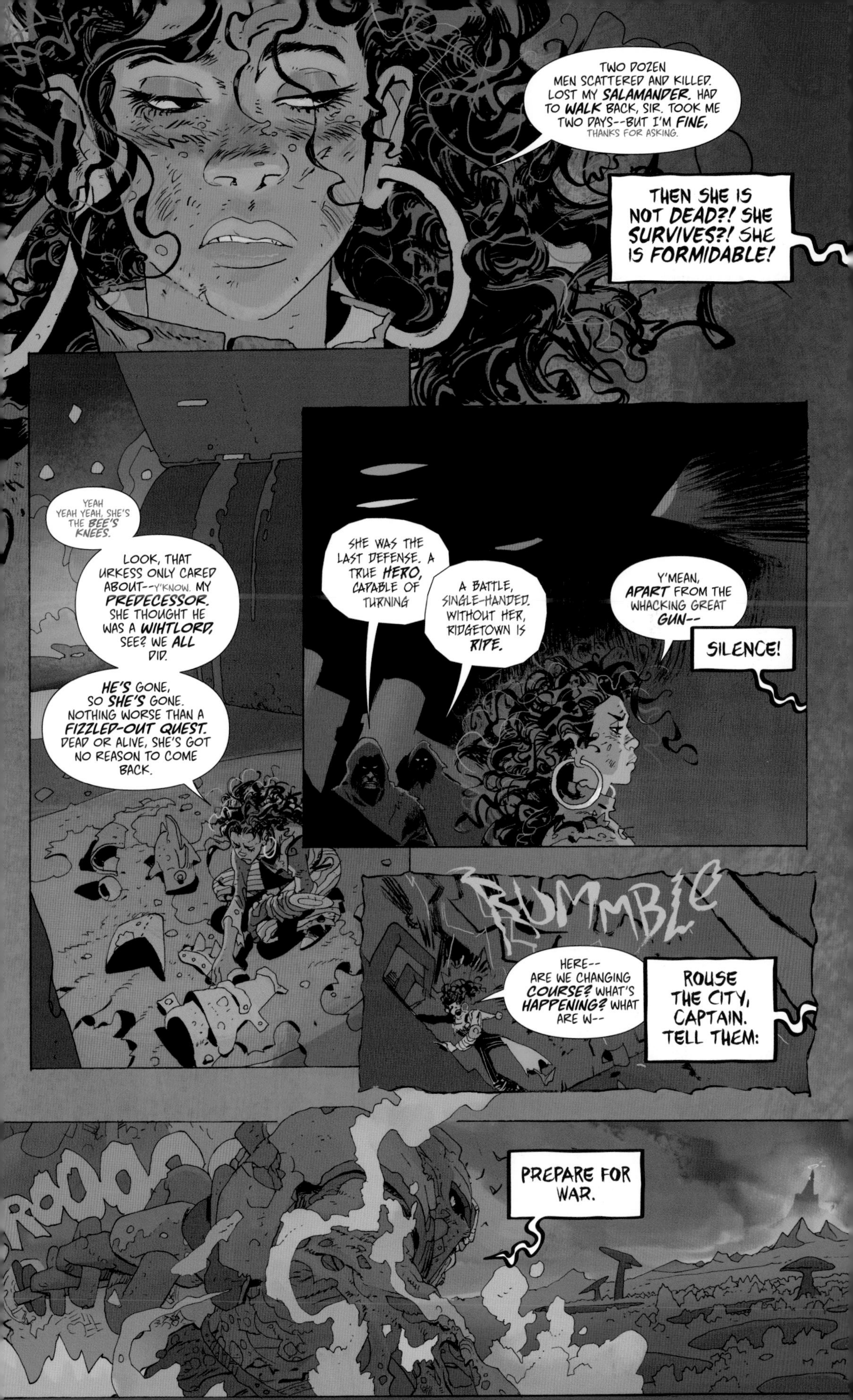
TWO DOZEN MEN SCATTERED AND KILLED. LOST MY SALAMANDER. HAD TO WALK BACK, SIR. TOOK ME TWO DAYS--BUT I'M FINE, THANKS FOR ASKING.
THEN SHE IS NOT DEAD?! SHE SURVIVES?! SHE IS FORMIDABLE!
YEAH YEAH YEAH, SHE'S THE BEE'S KNEES.
LOOK, THAT URKESS ONLY CARED ABOUT--Y'KNOW. MY PREDECESSOR. SHE THOUGHT HE WAS A WIHTLORD, SEE? WE ALL DID.
HE'S GONE, SO SHE'S GONE. NOTHING WORSE THAN A FIZZLED-OUT QUEST. DEAD OR ALIVE, SHE'S GOT NO REASON TO COME BACK.
SHE WAS THE LAST DEFENSE. A TRUE HERO, CAPABLE OF TURNING
A BATTLE, SINGLE-HANDED. WITHOUT HER, RIDGETOWN IS RIPE.
Y'MEAN, APART FROM THE WHACKING GREAT GUN--
SILENCE!
RUMMBLE
HERE-- ARE WE CHANGING COURSE? WHAT'S HAPPENING? WHAT ARE W--
ROUSE THE CITY, CAPTAIN. TELL THEM:
PREPARE FOR WAR.

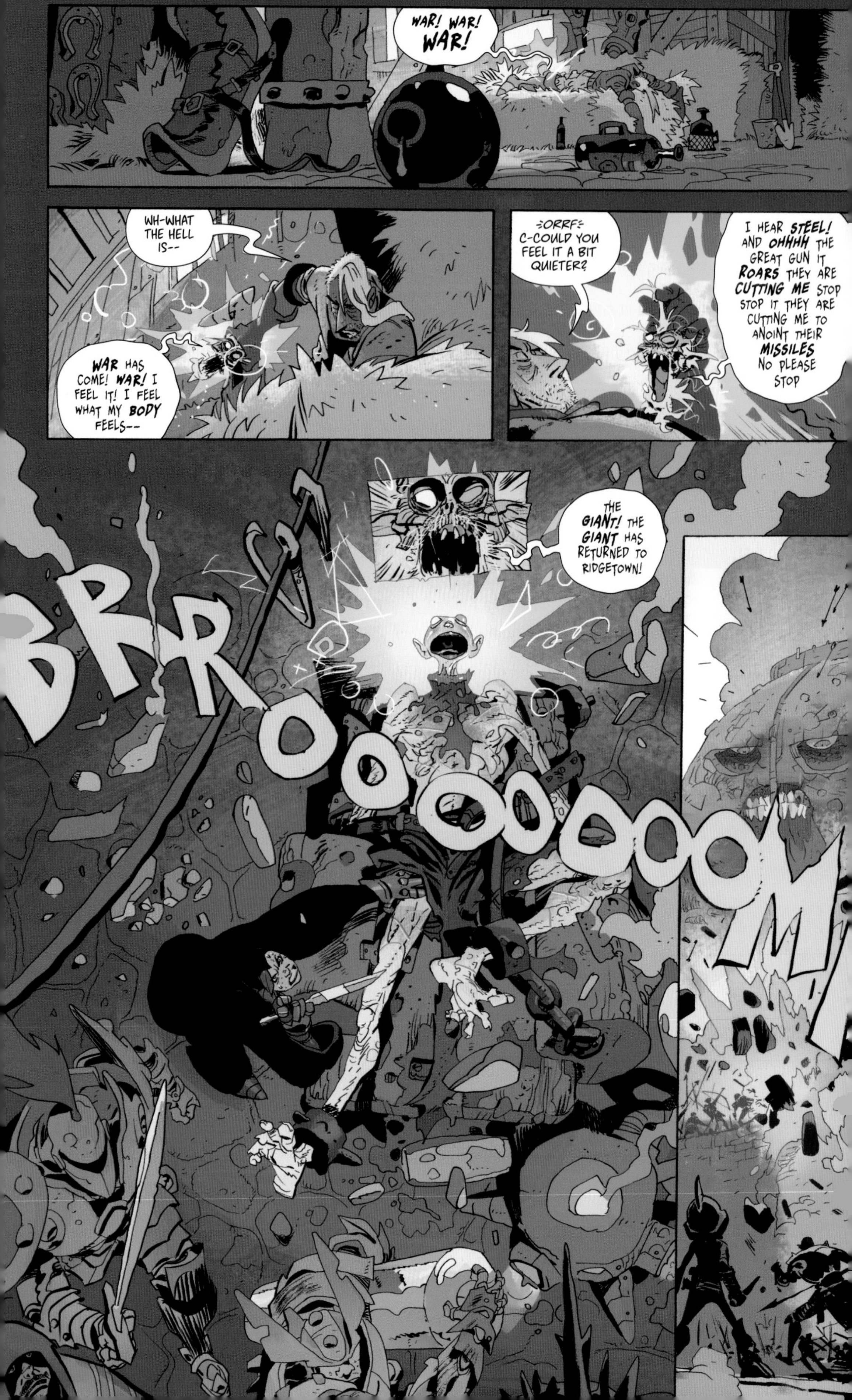
WAR! WAR! WAR!
WH-WHAT THE HELL IS--
WAR HAS COME! WAR! I FEEL IT! I FEEL WHAT MY BODY FEELS--
=ORRF= C-COULD YOU FEEL IT A BIT QUIETER?
I HEAR STEEL! AND OHHHH THE GREAT GUN IT ROARS THEY ARE CUTTING ME STOP STOP IT THEY ARE CUTTING ME TO ANOINT THEIR MISSILES NO PLEASE STOP
THE GIANT! THE GIANT HAS RETURNED TO RIDGETOWN!
BRROOOOOOOM

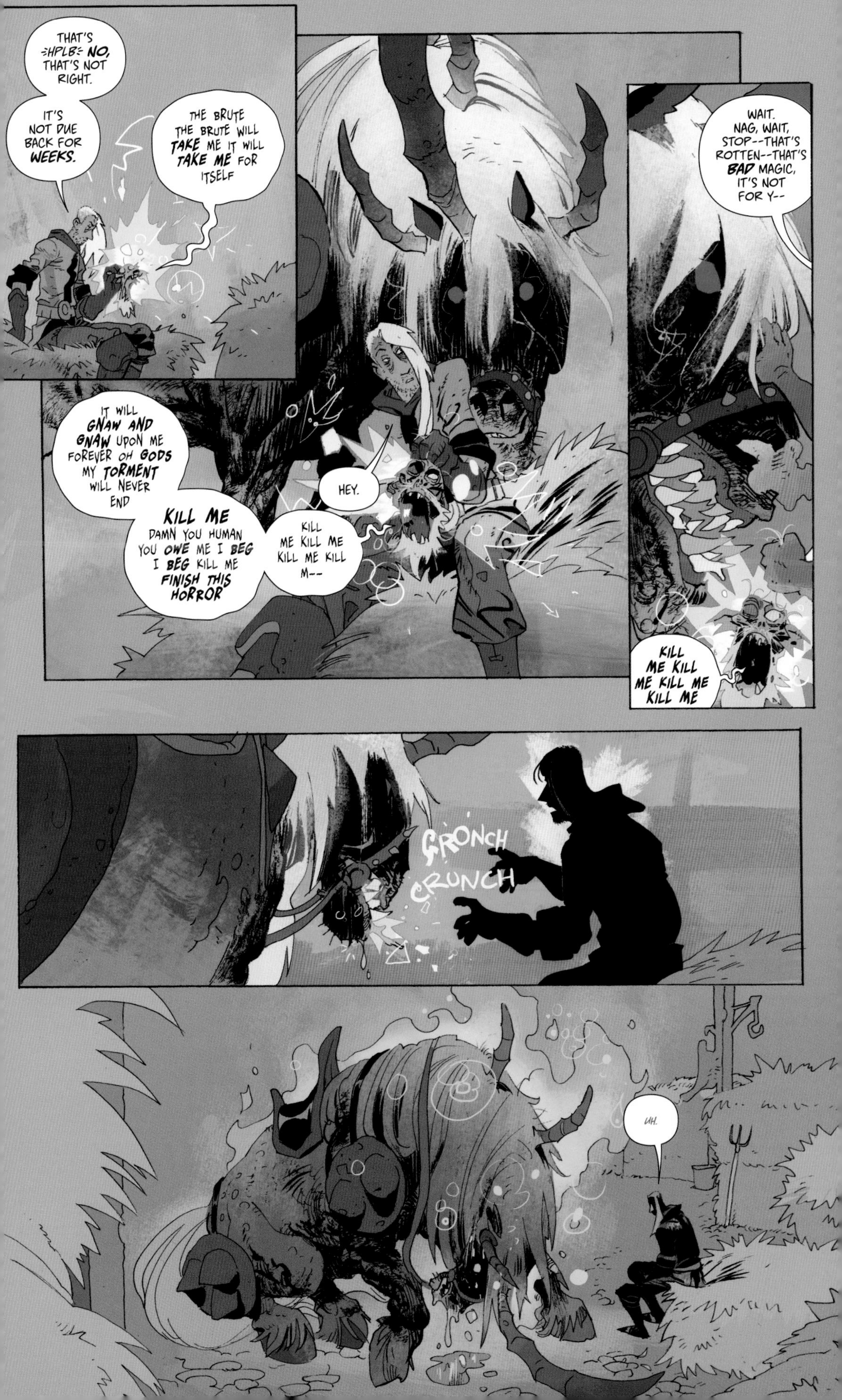
THAT'S =HPLB= NO, THAT'S NOT RIGHT.
IT'S NOT DUE BACK FOR WEEKS.
THE BRUTE THE BRUTE WILL TAKE ME IT WILL TAKE ME FOR ITSELF
IT WILL GNAW AND GNAW UPON ME FOREVER OH GODS MY TORMENT WILL NEVER END
KILL ME DAMN YOU HUMAN YOU OWE ME I BEG I BEG KILL ME FINISH THIS HORROR
HEY.
KILL ME KILL ME KILL ME KILL M--
WAIT. NAG, WAIT, STOP--THAT'S ROTTEN--THAT'S BAD MAGIC, IT'S NOT FOR Y--
KILL ME KILL ME KILL ME KILL ME
GRONCH
CRUNCH
UH.

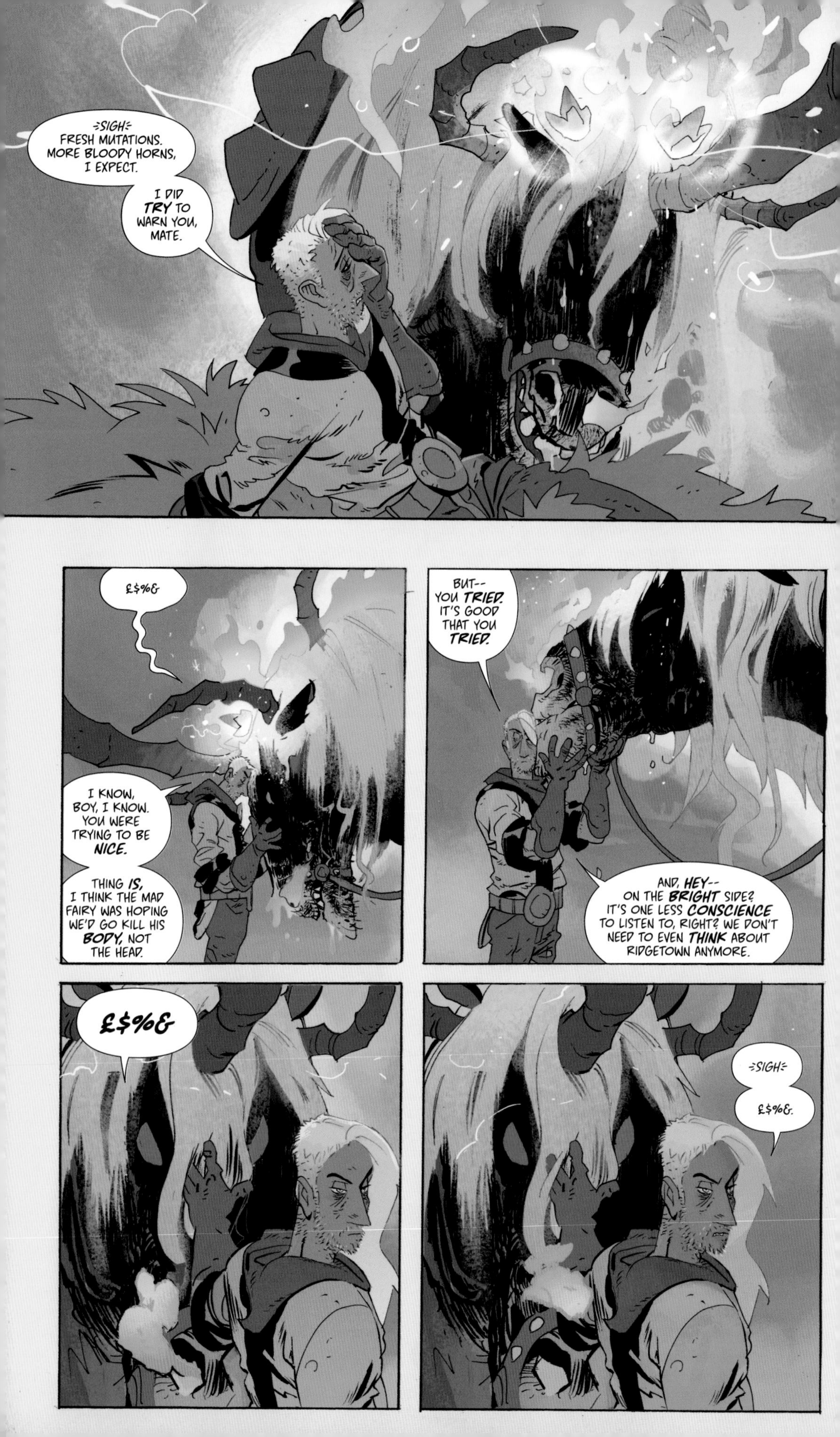

=SIGH= FRESH MUTATIONS. MORE BLOODY HORNS, I EXPECT.
I DID TRY TO WARN YOU, MATE.
£$%&
I KNOW, BOY, I KNOW. YOU WERE TRYING TO BE NICE.
THING IS, I THINK THE MAD FAIRY WAS HOPING WE'D GO KILL HIS BODY, NOT THE HEAD.
BUT-- YOU TRIED. IT'S GOOD THAT YOU TRIED.
AND, HEY-- ON THE BRIGHT SIDE? IT'S ONE LESS CONSCIENCE TO LISTEN TO, RIGHT? WE DON'T NEED TO EVEN THINK ABOUT RIDGETOWN ANYMORE.
£$%&
=SIGH=
£$%&.

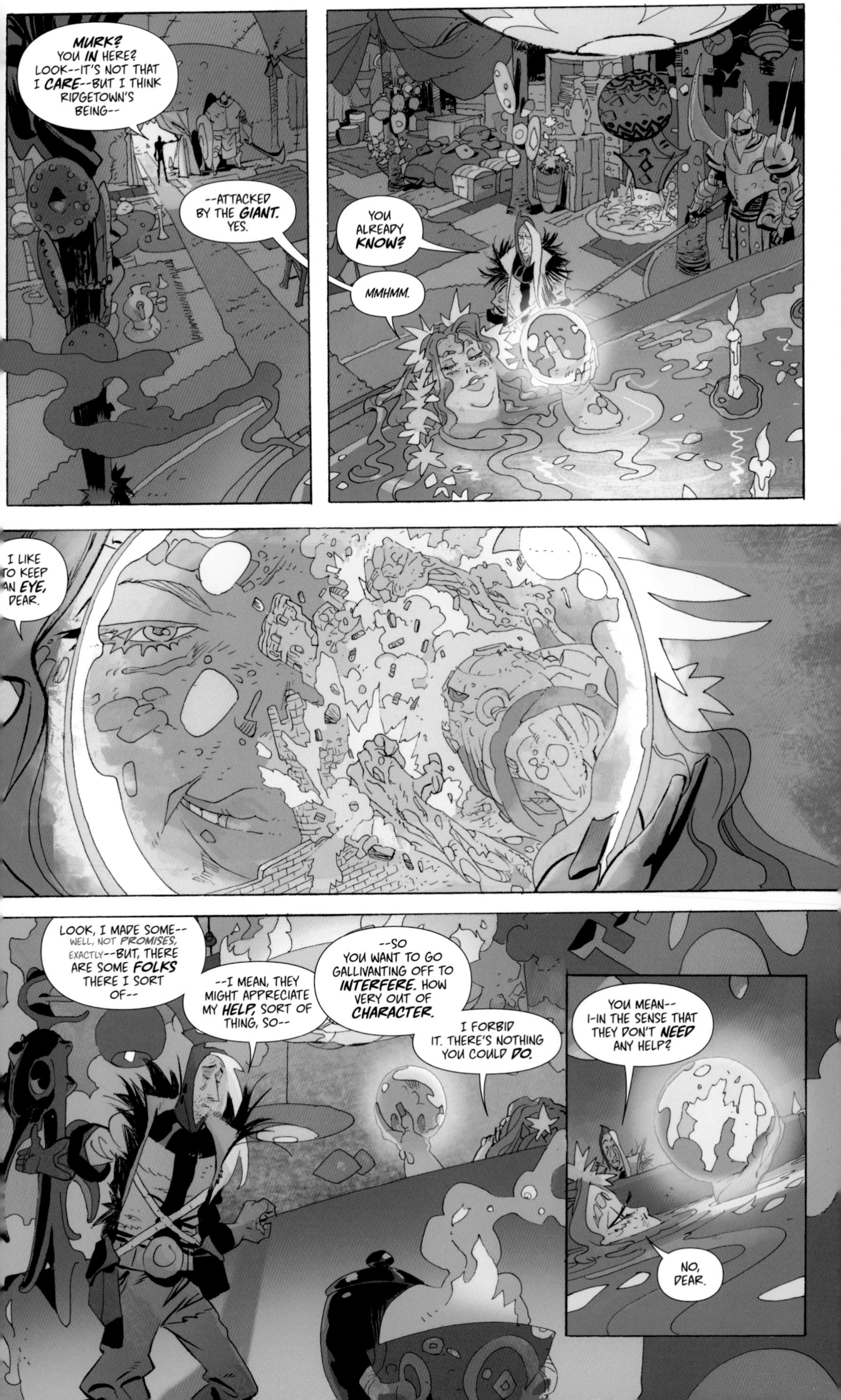
MURK? YOU IN HERE? LOOK--IT'S NOT THAT I CARE--BUT I THINK RIDGETOWN'S BEING--
--ATTACKED BY THE GIANT. YES.
YOU ALREADY KNOW?
MMHMM.
I LIKE TO KEEP AN EYE, DEAR.
LOOK, I MADE SOME-- WELL, NOT PROMISES, EXACTLY--BUT, THERE ARE SOME FOLKS THERE I SORT OF--
--I MEAN, THEY MIGHT APPRECIATE MY HELP, SORT OF THING, SO--
--SO YOU WANT TO GO GALLIVANTING OFF TO INTERFERE. HOW VERY OUT OF CHARACTER.
I FORBID IT. THERE'S NOTHING YOU COULD DO.
YOU MEAN-- I-IN THE SENSE THAT THEY DON'T NEED ANY HELP?
NO, DEAR.

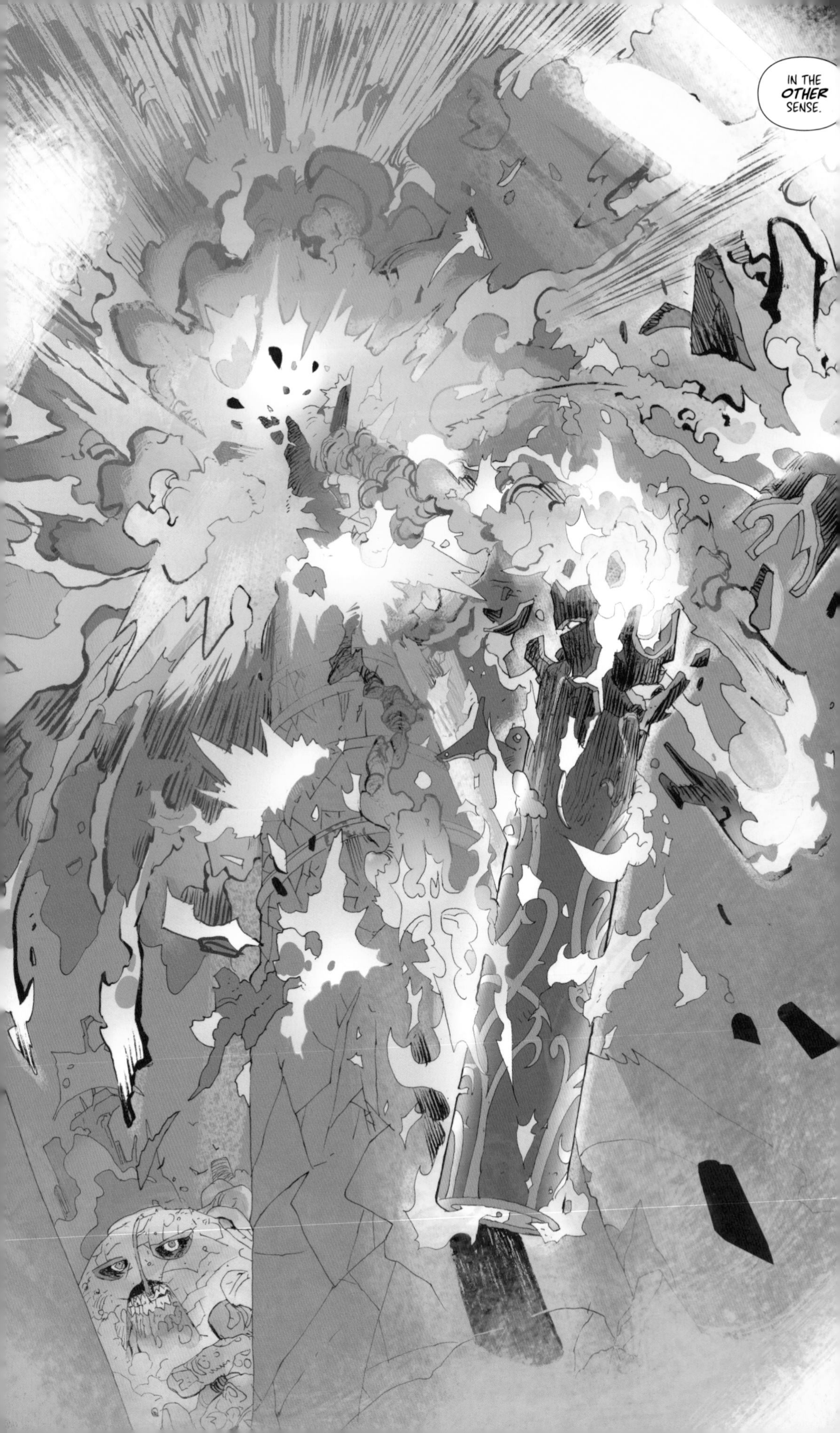
IN THE OTHER SENSE.

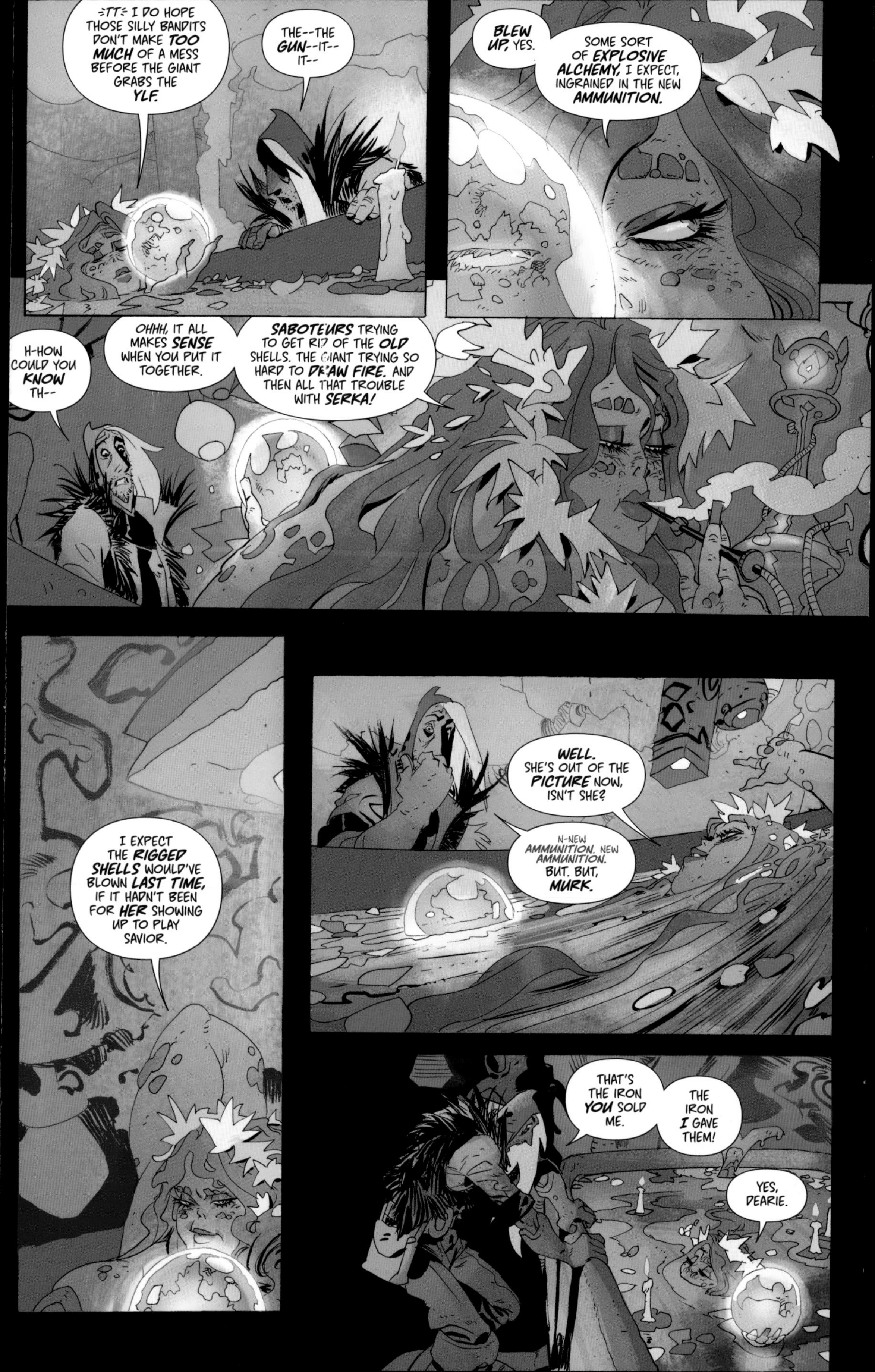

=TT= I DO HOPE THOSE SILLY BANDITS DON'T MAKE TOO MUCH OF A MESS BEFORE THE GIANT GRABS THE YLF.
THE--THE GUN--IT--IT--
BLEW UP, YES.
SOME SORT OF EXPLOSIVE ALCHEMY, I EXPECT, INGRAINED IN THE NEW AMMUNITION.
H-HOW COULD YOU KNOW TH--
OHHH, IT ALL MAKES SENSE WHEN YOU PUT IT TOGETHER.
SABOTEURS TRYING TO GET RID OF THE OLD SHELLS. THE GIANT TRYING SO HARD TO DRAW FIRE. AND THEN ALL THAT TROUBLE WITH SERKA!
I EXPECT THE RIGGED SHELLS WOULD'VE BLOWN LAST TIME, IF IT HADN'T BEEN FOR HER SHOWING UP TO PLAY SAVIOR.
WELL. SHE'S OUT OF THE PICTURE NOW, ISN'T SHE?
N-NEW AMMUNITION. NEW AMMUNITION. BUT. BUT, MURK.
THAT'S THE IRON YOU SOLD ME.
THE IRON I GAVE THEM!
YES, DEARIE.

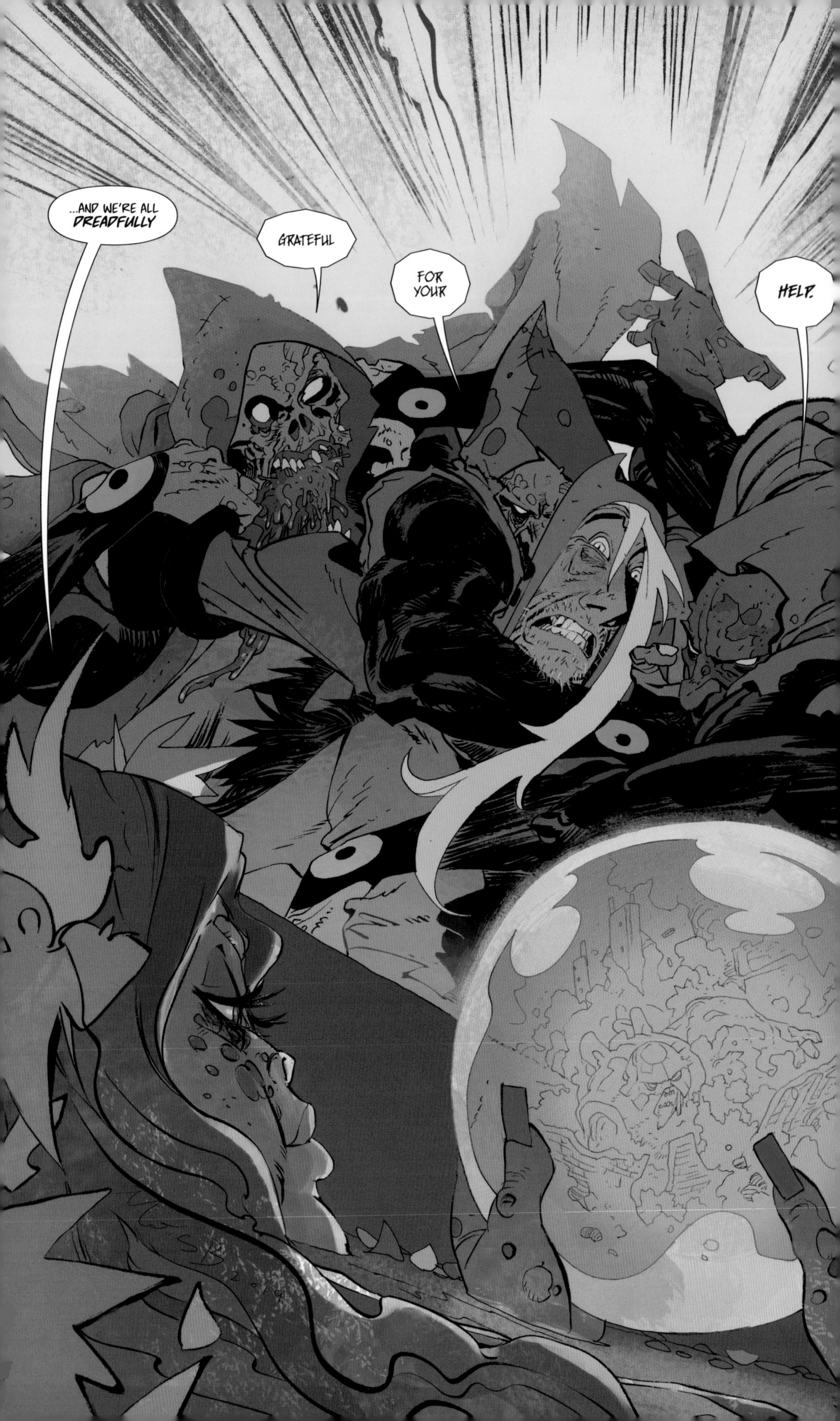
...AND WE'RE ALL DREADFULLY
GRATEFUL
FOR YOUR
HELP.

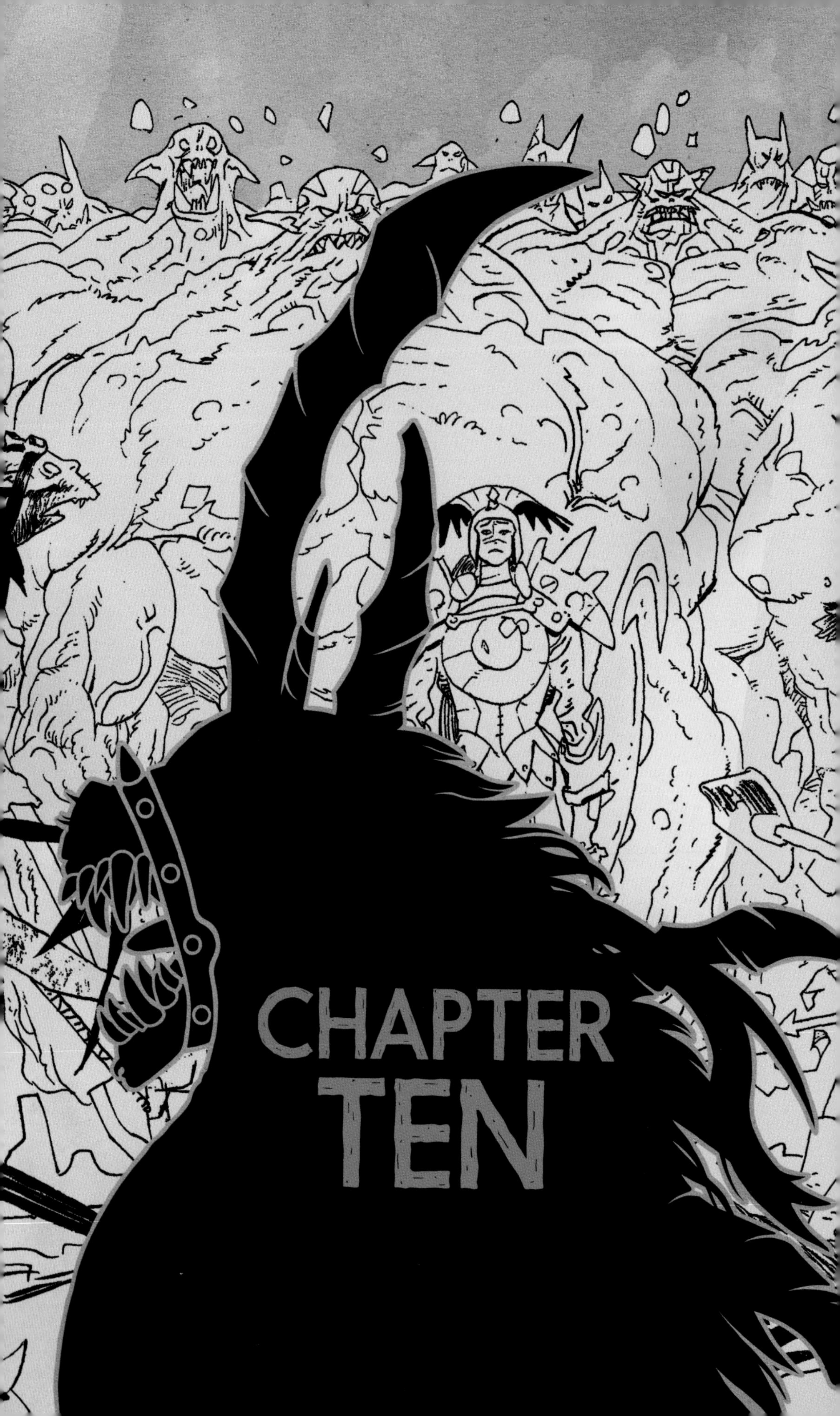
CHAPTER
TEN

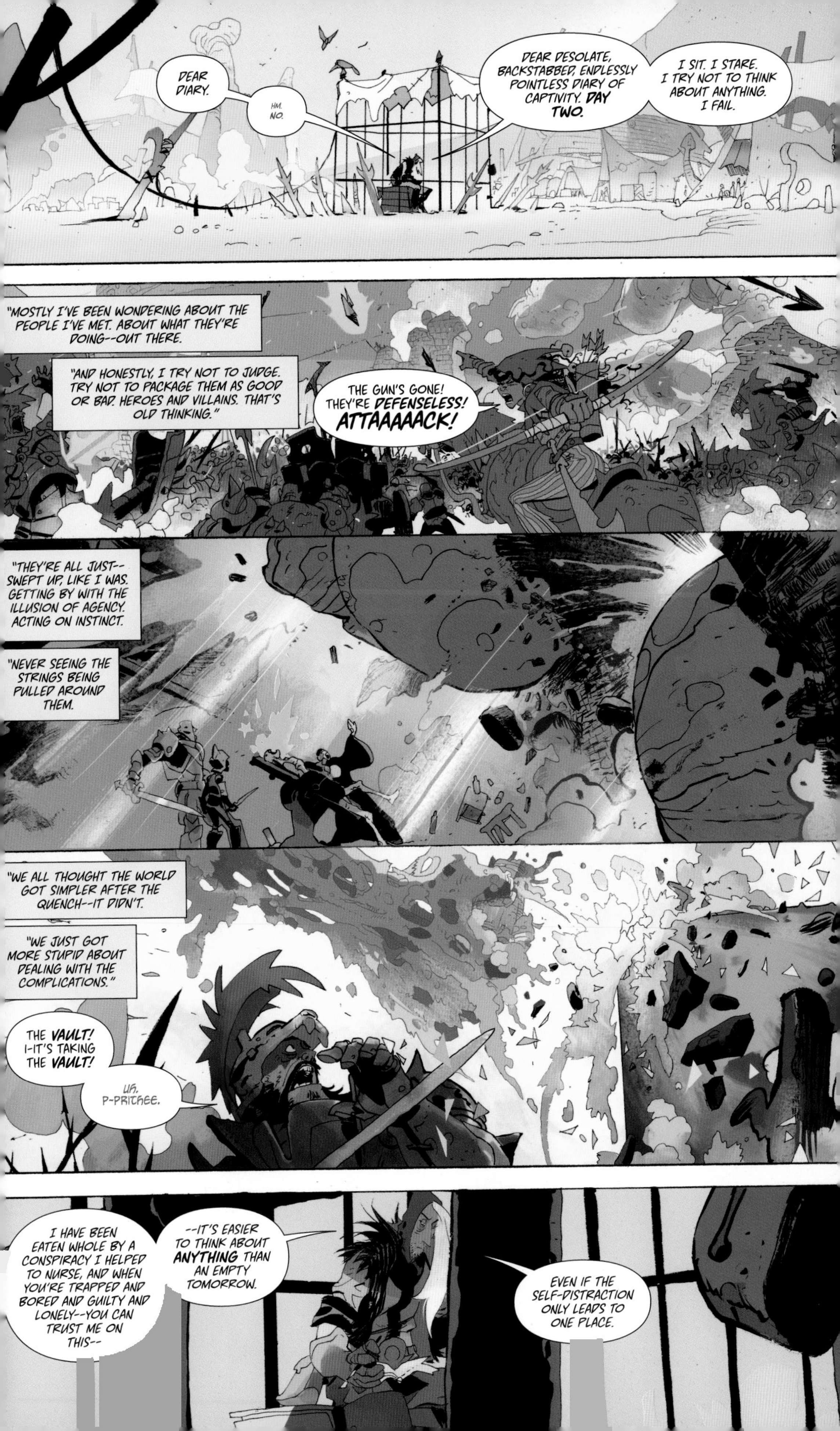
DEAR DIARY.
HM. NO.
DEAR DESOLATE, BACKSTABBED, ENDLESSLY POINTLESS DIARY OF CAPTIVITY. DAY TWO.
I SIT. I STARE. I TRY NOT TO THINK ABOUT ANYTHING. I FAIL.
"MOSTLY I'VE BEEN WONDERING ABOUT THE PEOPLE I'VE MET. ABOUT WHAT THEY'RE DOING--OUT THERE.
"AND HONESTLY, I TRY NOT TO JUDGE. TRY NOT TO PACKAGE THEM AS GOOD OR BAD. HEROES AND VILLAINS. THAT'S OLD THINKING."
THE GUN'S GONE! THEY'RE DEFENSELESS! ATTAAAAACK!
"THEY'RE ALL JUST--SWEPT UP, LIKE I WAS. GETTING BY WITH THE ILLUSION OF AGENCY. ACTING ON INSTINCT.
"NEVER SEEING THE STRINGS BEING PULLED AROUND THEM.
"WE ALL THOUGHT THE WORLD GOT SIMPLER AFTER THE QUENCH--IT DIDN'T.
"WE JUST GOT MORE STUPID ABOUT DEALING WITH THE COMPLICATIONS."
THE VAULT! I-IT'S TAKING THE VAULT!
UH. P-PRITHEE.
I HAVE BEEN EATEN WHOLE BY A CONSPIRACY I HELPED TO NURSE, AND WHEN YOU'RE TRAPPED AND BORED AND GUILTY AND LONELY--YOU CAN TRUST ME ON THIS--
--IT'S EASIER TO THINK ABOUT ANYTHING THAN AN EMPTY TOMORROW.
EVEN IF THE SELF-DISTRACTION ONLY LEADS TO ONE PLACE.

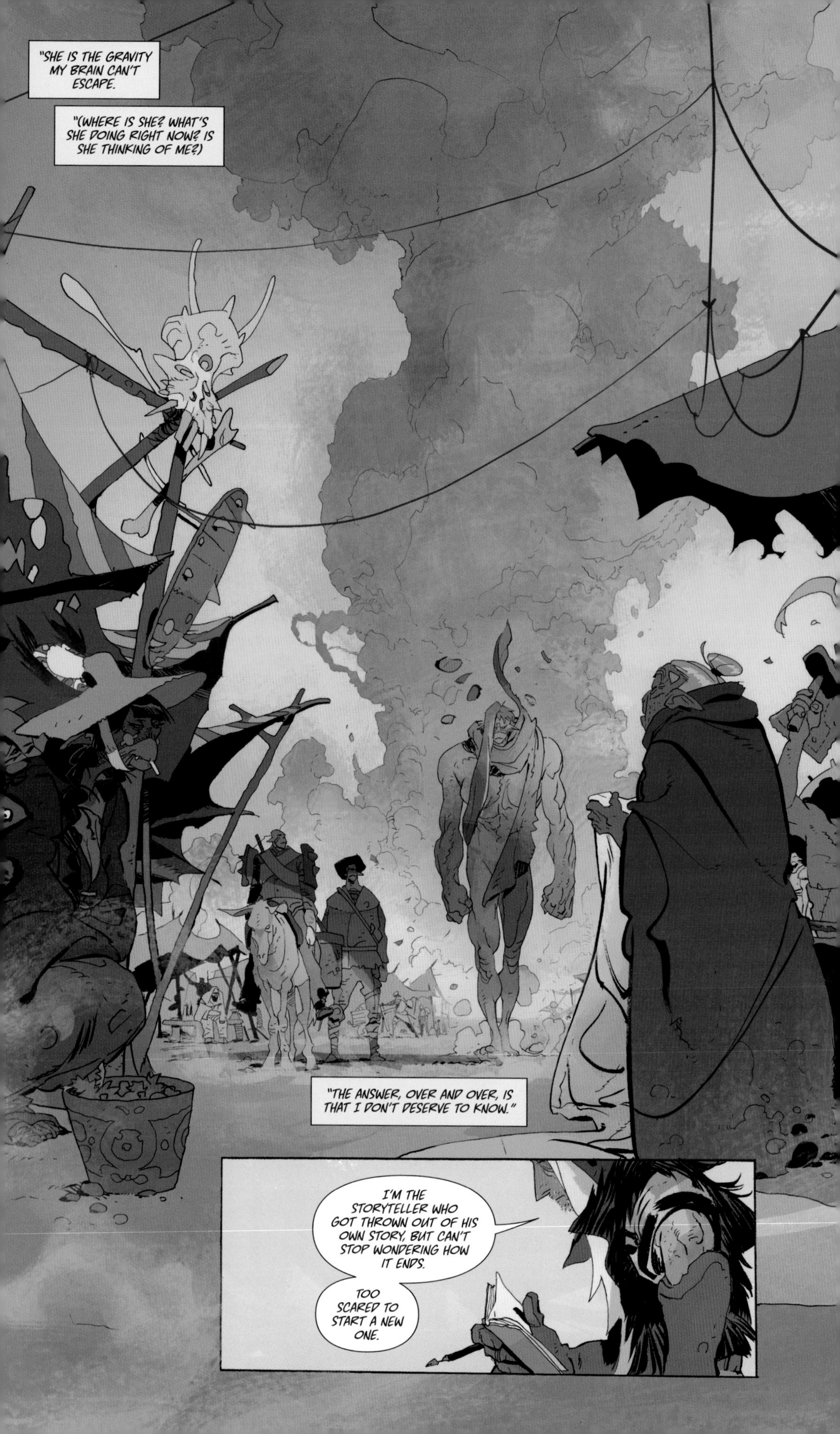
"SHE IS THE GRAVITY MY BRAIN CAN'T ESCAPE.
"(WHERE IS SHE? WHAT'S SHE DOING RIGHT NOW? IS SHE THINKING OF ME?)
"THE ANSWER, OVER AND OVER, IS THAT I DON'T DESERVE TO KNOW."
I'M THE STORYTELLER WHO GOT THROWN OUT OF HIS OWN STORY, BUT CAN'T STOP WONDERING HOW IT ENDS.
TOO SCARED TO START A NEW ONE.

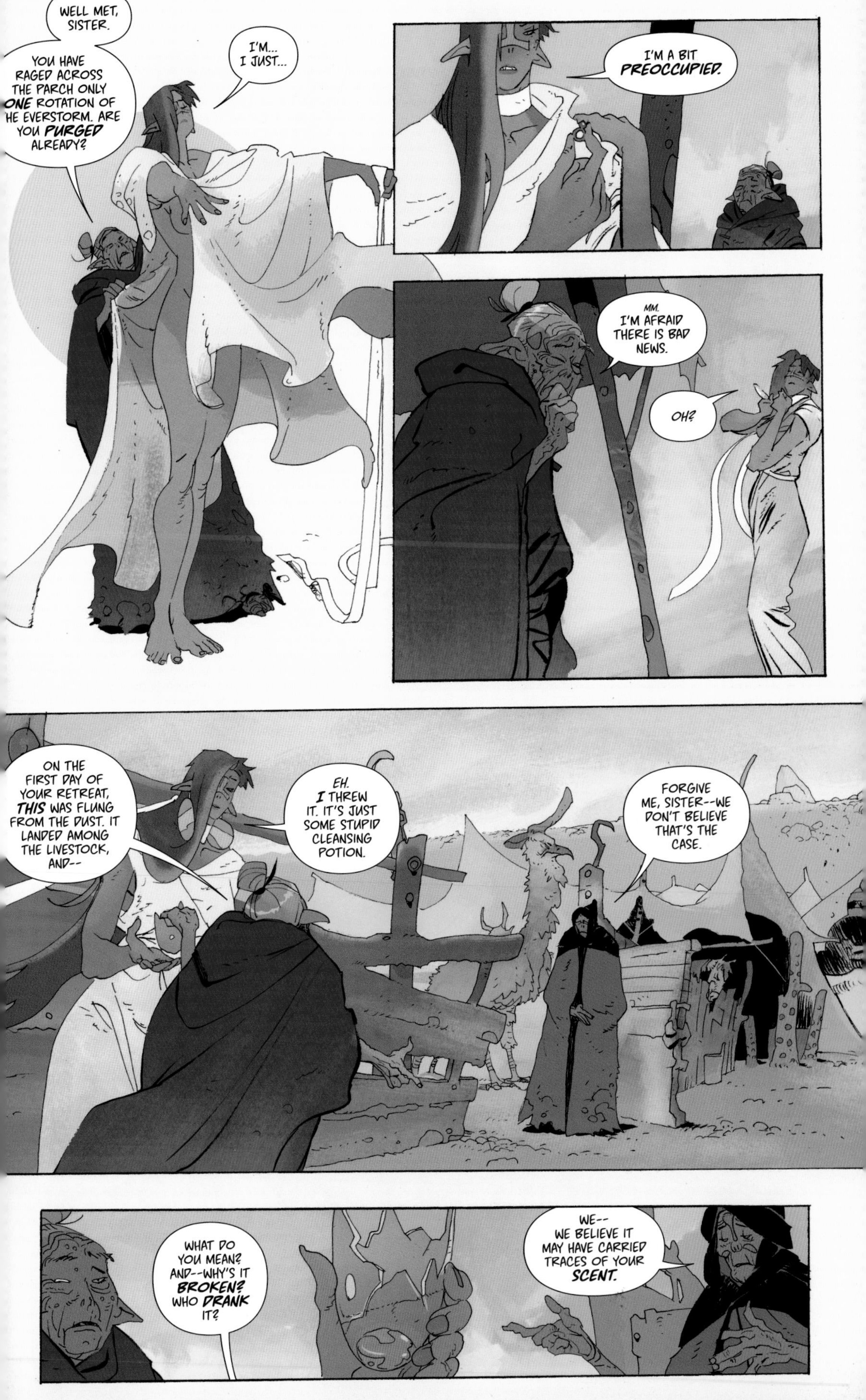
WELL MET, SISTER.
YOU HAVE RAGED ACROSS THE PARCH ONLY **ONE** ROTATION OF HE EVERSTORM. ARE YOU **PURGED** ALREADY?
I'M... I JUST...
I'M A BIT **PREOCCUPIED.**
MM. I'M AFRAID THERE IS BAD NEWS.
OH?
ON THE FIRST DAY OF YOUR RETREAT, **THIS** WAS FLUNG FROM THE DUST. IT LANDED AMONG THE LIVESTOCK, AND--
EH. **I** THREW IT. IT'S JUST SOME STUPID CLEANSING POTION.
FORGIVE ME, SISTER--WE DON'T BELIEVE THAT'S THE CASE.
WHAT DO YOU MEAN? AND--WHY'S IT **BROKEN?** WHO **DRANK** IT?
WE-- WE BELIEVE IT MAY HAVE CARRIED TRACES OF YOUR **SCENT.**

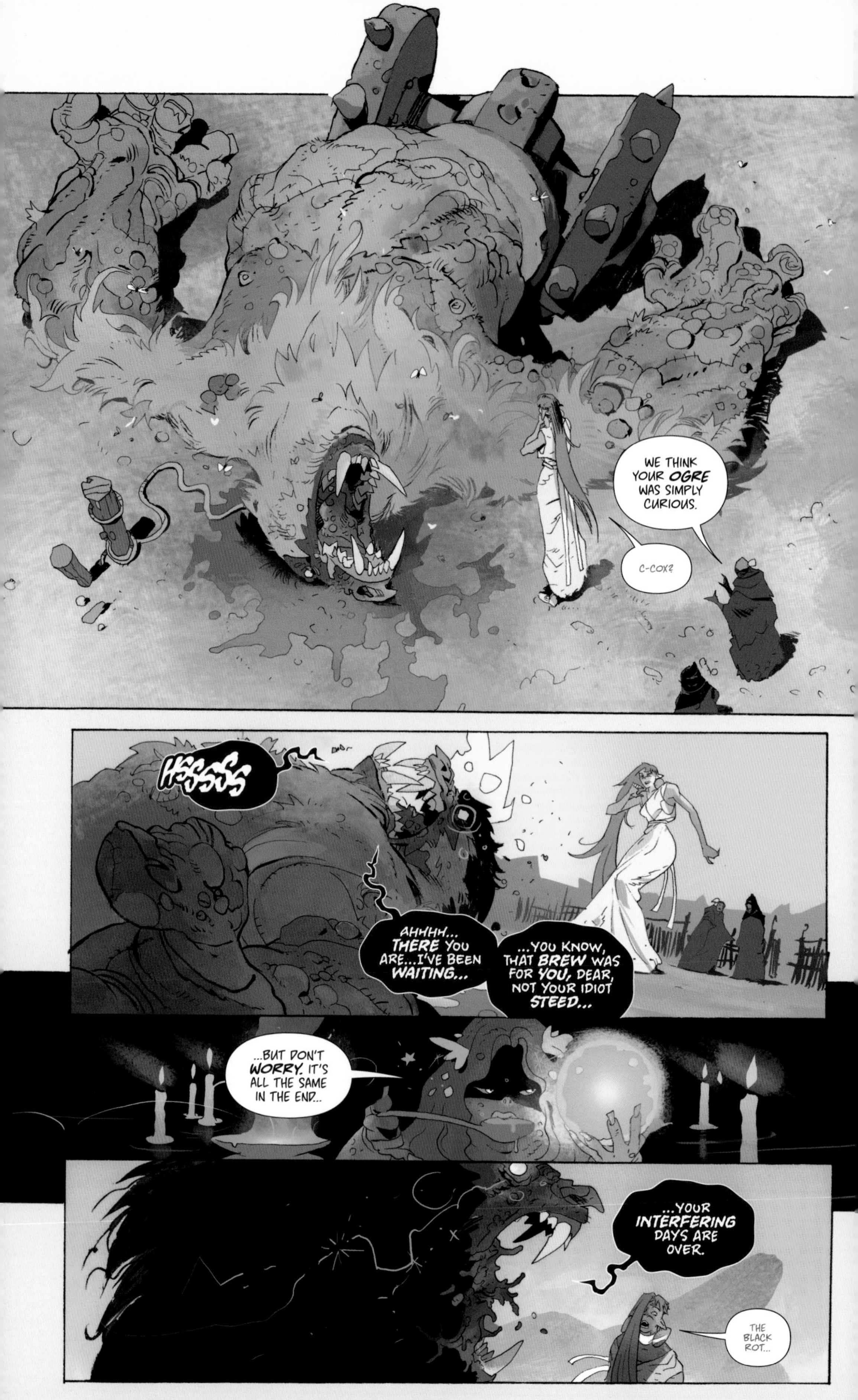
WE THINK YOUR OGRE WAS SIMPLY CURIOUS.
C-COX?
HSSSSS
AHHHH... THERE YOU ARE...I'VE BEEN WAITING...
...YOU KNOW, THAT BREW WAS FOR YOU, DEAR, NOT YOUR IDIOT STEED...
...BUT DON'T WORRY. IT'S ALL THE SAME IN THE END...
...YOUR INTERFERING DAYS ARE OVER.
THE BLACK ROT...

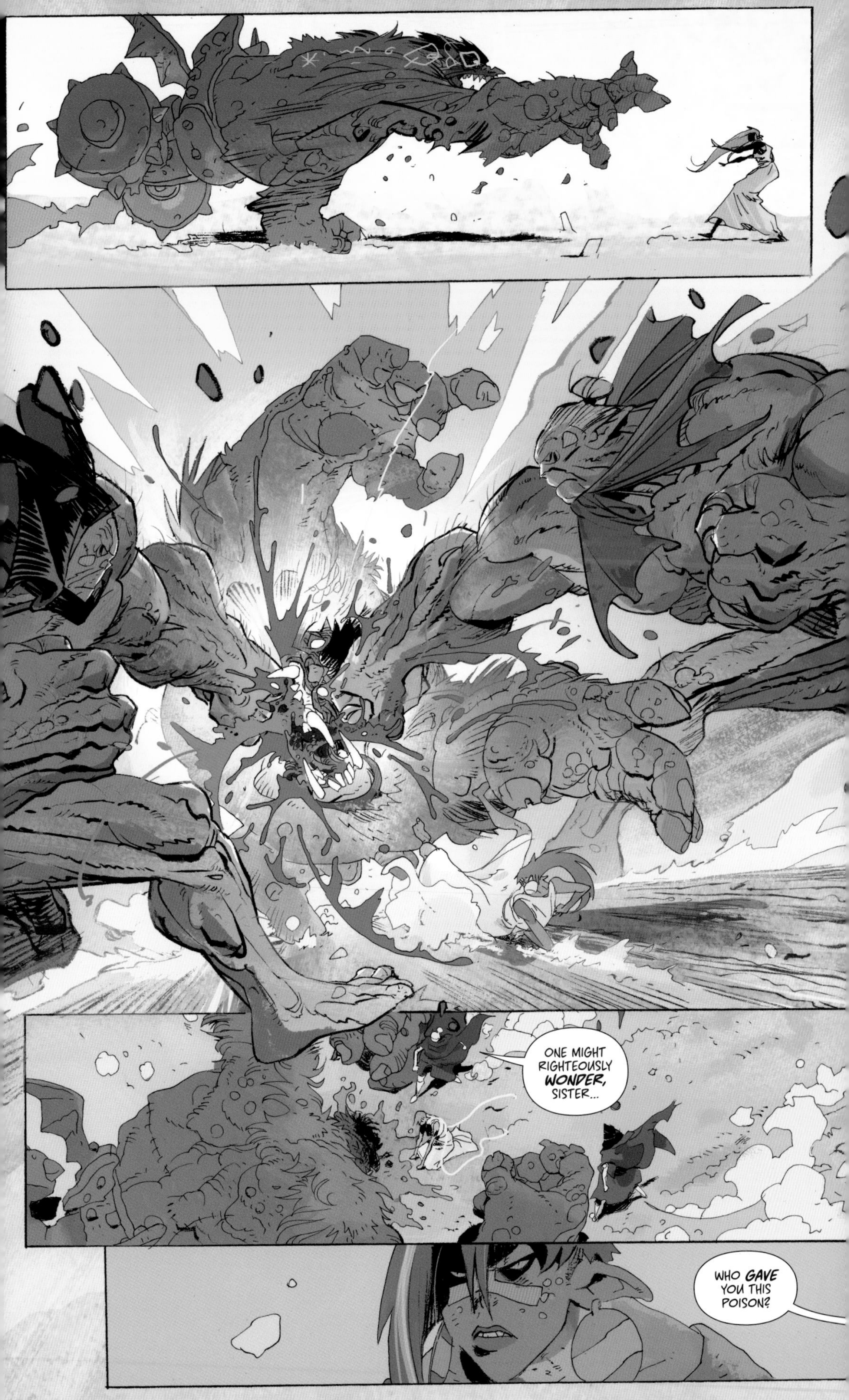
ONE MIGHT RIGHTEOUSLY **WONDER,** SISTER...
WHO **GAVE** YOU THIS POISON?

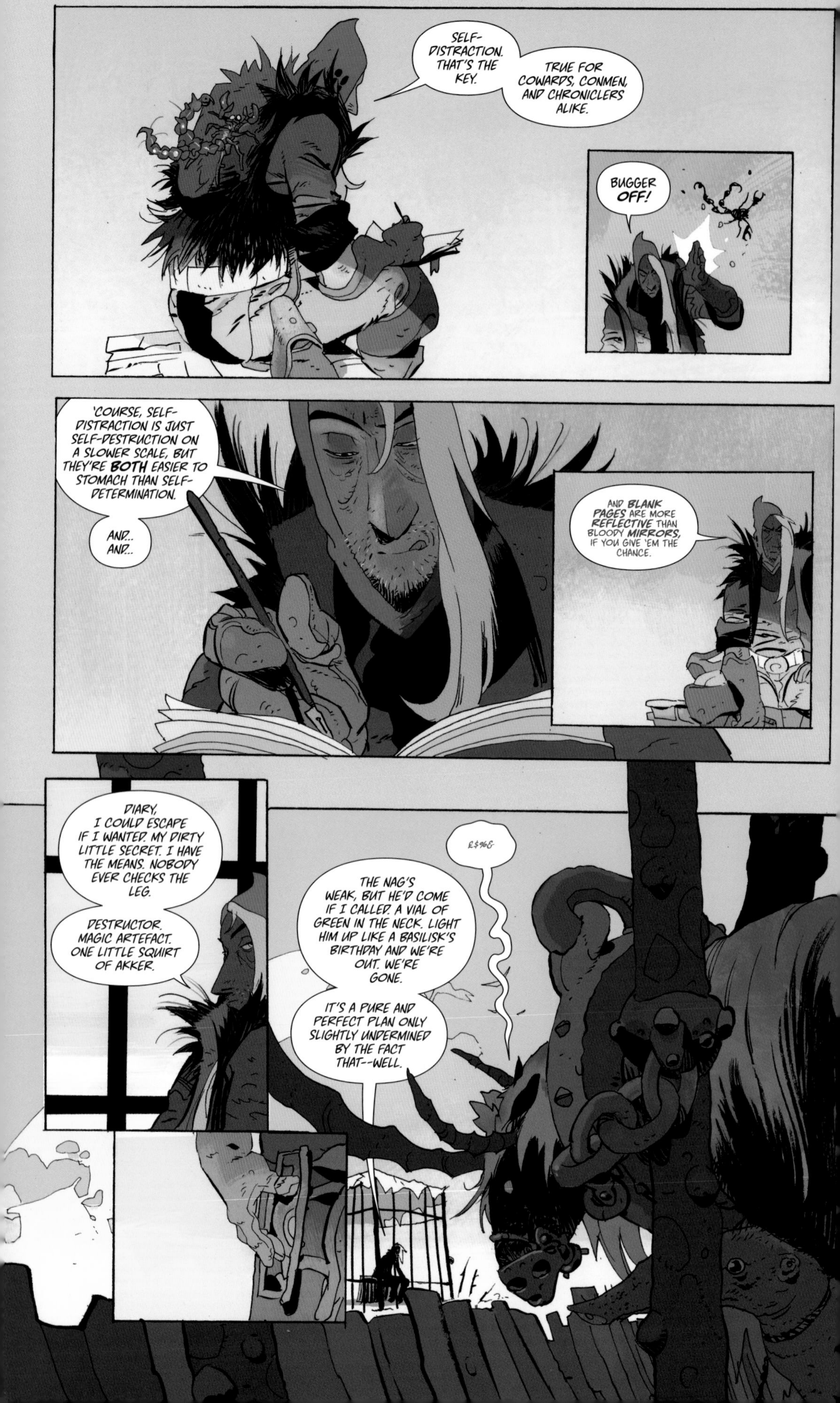
SELF-DISTRACTION. THAT'S THE KEY.
TRUE FOR COWARDS, CONMEN, AND CHRONICLERS ALIKE.
BUGGER OFF!
'COURSE, SELF-DISTRACTION IS JUST SELF-DESTRUCTION ON A SLOWER SCALE, BUT THEY'RE BOTH EASIER TO STOMACH THAN SELF-DETERMINATION.
AND.. AND..
AND BLANK PAGES ARE MORE REFLECTIVE THAN BLOODY MIRRORS, IF YOU GIVE 'EM THE CHANCE.
DIARY, I COULD ESCAPE IF I WANTED. MY DIRTY LITTLE SECRET. I HAVE THE MEANS. NOBODY EVER CHECKS THE LEG.
DESTRUCTOR. MAGIC ARTEFACT. ONE LITTLE SQUIRT OF AKKER.
THE NAG'S WEAK, BUT HE'D COME IF I CALLED. A VIAL OF GREEN IN THE NECK. LIGHT HIM UP LIKE A BASILISK'S BIRTHDAY AND WE'RE OUT. WE'RE GONE.
IT'S A PURE AND PERFECT PLAN ONLY SLIGHTLY UNDERMINED BY THE FACT THAT--WELL.
£$%&

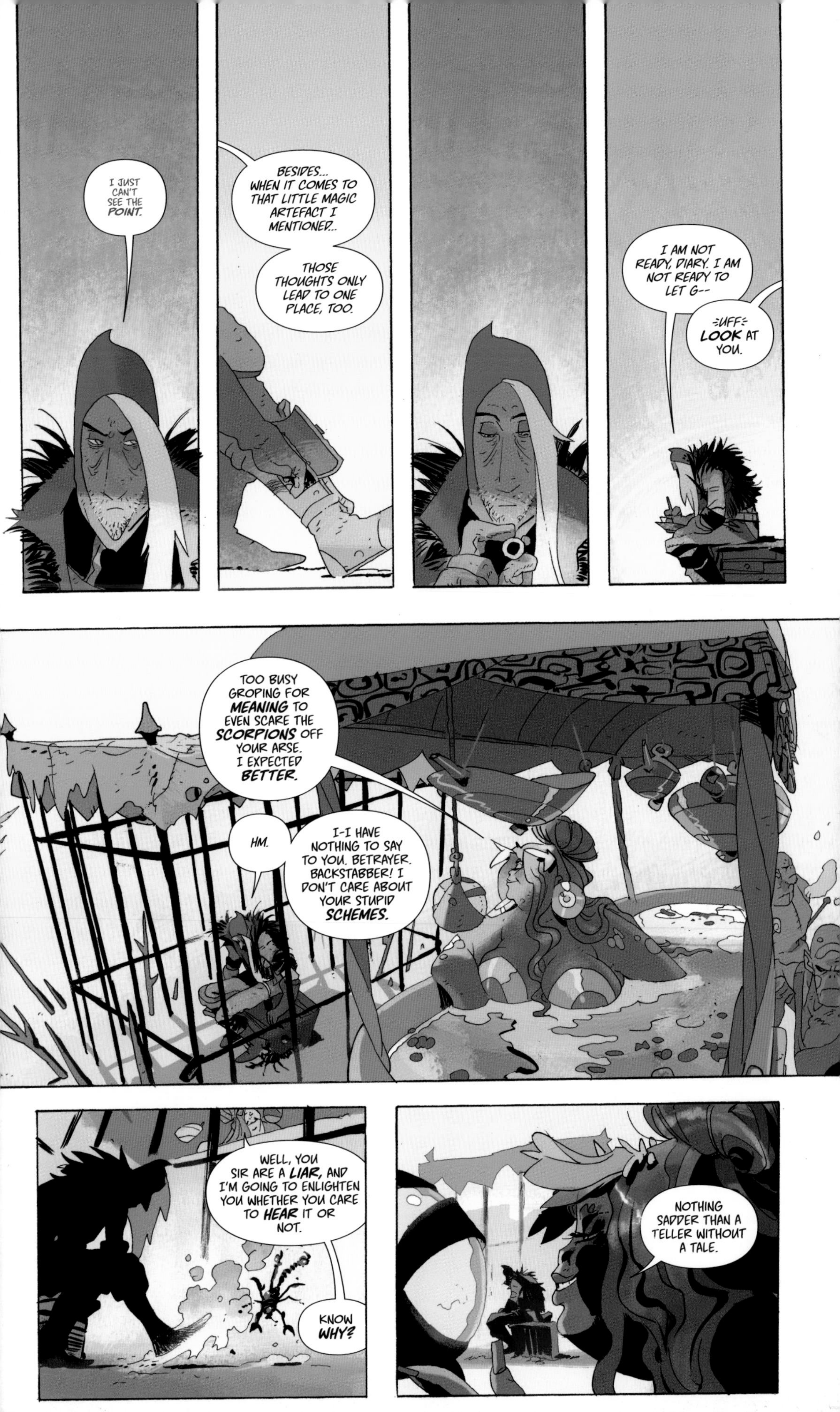

I JUST CAN'T SEE THE POINT.
BESIDES... WHEN IT COMES TO THAT LITTLE MAGIC ARTEFACT I MENTIONED...
THOSE THOUGHTS ONLY LEAD TO ONE PLACE, TOO.
I AM NOT READY, DIARY. I AM NOT READY TO LET G--
UFF LOOK AT YOU.
TOO BUSY GROPING FOR MEANING TO EVEN SCARE THE SCORPIONS OFF YOUR ARSE. I EXPECTED BETTER.
HM.
I-I HAVE NOTHING TO SAY TO YOU. BETRAYER. BACKSTABBER! I DON'T CARE ABOUT YOUR STUPID SCHEMES.
WELL, YOU SIR ARE A LIAR, AND I'M GOING TO ENLIGHTEN YOU WHETHER YOU CARE TO HEAR IT OR NOT.
KNOW WHY?
NOTHING SADDER THAN A TELLER WITHOUT A TALE.

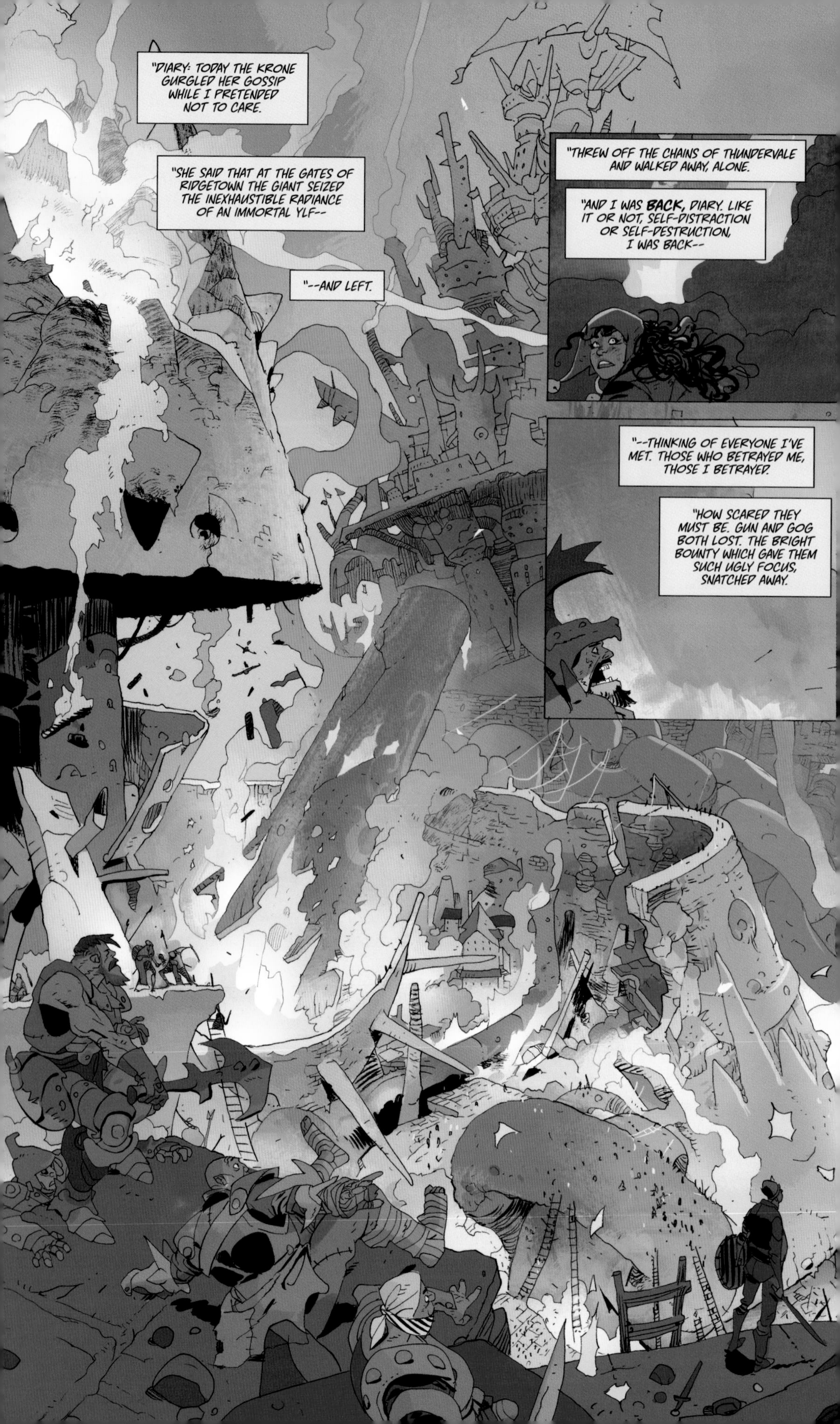
"DIARY: TODAY THE KRONE GURGLED HER GOSSIP WHILE I PRETENDED NOT TO CARE.
"SHE SAID THAT AT THE GATES OF RIDGETOWN THE GIANT SEIZED THE INEXHAUSTIBLE RADIANCE OF AN IMMORTAL YLF--
"--AND LEFT.
"THREW OFF THE CHAINS OF THUNDERVALE AND WALKED AWAY, ALONE.
"AND I WAS **BACK,** DIARY. LIKE IT OR NOT, SELF-DISTRACTION OR SELF-DESTRUCTION, I WAS BACK--
"--THINKING OF EVERYONE I'VE MET. THOSE WHO BETRAYED ME, THOSE I BETRAYED.
"HOW SCARED THEY MUST BE. GUN AND GOG BOTH LOST. THE BRIGHT BOUNTY WHICH GAVE THEM SUCH UGLY FOCUS, SNATCHED AWAY.

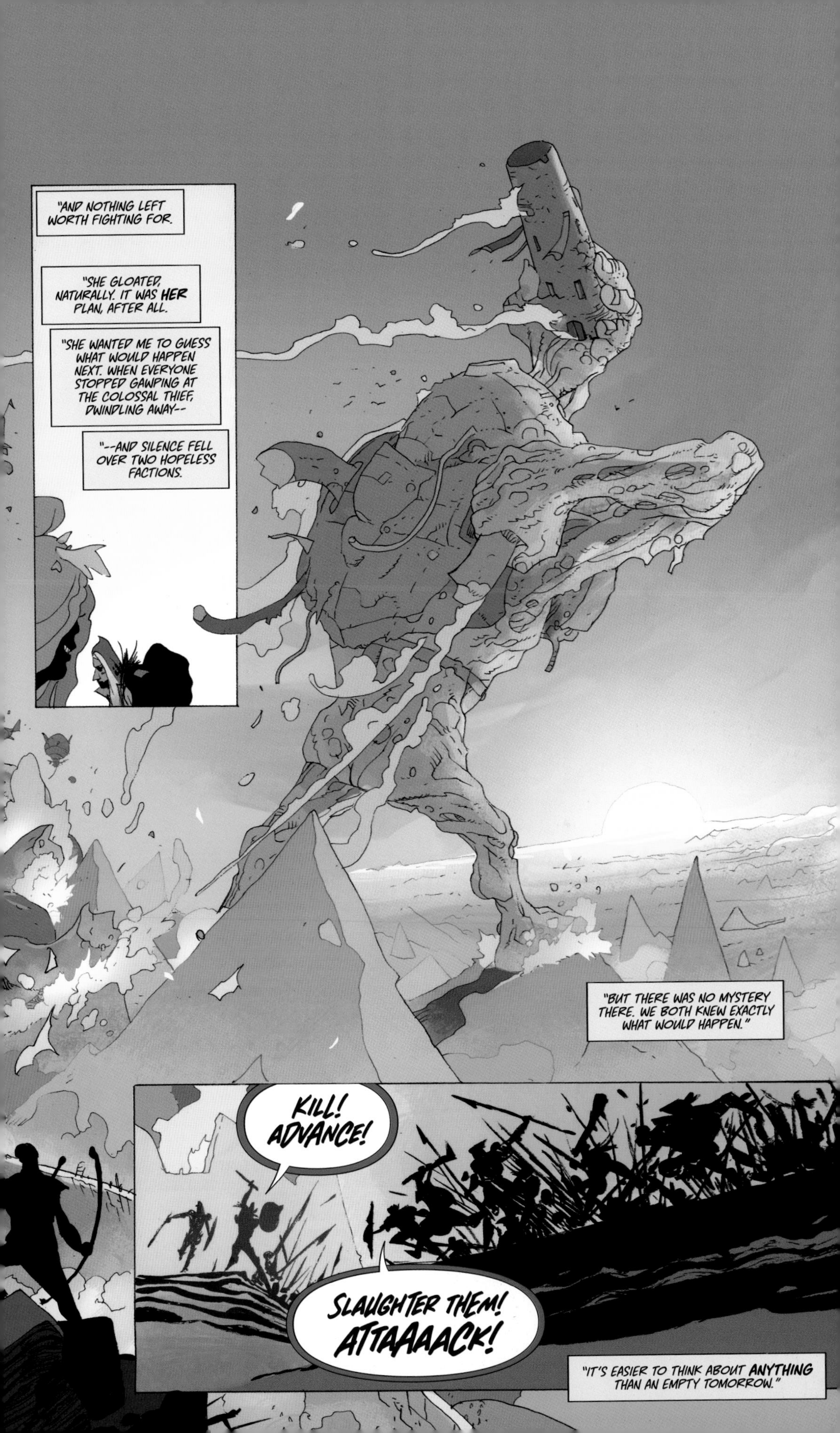
"AND NOTHING LEFT WORTH FIGHTING FOR.
"SHE GLOATED, NATURALLY. IT WAS HER PLAN, AFTER ALL.
"SHE WANTED ME TO GUESS WHAT WOULD HAPPEN NEXT. WHEN EVERYONE STOPPED GAWPING AT THE COLOSSAL THIEF, DWINDLING AWAY--
"--AND SILENCE FELL OVER TWO HOPELESS FACTIONS.
"BUT THERE WAS NO MYSTERY THERE. WE BOTH KNEW EXACTLY WHAT WOULD HAPPEN."
KILL! ADVANCE!
SLAUGHTER THEM! ATTAAAACK!
"IT'S EASIER TO THINK ABOUT ANYTHING THAN AN EMPTY TOMORROW."

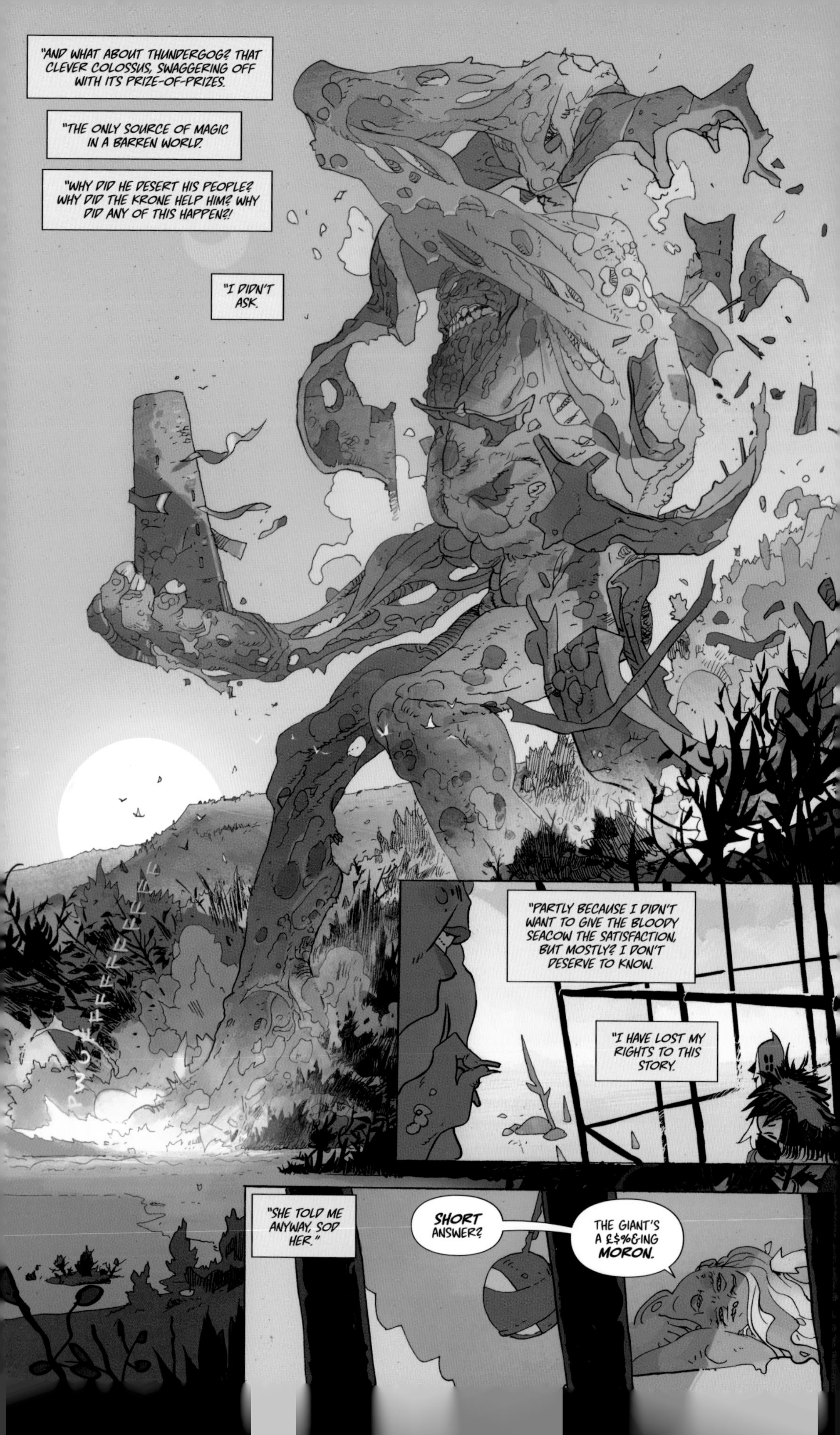
"AND WHAT ABOUT THUNDERGOG? THAT CLEVER COLOSSUS, SWAGGERING OFF WITH ITS PRIZE-OF-PRIZES.
"THE ONLY SOURCE OF MAGIC IN A BARREN WORLD.
"WHY DID HE DESERT HIS PEOPLE? WHY DID THE KRONE HELP HIM? WHY DID ANY OF THIS HAPPEN?!
"I DIDN'T ASK.
PWOFFFFFFFFF
"PARTLY BECAUSE I DIDN'T WANT TO GIVE THE BLOODY SEACOW THE SATISFACTION, BUT MOSTLY? I DON'T DESERVE TO KNOW.
"I HAVE LOST MY RIGHTS TO THIS STORY.
"SHE TOLD ME ANYWAY, SOD HER."
SHORT ANSWER?
THE GIANT'S A £$%&ING MORON.

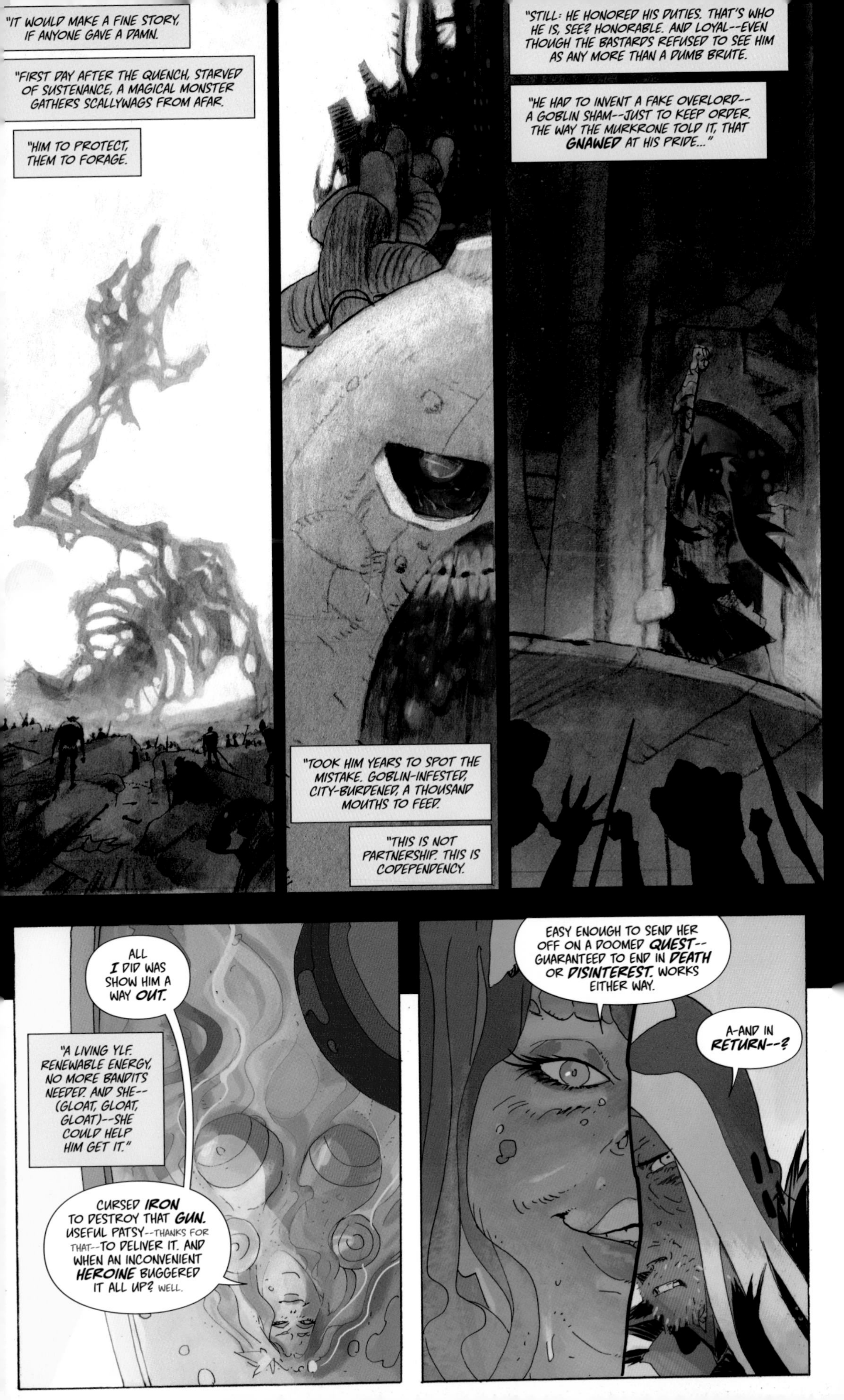
"IT WOULD MAKE A FINE STORY, IF ANYONE GAVE A DAMN.
"FIRST DAY AFTER THE QUENCH, STARVED OF SUSTENANCE, A MAGICAL MONSTER GATHERS SCALLYWAGS FROM AFAR.
"HIM TO PROTECT, THEM TO FORAGE.
"TOOK HIM YEARS TO SPOT THE MISTAKE. GOBLIN-INFESTED, CITY-BURDENED, A THOUSAND MOUTHS TO FEED.
"THIS IS NOT PARTNERSHIP. THIS IS CODEPENDENCY.
"STILL: HE HONORED HIS DUTIES. THAT'S WHO HE IS, SEE? HONORABLE. AND LOYAL--EVEN THOUGH THE BASTARDS REFUSED TO SEE HIM AS ANY MORE THAN A DUMB BRUTE.
"HE HAD TO INVENT A FAKE OVERLORD--A GOBLIN SHAM--JUST TO KEEP ORDER. THE WAY THE MURKRONE TOLD IT, THAT GNAWED AT HIS PRIDE..."
ALL I DID WAS SHOW HIM A WAY OUT.
"A LIVING YLF. RENEWABLE ENERGY, NO MORE BANDITS NEEDED. AND SHE--(GLOAT, GLOAT, GLOAT)--SHE COULD HELP HIM GET IT."
CURSED IRON TO DESTROY THAT GUN. USEFUL PATSY--THANKS FOR THAT--TO DELIVER IT. AND WHEN AN INCONVENIENT HEROINE BUGGERED IT ALL UP? WELL.
EASY ENOUGH TO SEND HER OFF ON A DOOMED QUEST--GUARANTEED TO END IN DEATH OR DISINTEREST. WORKS EITHER WAY.
A-AND IN RETURN--?

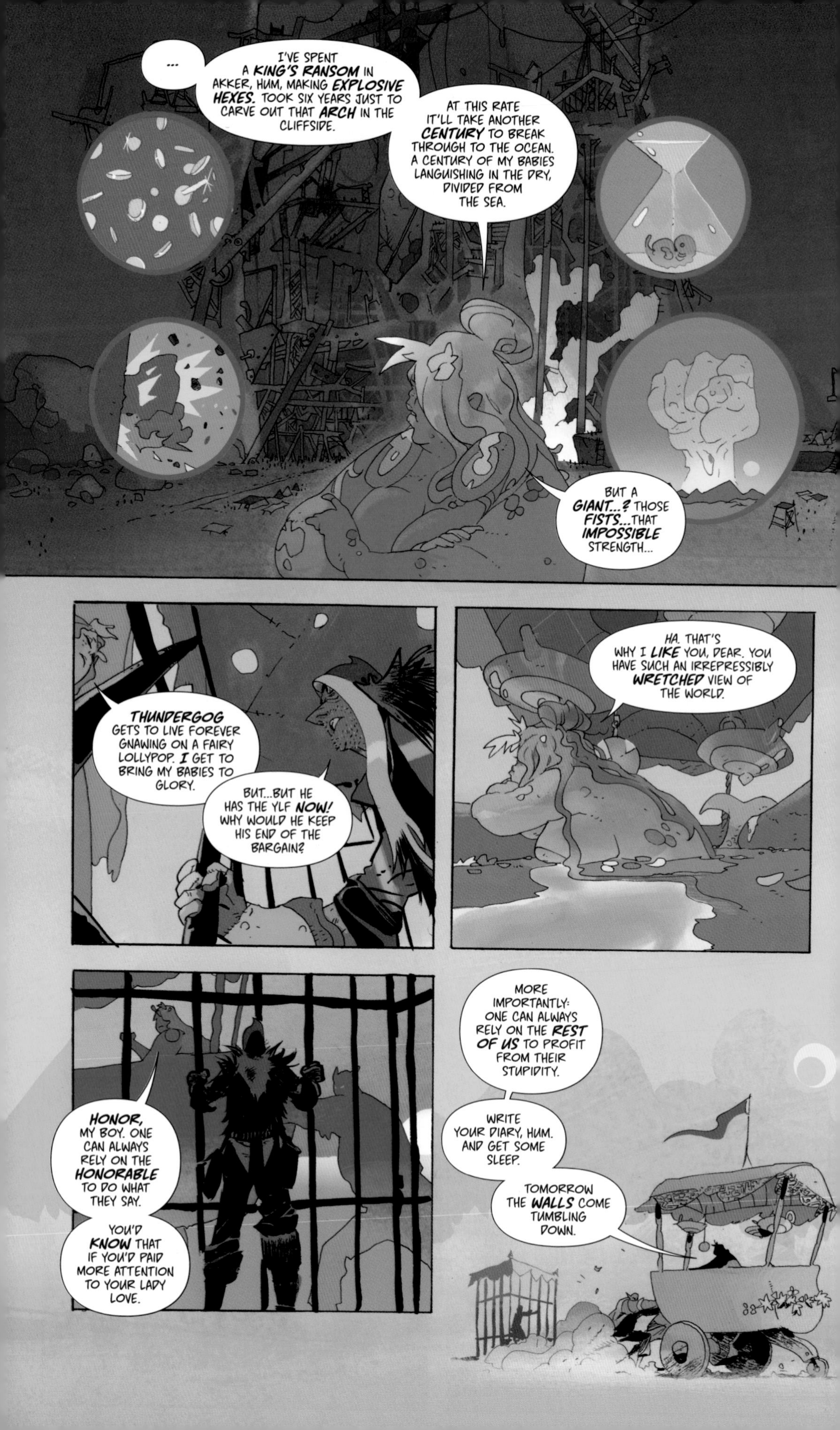
...
I'VE SPENT A KING'S RANSOM IN AKKER, HUM, MAKING EXPLOSIVE HEXES. TOOK SIX YEARS JUST TO CARVE OUT THAT ARCH IN THE CLIFFSIDE.
AT THIS RATE IT'LL TAKE ANOTHER CENTURY TO BREAK THROUGH TO THE OCEAN. A CENTURY OF MY BABIES LANGUISHING IN THE DRY, DIVIDED FROM THE SEA.
BUT A GIANT...? THOSE FISTS...THAT IMPOSSIBLE STRENGTH...
THUNDERGOG GETS TO LIVE FOREVER GNAWING ON A FAIRY LOLLYPOP. I GET TO BRING MY BABIES TO GLORY.
BUT...BUT HE HAS THE YLF NOW! WHY WOULD HE KEEP HIS END OF THE BARGAIN?
HA. THAT'S WHY I LIKE YOU, DEAR. YOU HAVE SUCH AN IRREPRESSIBLY WRETCHED VIEW OF THE WORLD.
HONOR, MY BOY. ONE CAN ALWAYS RELY ON THE HONORABLE TO DO WHAT THEY SAY.
YOU'D KNOW THAT IF YOU'D PAID MORE ATTENTION TO YOUR LADY LOVE.
MORE IMPORTANTLY: ONE CAN ALWAYS RELY ON THE REST OF US TO PROFIT FROM THEIR STUPIDITY.
WRITE YOUR DIARY, HUM. AND GET SOME SLEEP.
TOMORROW THE WALLS COME TUMBLING DOWN.

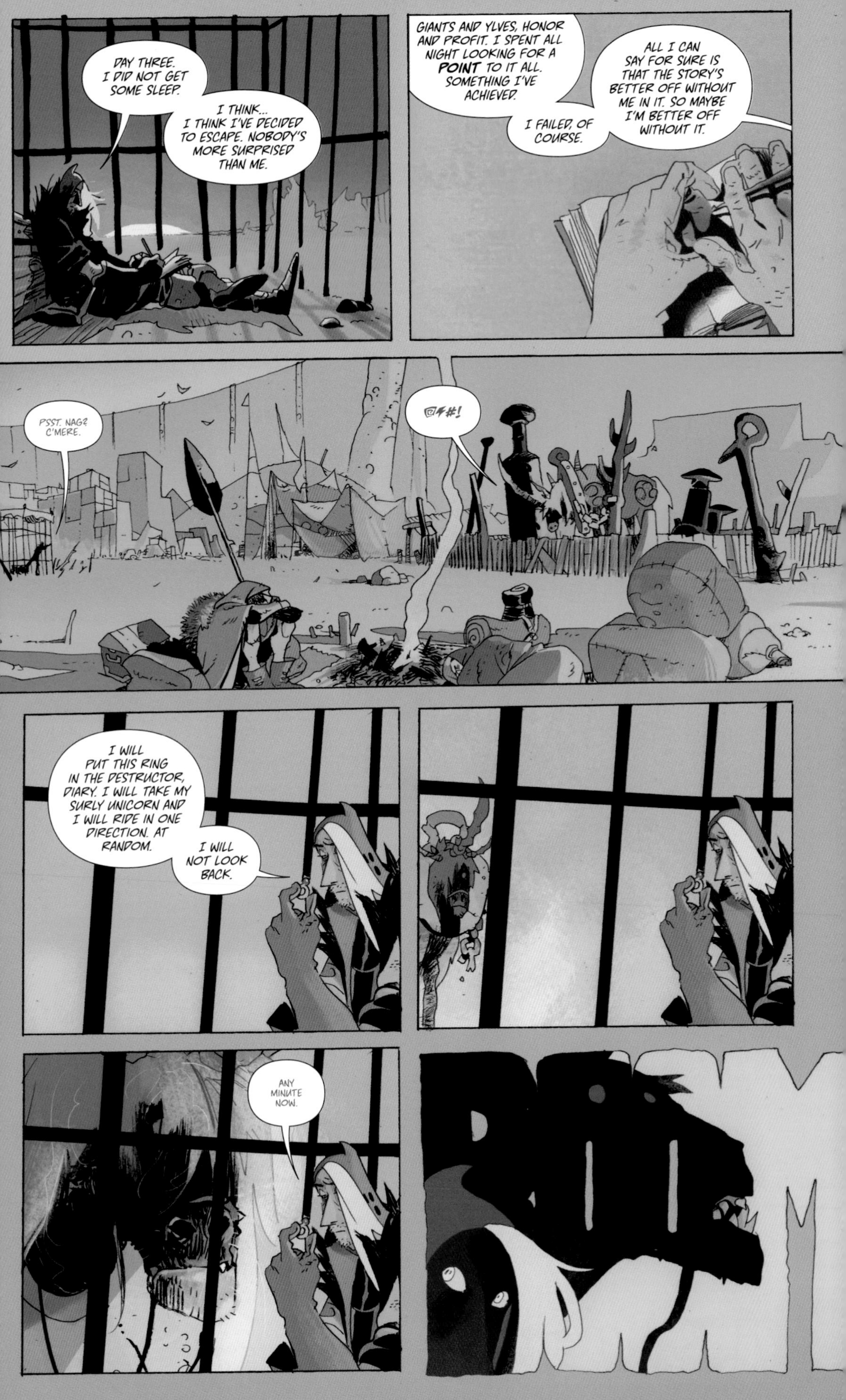
DAY THREE. I DID NOT GET SOME SLEEP.
I THINK... I THINK I'VE DECIDED TO ESCAPE. NOBODY'S MORE SURPRISED THAN ME.
GIANTS AND YLVES, HONOR AND PROFIT. I SPENT ALL NIGHT LOOKING FOR A **POINT** TO IT ALL. SOMETHING I'VE ACHIEVED.
I FAILED, OF COURSE.
ALL I CAN SAY FOR SURE IS THAT THE STORY'S BETTER OFF WITHOUT ME IN IT. SO MAYBE I'M BETTER OFF WITHOUT IT.
PSST. NAG? C'MERE.
I WILL PUT THIS RING IN THE DESTRUCTOR, DIARY. I WILL TAKE MY SURLY UNICORN AND I WILL RIDE IN ONE DIRECTION. AT RANDOM.
I WILL NOT LOOK BACK.
ANY MINUTE NOW.
BOOM

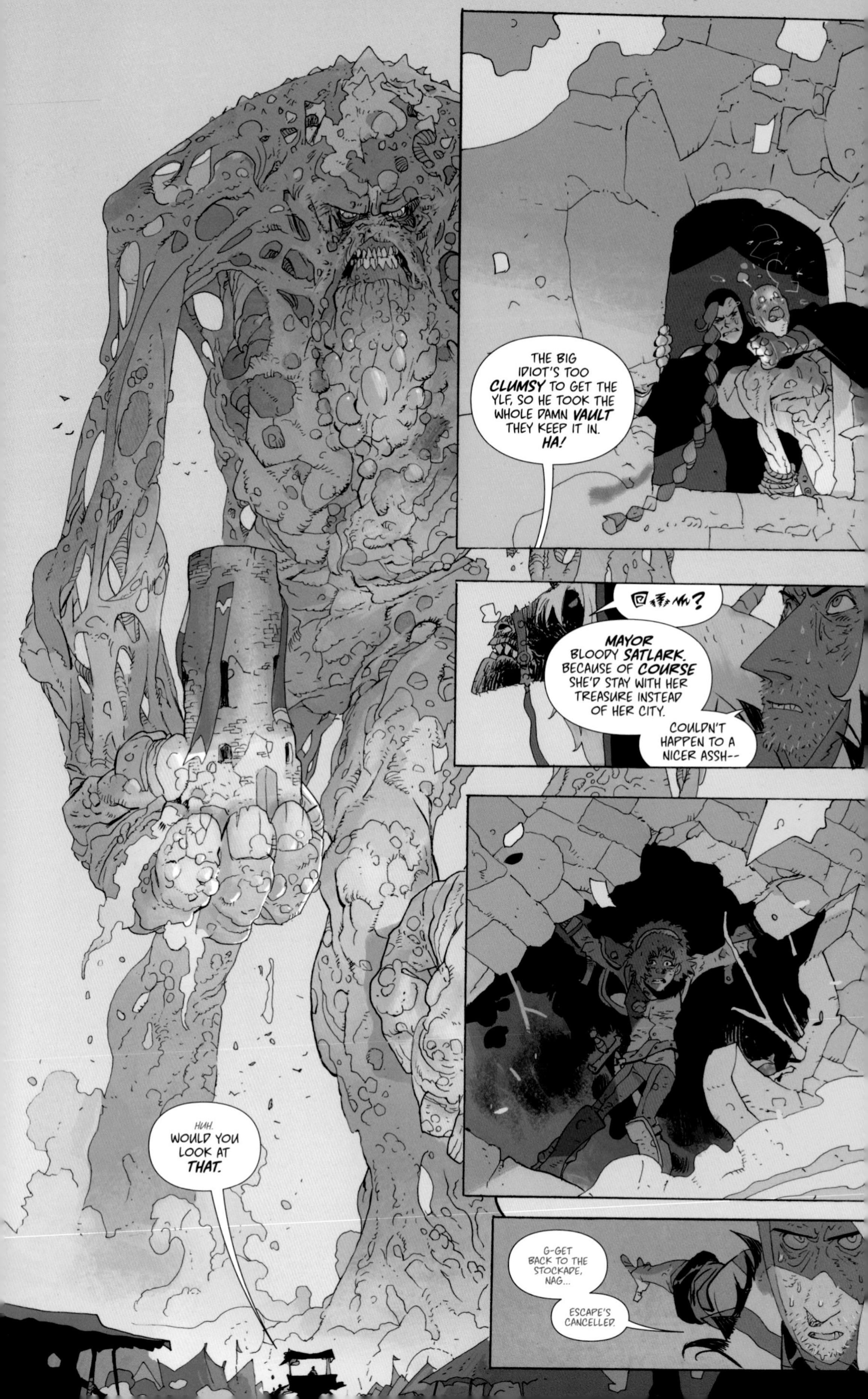
THE BIG IDIOT'S TOO CLUMSY TO GET THE YLF, SO HE TOOK THE WHOLE DAMN VAULT THEY KEEP IT IN. HA!
MAYOR BLOODY SATLARK. BECAUSE OF COURSE SHE'D STAY WITH HER TREASURE INSTEAD OF HER CITY.
COULDN'T HAPPEN TO A NICER ASSH--
HUH. WOULD YOU LOOK AT THAT.
G-GET BACK TO THE STOCKADE, NAG...
ESCAPE'S CANCELLED.

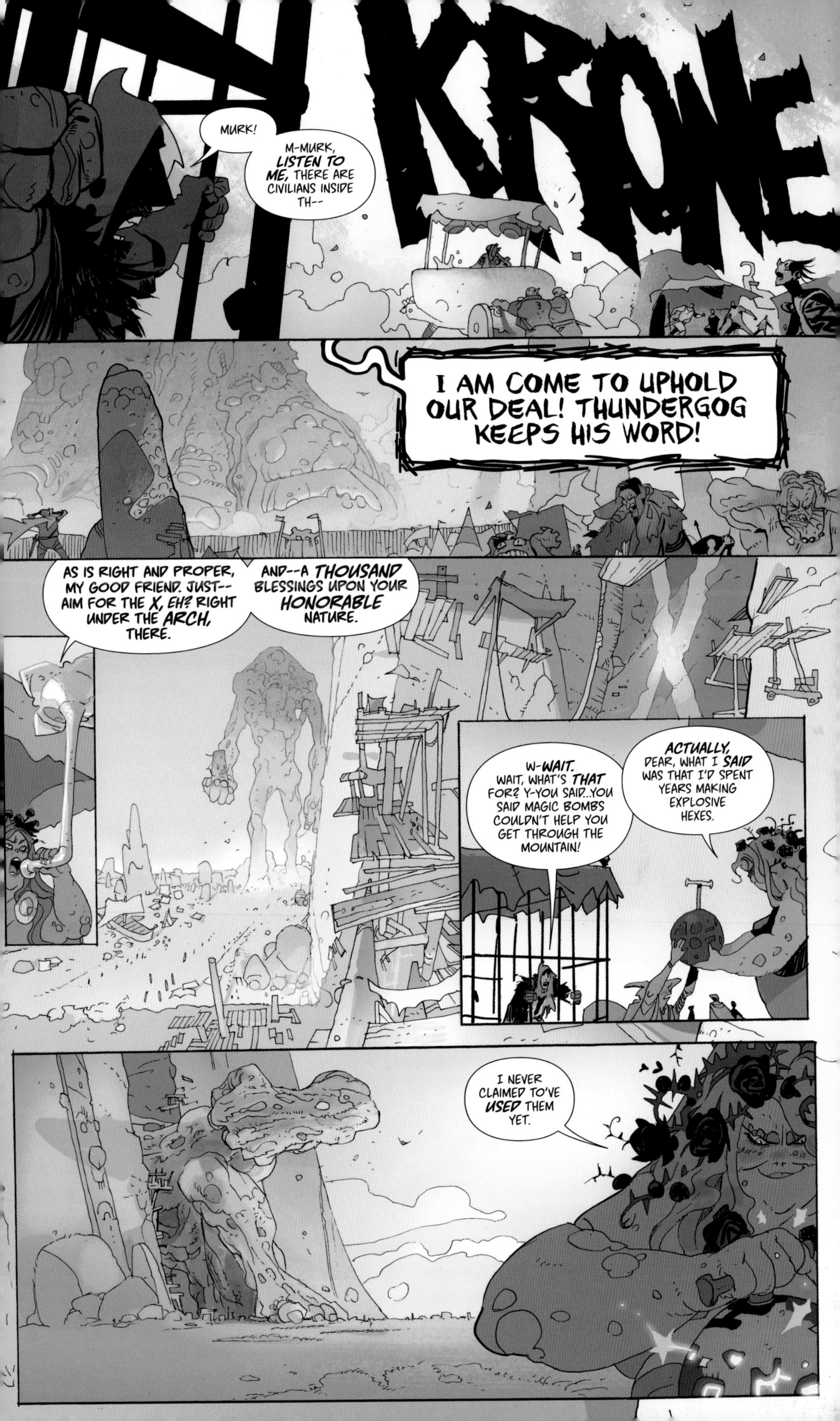
KRONE
MURK!
M-MURK, LISTEN TO ME, THERE ARE CIVILIANS INSIDE TH--
I AM COME TO UPHOLD OUR DEAL! THUNDERGOG KEEPS HIS WORD!
AS IS RIGHT AND PROPER, MY GOOD FRIEND. JUST--AIM FOR THE X, EH? RIGHT UNDER THE ARCH, THERE.
AND--A THOUSAND BLESSINGS UPON YOUR HONORABLE NATURE.
W-WAIT. WAIT, WHAT'S THAT FOR? Y-YOU SAID...YOU SAID MAGIC BOMBS COULDN'T HELP YOU GET THROUGH THE MOUNTAIN!
ACTUALLY, DEAR, WHAT I SAID WAS THAT I'D SPENT YEARS MAKING EXPLOSIVE HEXES.
I NEVER CLAIMED TO'VE USED THEM YET.

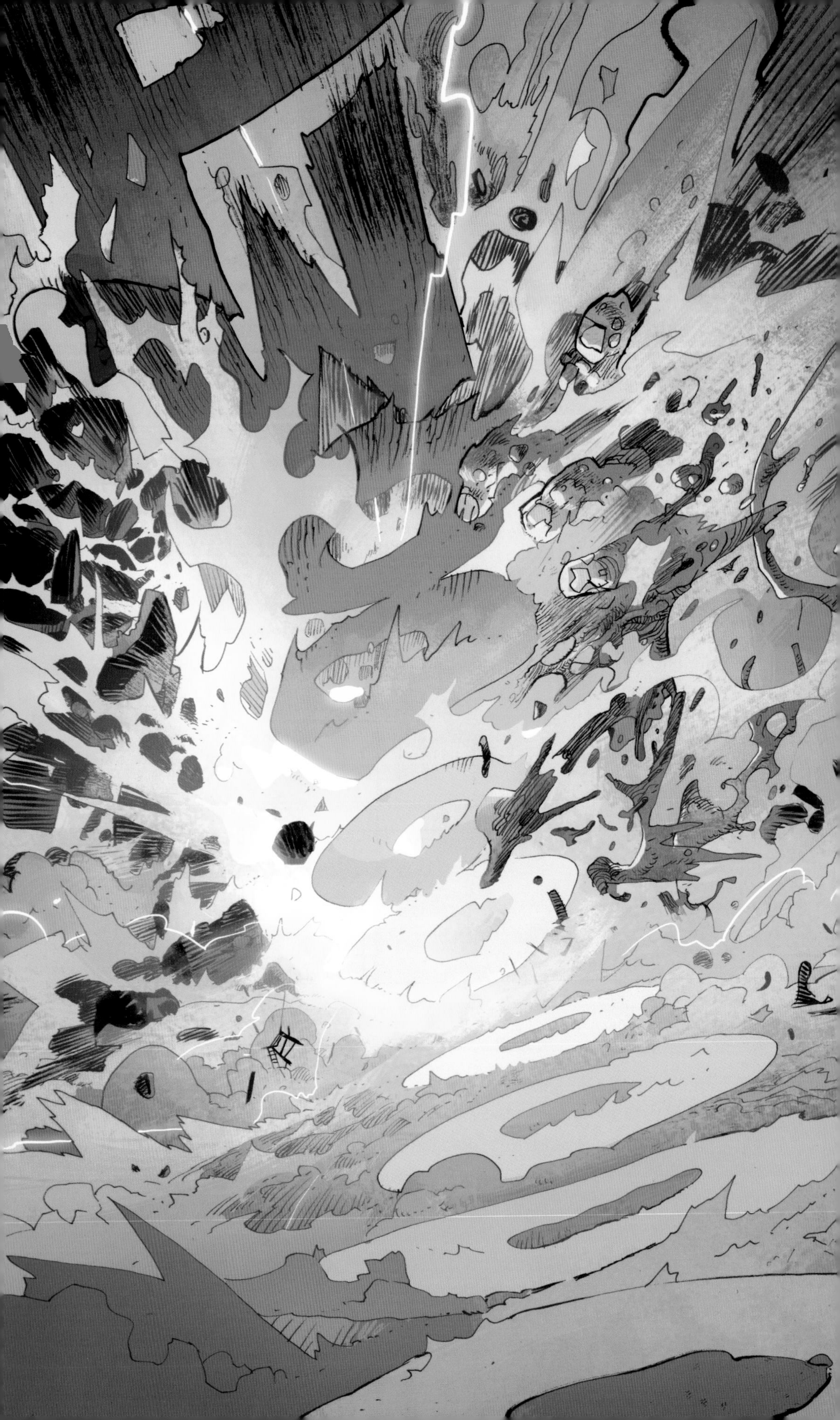

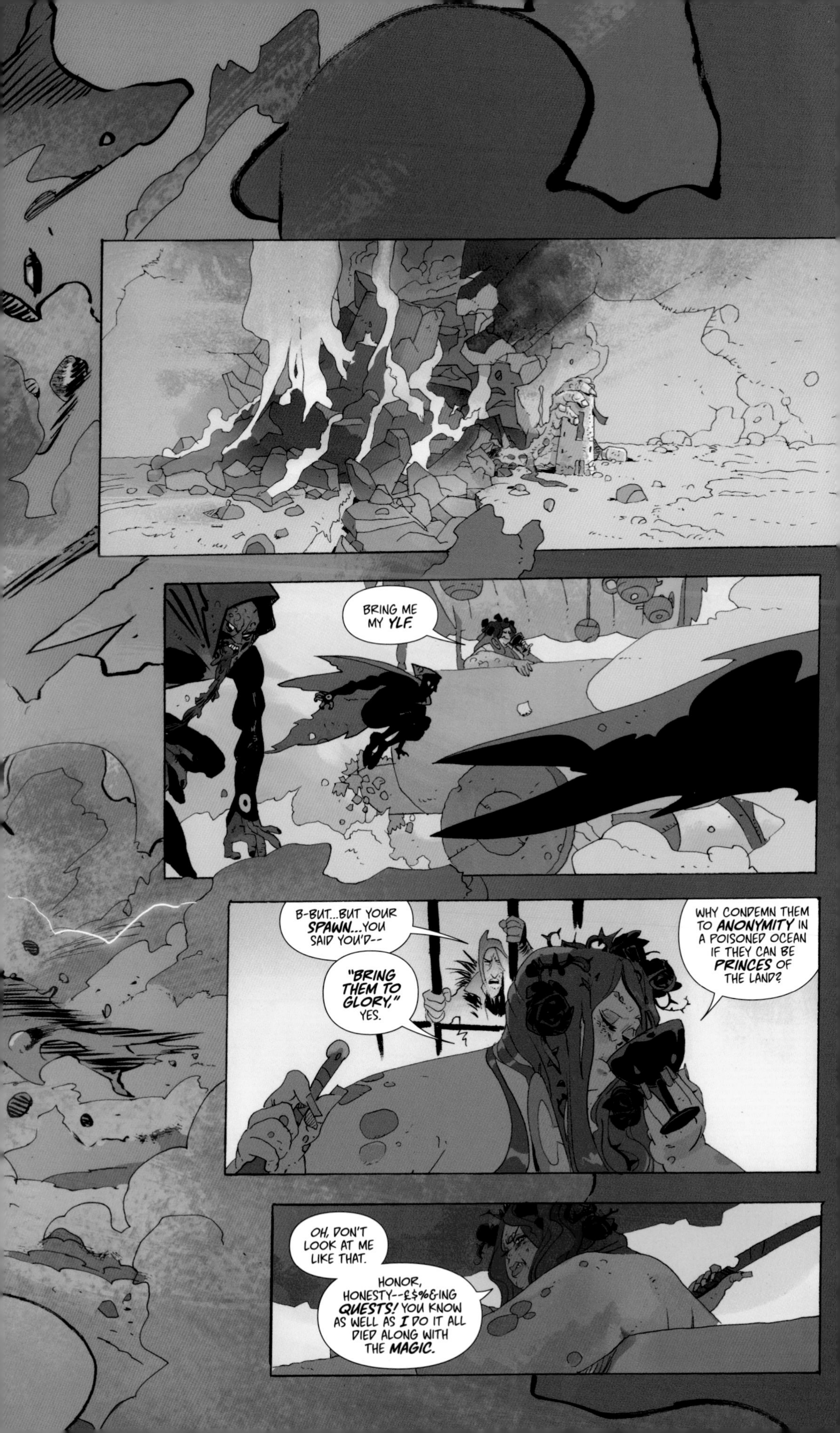
BRING ME MY YLF.
B-BUT...BUT YOUR SPAWN...YOU SAID YOU'D--
"BRING THEM TO GLORY," YES.
WHY CONDEMN THEM TO ANONYMITY IN A POISONED OCEAN IF THEY CAN BE PRINCES OF THE LAND?
OH, DON'T LOOK AT ME LIKE THAT.
HONOR, HONESTY--£$%&ING QUESTS! YOU KNOW AS WELL AS I DO IT ALL DIED ALONG WITH THE MAGIC.

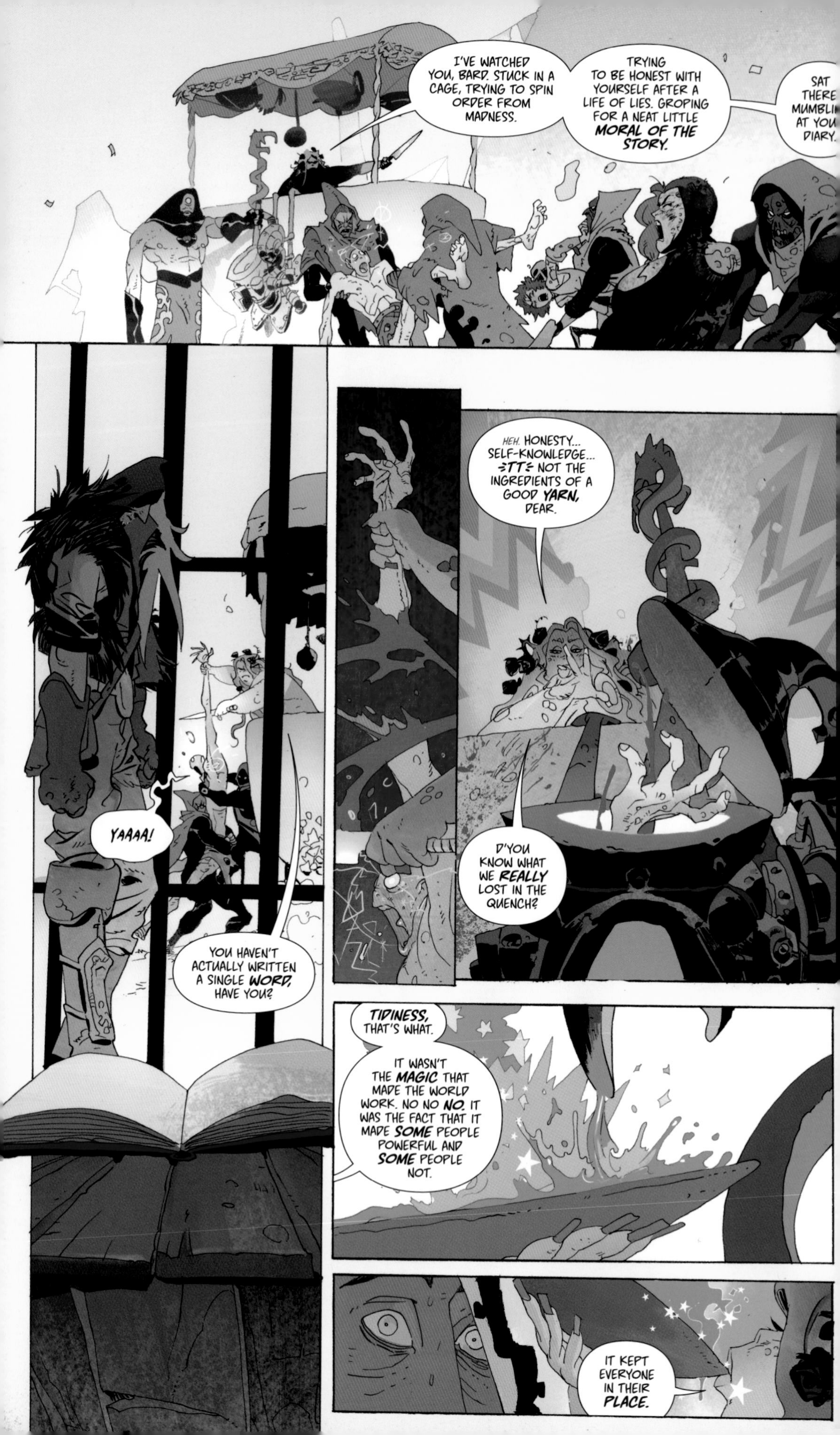

I'VE WATCHED YOU, BARD. STUCK IN A CAGE, TRYING TO SPIN ORDER FROM MADNESS.
TRYING TO BE HONEST WITH YOURSELF AFTER A LIFE OF LIES. GROPING FOR A NEAT LITTLE ***MORAL OF THE STORY.***
SAT THERE MUMBLI AT YOU DIARY.
YAAAA!
YOU HAVEN'T ACTUALLY WRITTEN A SINGLE ***WORD,*** HAVE YOU?
HEH. HONESTY... SELF-KNOWLEDGE... ***TT*** NOT THE INGREDIENTS OF A GOOD **YARN,** DEAR.
D'YOU KNOW WHAT WE ***REALLY*** LOST IN THE QUENCH?
TIDINESS, THAT'S WHAT.
IT WASN'T THE ***MAGIC*** THAT MADE THE WORLD WORK. NO NO ***NO,*** IT WAS THE FACT THAT IT MADE ***SOME*** PEOPLE POWERFUL AND ***SOME*** PEOPLE NOT.
IT KEPT EVERYONE IN THEIR ***PLACE.***

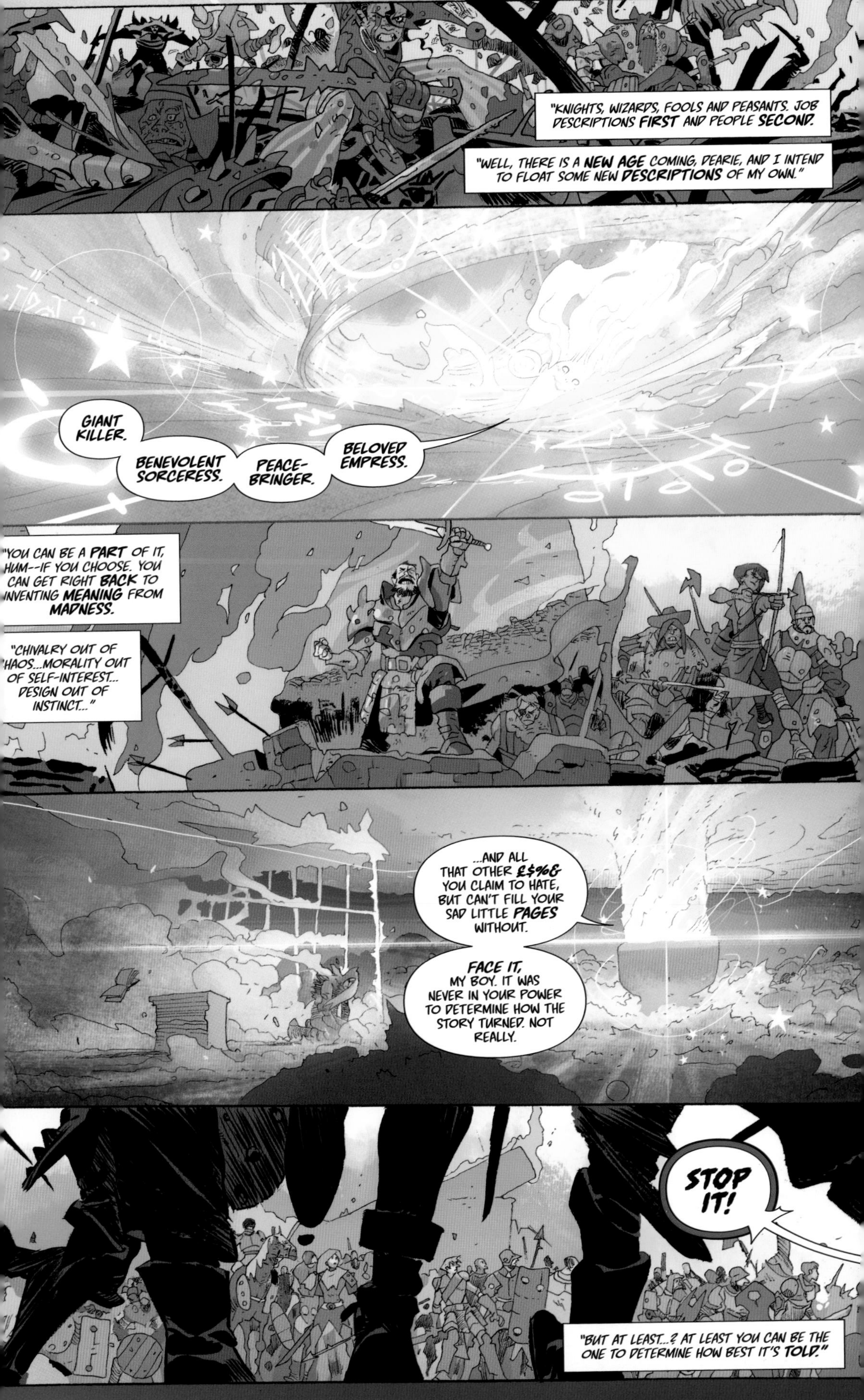
"KNIGHTS, WIZARDS, FOOLS AND PEASANTS. JOB DESCRIPTIONS FIRST AND PEOPLE SECOND.
"WELL, THERE IS A NEW AGE COMING, DEARIE, AND I INTEND TO FLOAT SOME NEW DESCRIPTIONS OF MY OWN."
GIANT KILLER.
BENEVOLENT SORCERESS.
PEACE-BRINGER.
BELOVED EMPRESS.
"YOU CAN BE A PART OF IT, HUM--IF YOU CHOOSE. YOU CAN GET RIGHT BACK TO INVENTING MEANING FROM MADNESS.
"CHIVALRY OUT OF CHAOS...MORALITY OUT OF SELF-INTEREST... DESIGN OUT OF INSTINCT..."
...AND ALL THAT OTHER £$%& YOU CLAIM TO HATE, BUT CAN'T FILL YOUR SAD LITTLE PAGES WITHOUT.
FACE IT, MY BOY. IT WAS NEVER IN YOUR POWER TO DETERMINE HOW THE STORY TURNED. NOT REALLY.
STOP IT!
"BUT AT LEAST...? AT LEAST YOU CAN BE THE ONE TO DETERMINE HOW BEST IT'S TOLD."

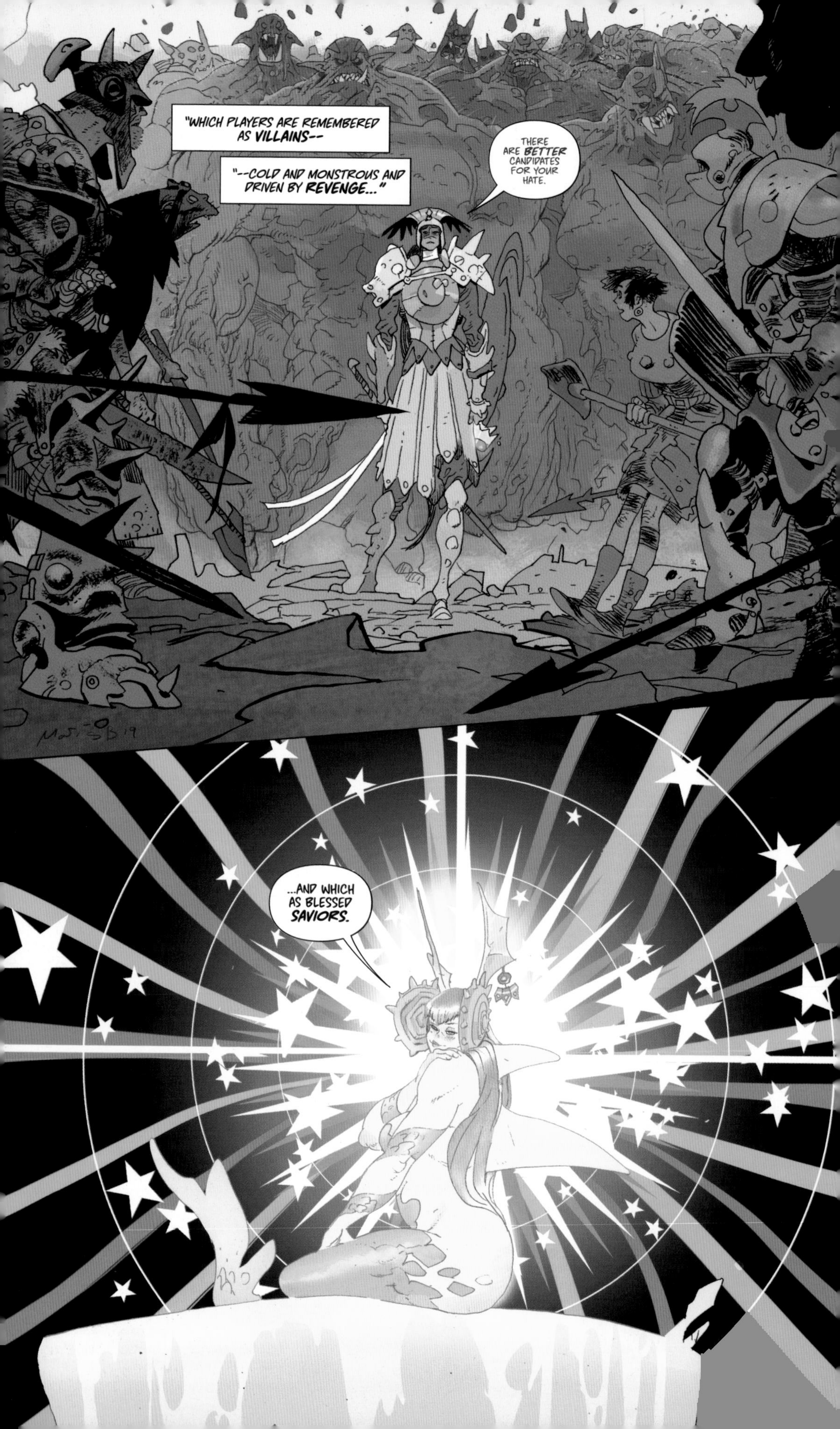
"WHICH PLAYERS ARE REMEMBERED AS VILLAINS--
"--COLD AND MONSTROUS AND DRIVEN BY REVENGE..."
THERE ARE BETTER CANDIDATES FOR YOUR HATE.
...AND WHICH AS BLESSED SAVIORS.

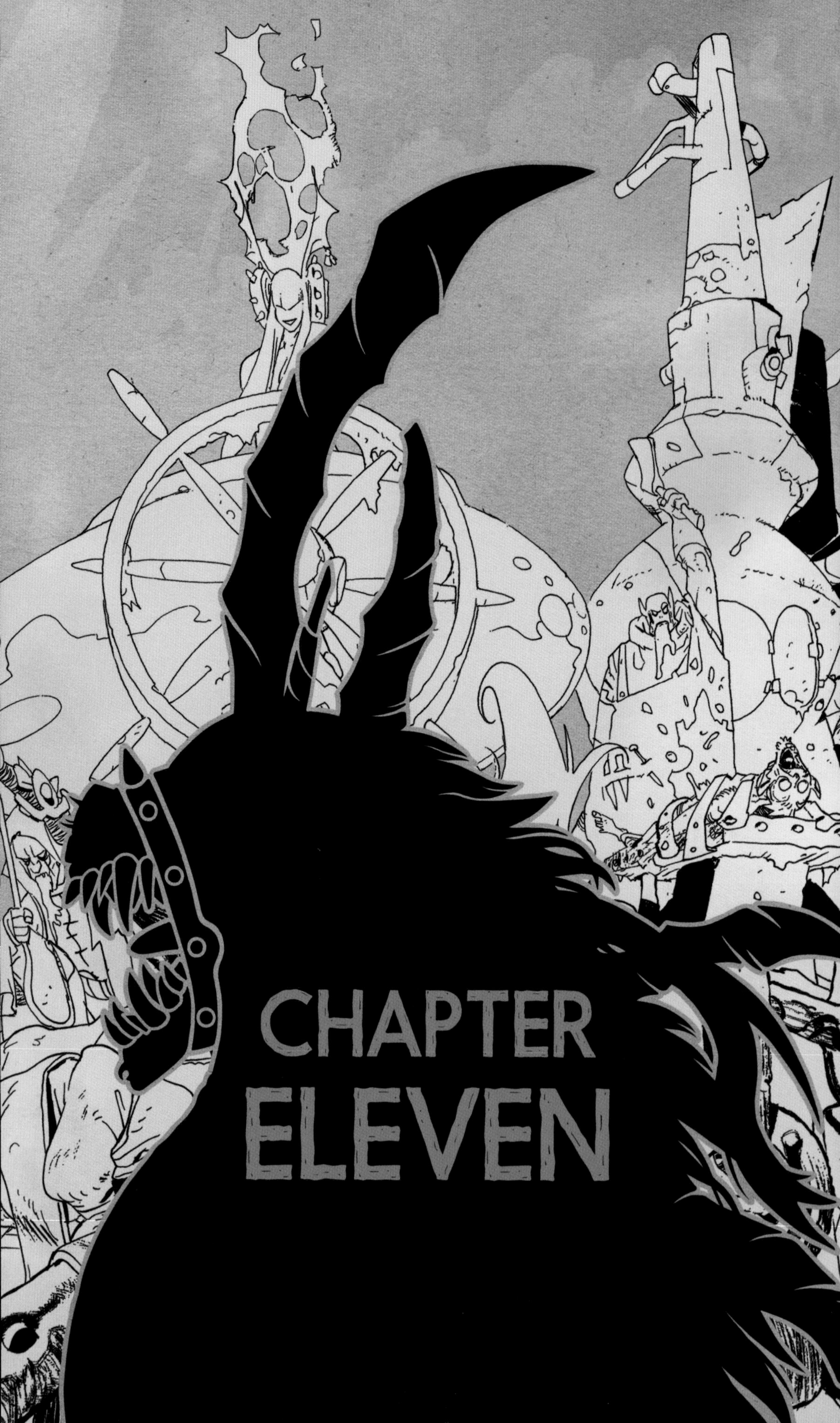
CHAPTER
ELEVEN

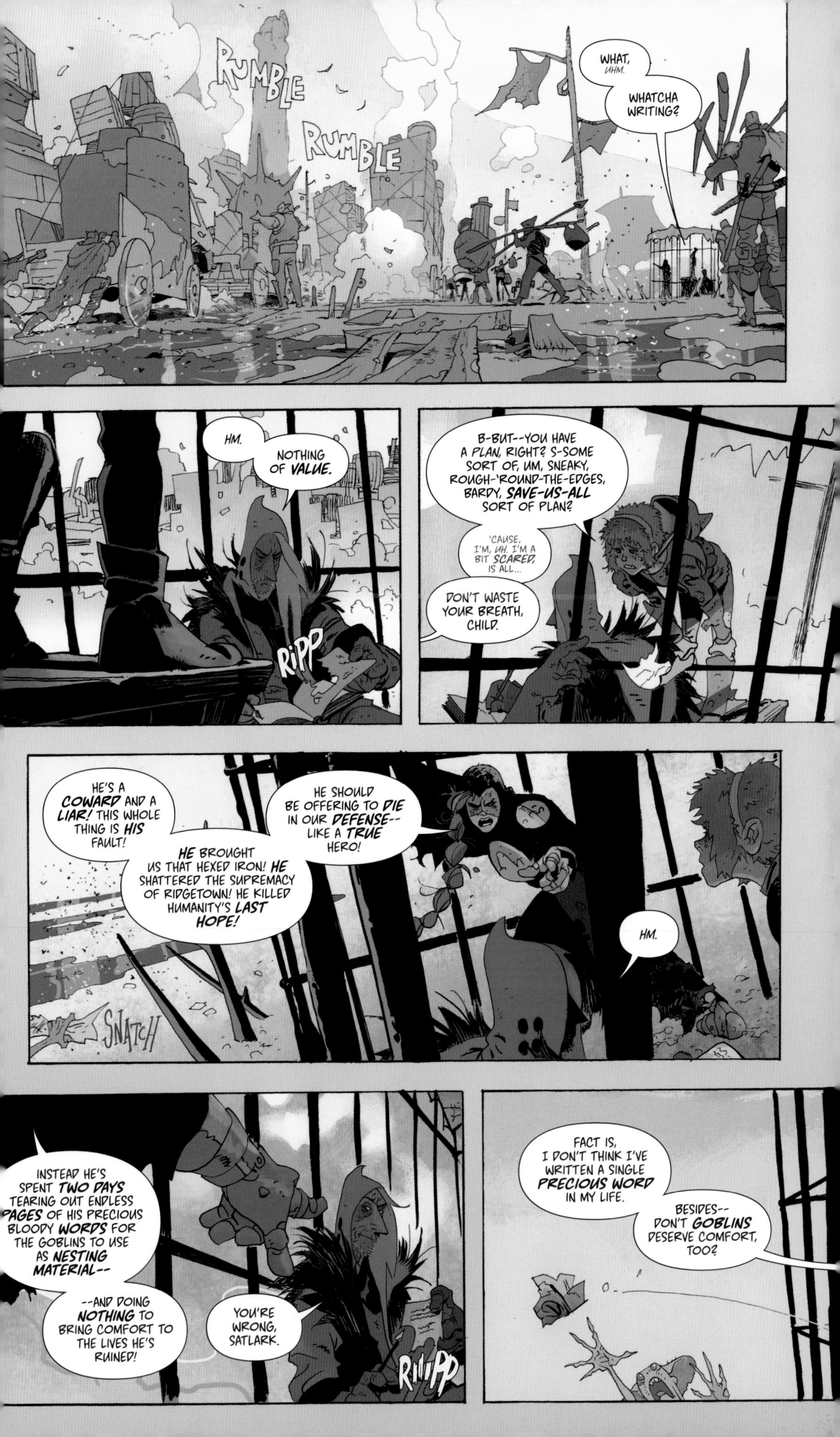
RUMBLE
RUMBLE
WHAT, UHM.
WHATCHA WRITING?
HM.
NOTHING OF VALUE.
RIPP
B-BUT--YOU HAVE A PLAN, RIGHT? S-SOME SORT OF, UM, SNEAKY, ROUGH-'ROUND-THE-EDGES, BARDY, SAVE-US-ALL SORT OF PLAN?
'CAUSE, I'M, UH, I'M A BIT SCARED, IS ALL...
DON'T WASTE YOUR BREATH, CHILD.
HE'S A COWARD AND A LIAR! THIS WHOLE THING IS HIS FAULT!
HE BROUGHT US THAT HEXED IRON! HE SHATTERED THE SUPREMACY OF RIDGETOWN! HE KILLED HUMANITY'S LAST HOPE!
HE SHOULD BE OFFERING TO DIE IN OUR DEFENSE--LIKE A TRUE HERO!
HM.
SNATCH
INSTEAD HE'S SPENT TWO DAYS TEARING OUT ENDLESS PAGES OF HIS PRECIOUS BLOODY WORDS FOR THE GOBLINS TO USE AS NESTING MATERIAL--
--AND DOING NOTHING TO BRING COMFORT TO THE LIVES HE'S RUINED!
YOU'RE WRONG, SATLARK.
RIIIPP
FACT IS, I DON'T THINK I'VE WRITTEN A SINGLE PRECIOUS WORD IN MY LIFE.
BESIDES--DON'T GOBLINS DESERVE COMFORT, TOO?

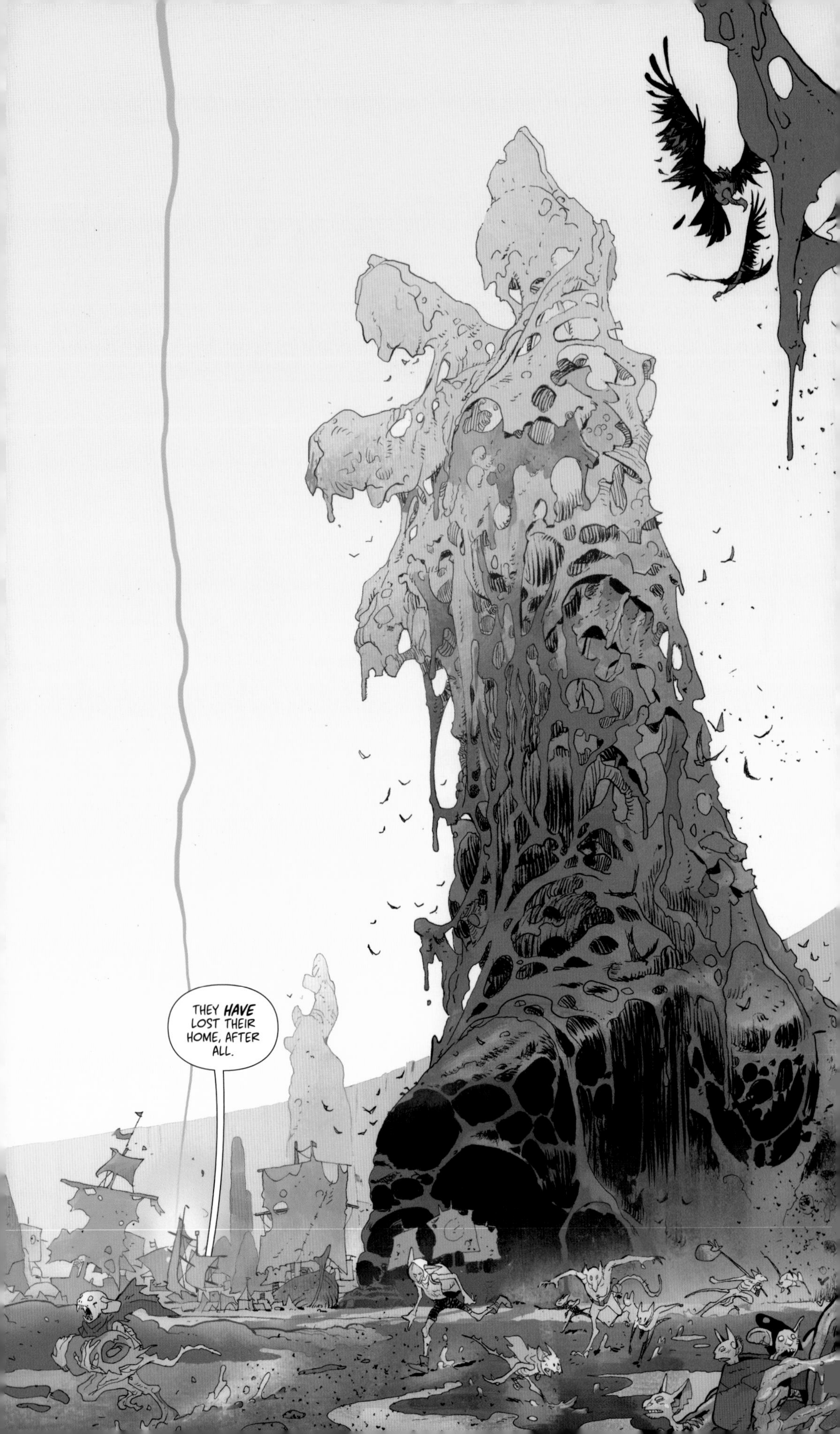
THEY HAVE LOST THEIR HOME, AFTER ALL.

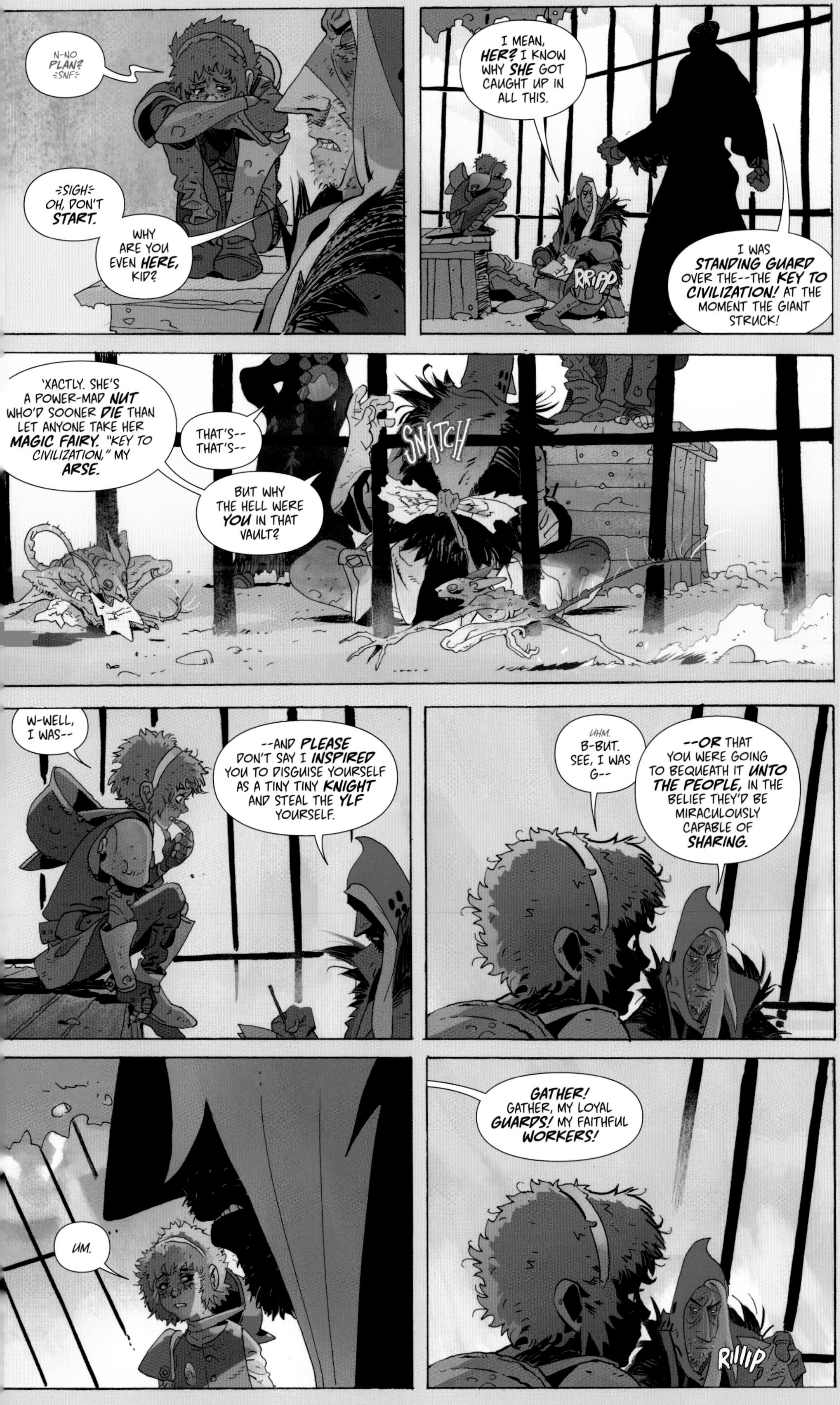

N-NO PLAN? ≈SNF≈
≈SIGH≈ OH, DON'T START.
WHY ARE YOU EVEN HERE, KID?
I MEAN, HER? I KNOW WHY SHE GOT CAUGHT UP IN ALL THIS.
RRIPP
I WAS STANDING GUARD OVER THE--THE KEY TO CIVILIZATION! AT THE MOMENT THE GIANT STRUCK!
'XACTLY. SHE'S A POWER-MAD NUT WHO'D SOONER DIE THAN LET ANYONE TAKE HER MAGIC FAIRY. "KEY TO CIVILIZATION," MY ARSE.
THAT'S-- THAT'S--
SNATCH
BUT WHY THE HELL WERE YOU IN THAT VAULT?
W-WELL, I WAS--
--AND PLEASE DON'T SAY I INSPIRED YOU TO DISGUISE YOURSELF AS A TINY TINY KNIGHT AND STEAL THE YLF YOURSELF.
UHM. B-BUT. SEE, I WAS G--
--OR THAT YOU WERE GOING TO BEQUEATH IT UNTO THE PEOPLE, IN THE BELIEF THEY'D BE MIRACULOUSLY CAPABLE OF SHARING.
UM.
GATHER! GATHER, MY LOYAL GUARDS! MY FAITHFUL WORKERS!
RIIIIP

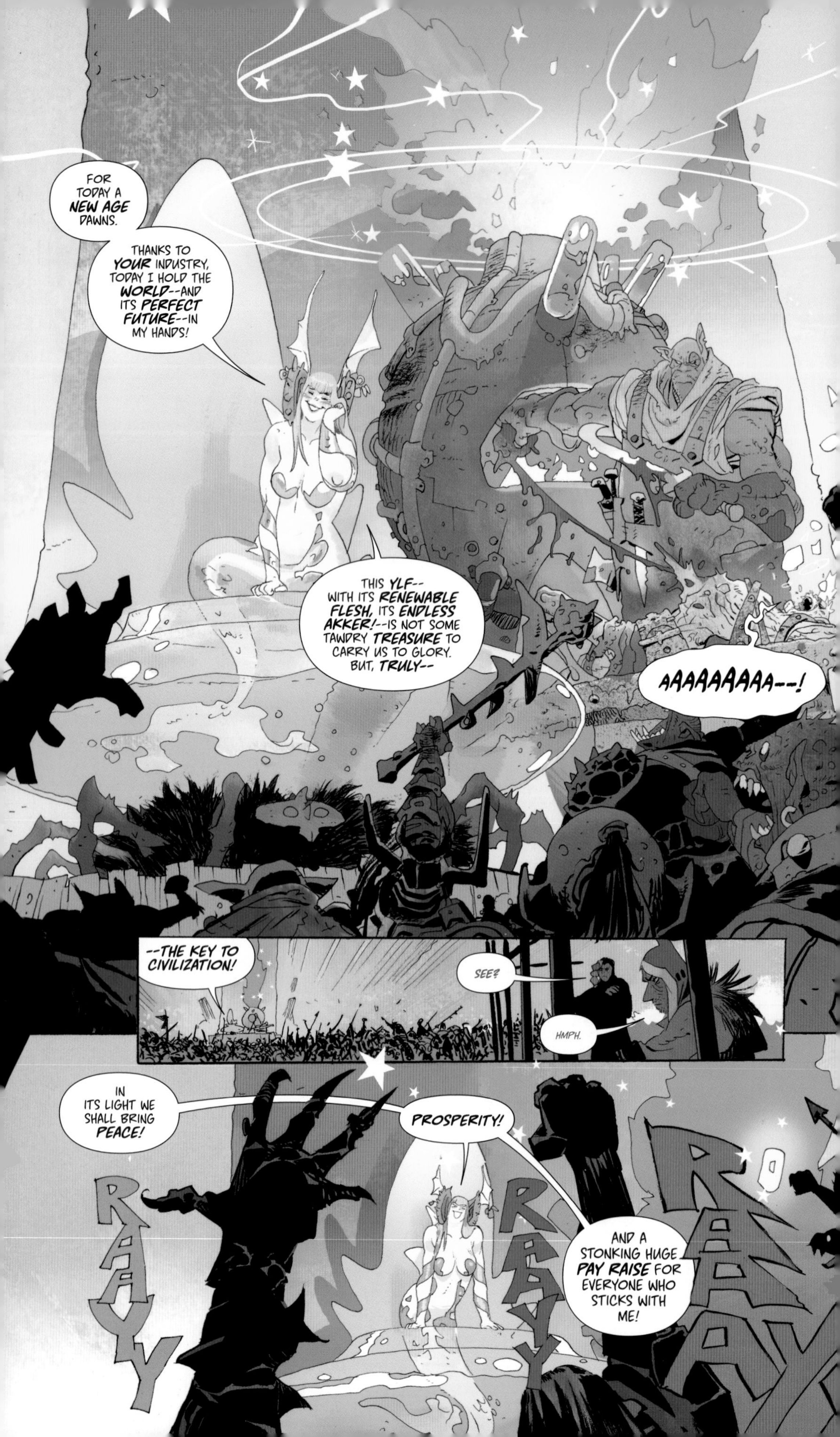

FOR TODAY A NEW AGE DAWNS.
THANKS TO YOUR INDUSTRY, TODAY I HOLD THE WORLD--AND ITS PERFECT FUTURE--IN MY HANDS!
THIS YLF--WITH ITS RENEWABLE FLESH, ITS ENDLESS AKKER!--IS NOT SOME TAWDRY TREASURE TO CARRY US TO GLORY. BUT, TRULY--
AAAAAAAAA--!
--THE KEY TO CIVILIZATION!
SEE?
HMPH.
IN ITS LIGHT WE SHALL BRING PEACE!
PROSPERITY!
AND A STONKING HUGE PAY RAISE FOR EVERYONE WHO STICKS WITH ME!
RAAAY
RAAAY
ROAAAY

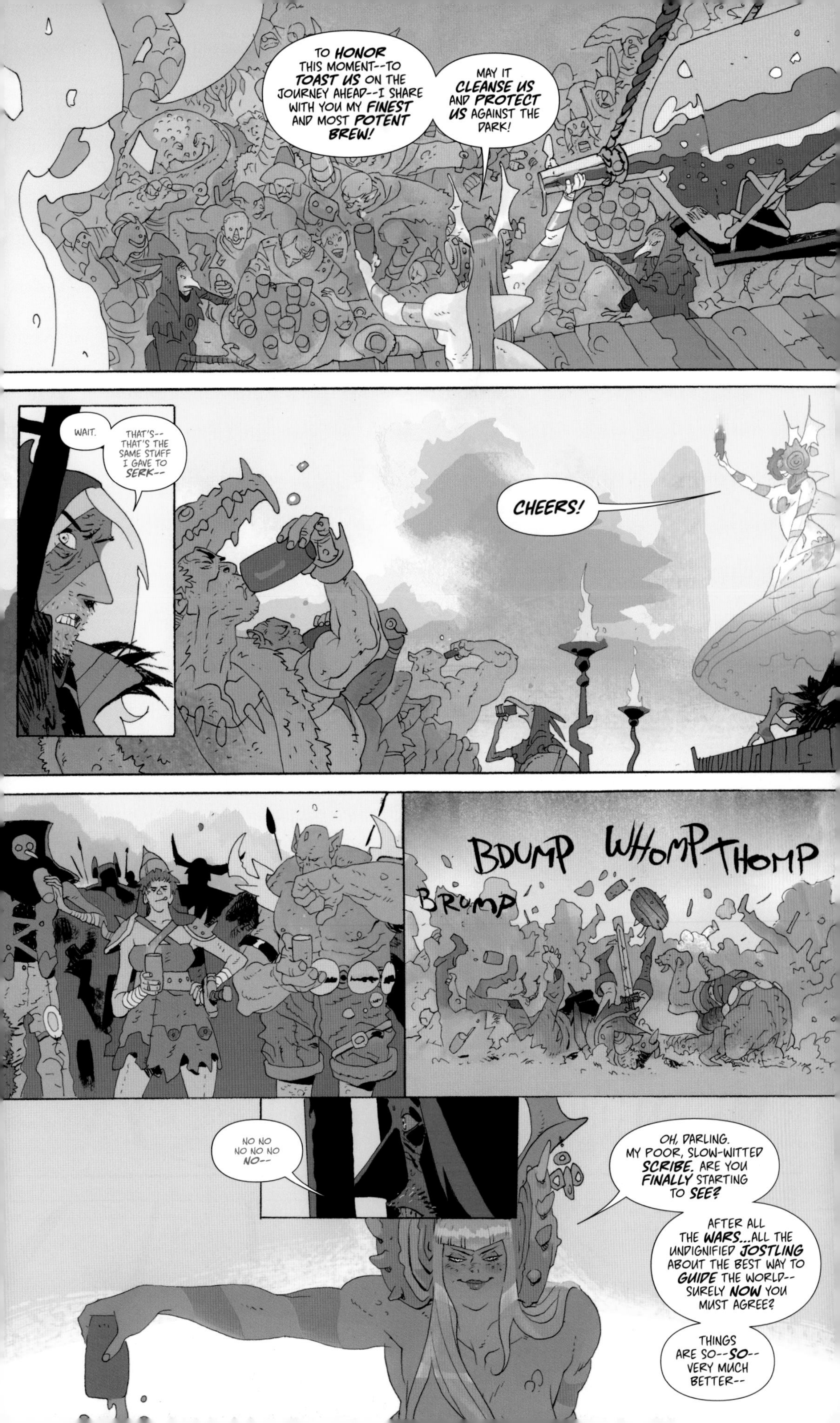
TO HONOR THIS MOMENT--TO TOAST US ON THE JOURNEY AHEAD--I SHARE WITH YOU MY FINEST AND MOST POTENT BREW!
MAY IT CLEANSE US AND PROTECT US AGAINST THE DARK!
WAIT.
THAT'S-- THAT'S THE SAME STUFF I GAVE TO SERK--
CHEERS!
BDUMP WHOMP THOMP
BRUMP
NO NO NO NO NO NO--
OH, DARLING. MY POOR, SLOW-WITTED SCRIBE. ARE YOU FINALLY STARTING TO SEE?
AFTER ALL THE WARS...ALL THE UNDIGNIFIED JOSTLING ABOUT THE BEST WAY TO GUIDE THE WORLD-- SURELY NOW YOU MUST AGREE?
THINGS ARE SO--SO-- VERY MUCH BETTER--

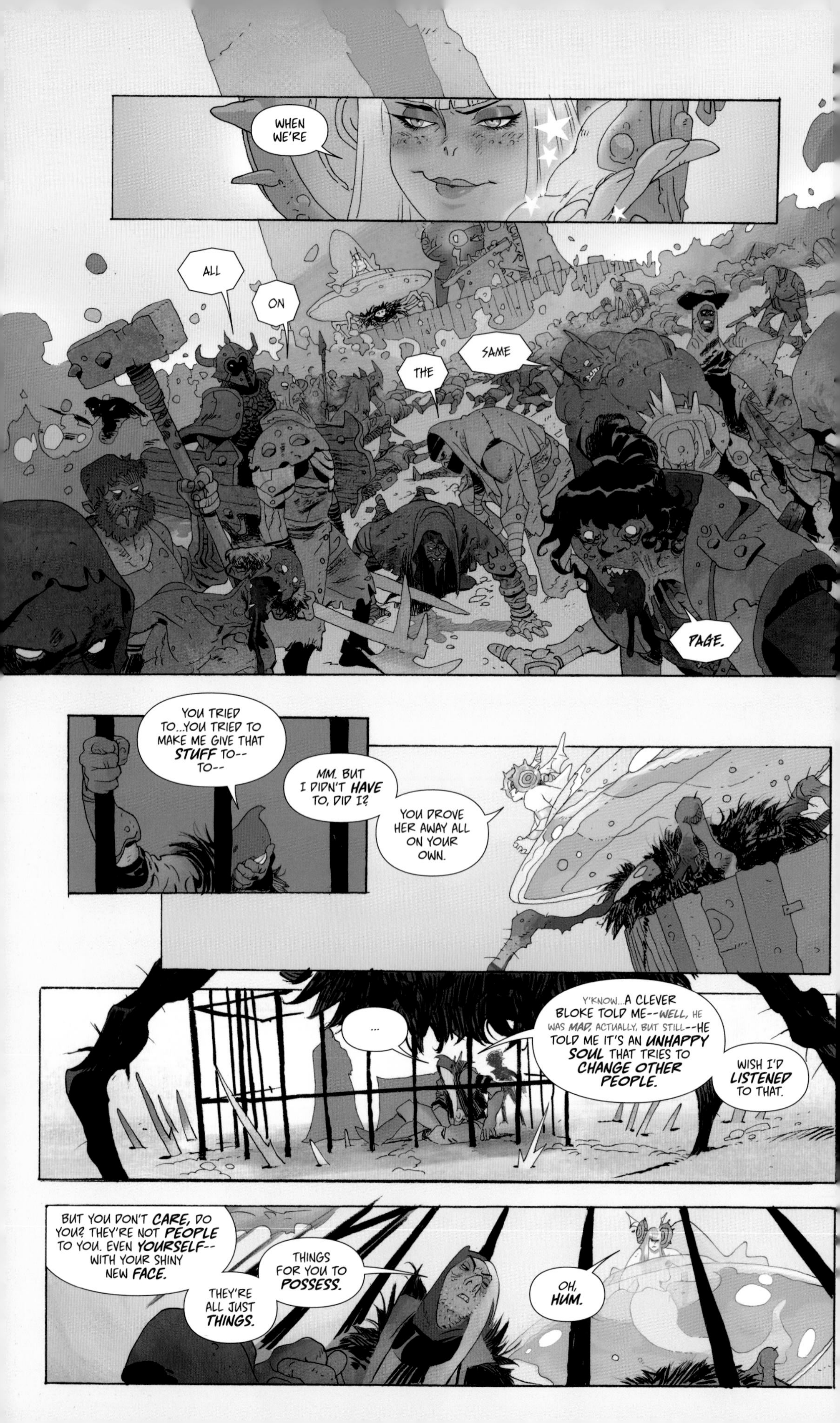

WHEN WE'RE
ALL
ON
THE
SAME
PAGE.
YOU TRIED TO...YOU TRIED TO MAKE ME GIVE THAT STUFF TO-- TO--
MM. BUT I DIDN'T HAVE TO, DID I?
YOU DROVE HER AWAY ALL ON YOUR OWN.
...
Y'KNOW...A CLEVER BLOKE TOLD ME--WELL, HE WAS MAD, ACTUALLY, BUT STILL--HE TOLD ME IT'S AN UNHAPPY SOUL THAT TRIES TO CHANGE OTHER PEOPLE.
WISH I'D LISTENED TO THAT.
BUT YOU DON'T CARE, DO YOU? THEY'RE NOT PEOPLE TO YOU. EVEN YOURSELF-- WITH YOUR SHINY NEW FACE.
THEY'RE ALL JUST THINGS.
THINGS FOR YOU TO POSSESS.
OH, HUM.

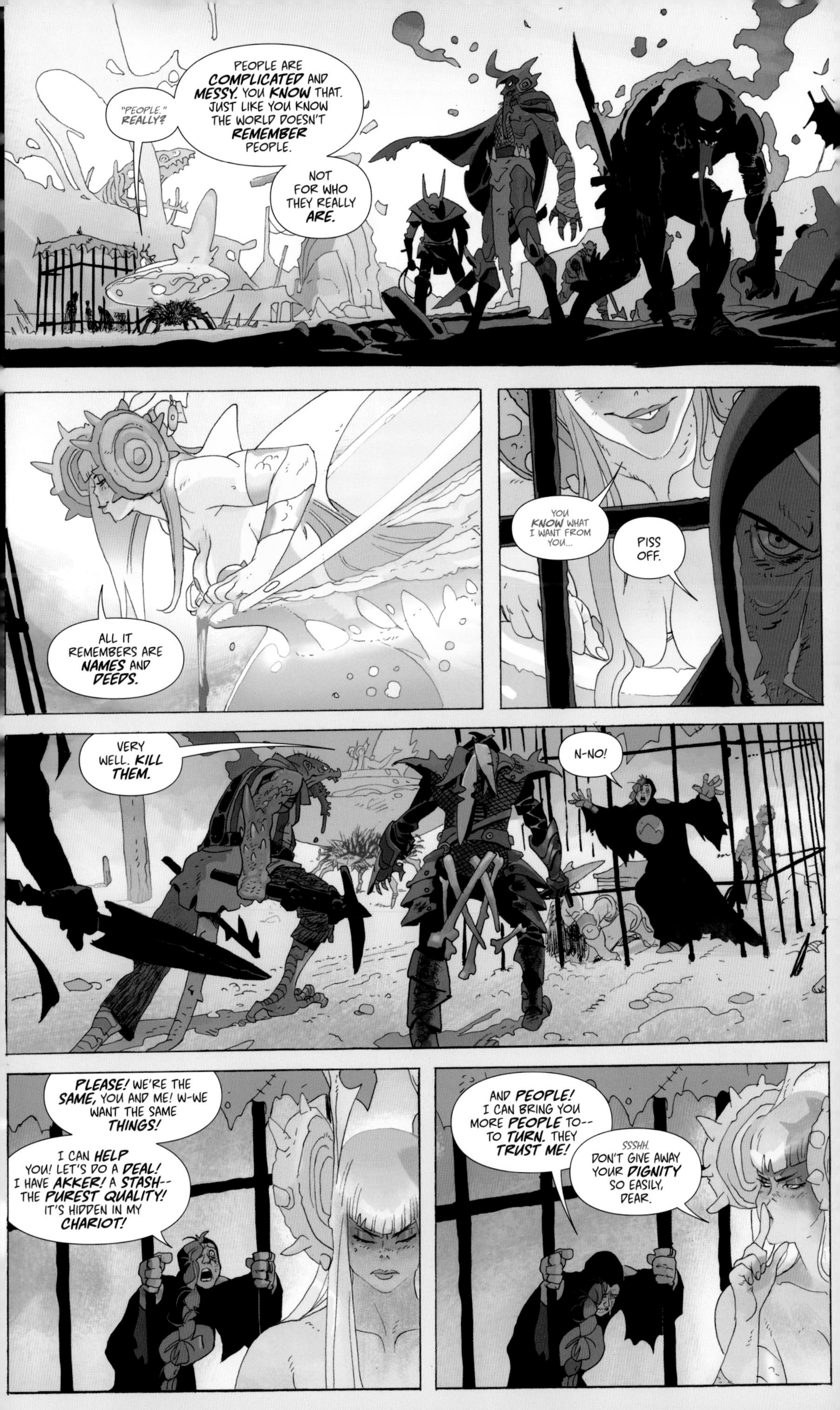
"PEOPLE." REALLY?
PEOPLE ARE COMPLICATED AND MESSY. YOU KNOW THAT. JUST LIKE YOU KNOW THE WORLD DOESN'T REMEMBER PEOPLE.
NOT FOR WHO THEY REALLY ARE.
ALL IT REMEMBERS ARE NAMES AND DEEDS.
YOU KNOW WHAT I WANT FROM YOU...
PISS OFF.
VERY WELL. KILL THEM.
N-NO!
PLEASE! WE'RE THE SAME, YOU AND ME! W-WE WANT THE SAME THINGS!
I CAN HELP YOU! LET'S DO A DEAL! I HAVE AKKER! A STASH--THE PUREST QUALITY! IT'S HIDDEN IN MY CHARIOT!
AND PEOPLE! I CAN BRING YOU MORE PEOPLE TO--TO TURN. THEY TRUST ME!
SSSHH. DON'T GIVE AWAY YOUR DIGNITY SO EASILY, DEAR.

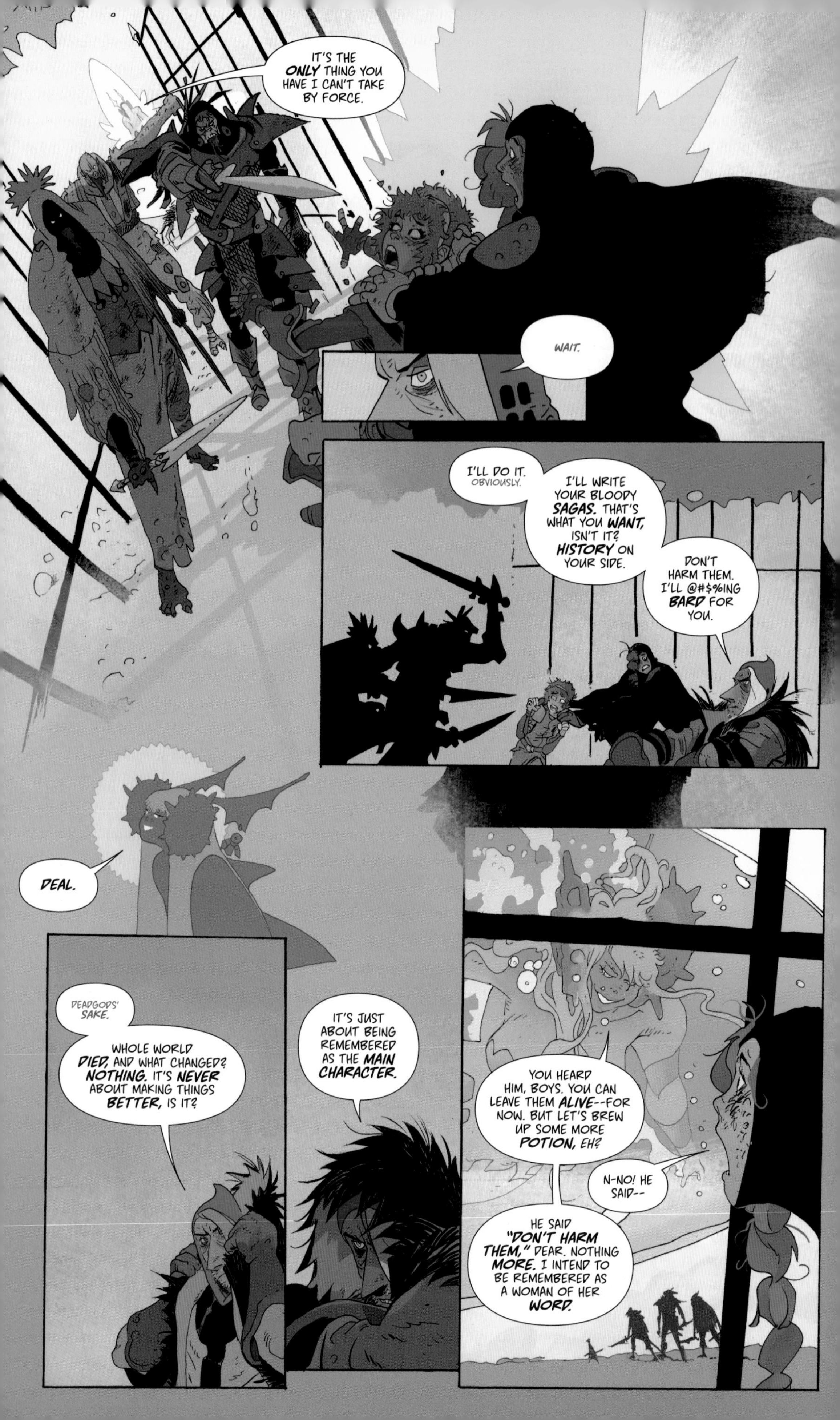
IT'S THE ONLY THING YOU HAVE I CAN'T TAKE BY FORCE.
WAIT.
I'LL DO IT. OBVIOUSLY.
I'LL WRITE YOUR BLOODY SAGAS. THAT'S WHAT YOU WANT, ISN'T IT? HISTORY ON YOUR SIDE.
DON'T HARM THEM. I'LL @#$%ING BARD FOR YOU.
DEAL.
DEADGODS' SAKE.
WHOLE WORLD DIED, AND WHAT CHANGED? NOTHING. IT'S NEVER ABOUT MAKING THINGS BETTER, IS IT?
IT'S JUST ABOUT BEING REMEMBERED AS THE MAIN CHARACTER.
YOU HEARD HIM, BOYS. YOU CAN LEAVE THEM ALIVE--FOR NOW. BUT LET'S BREW UP SOME MORE POTION, EH?
N-NO! HE SAID--
HE SAID "DON'T HARM THEM," DEAR. NOTHING MORE. I INTEND TO BE REMEMBERED AS A WOMAN OF HER WORD.

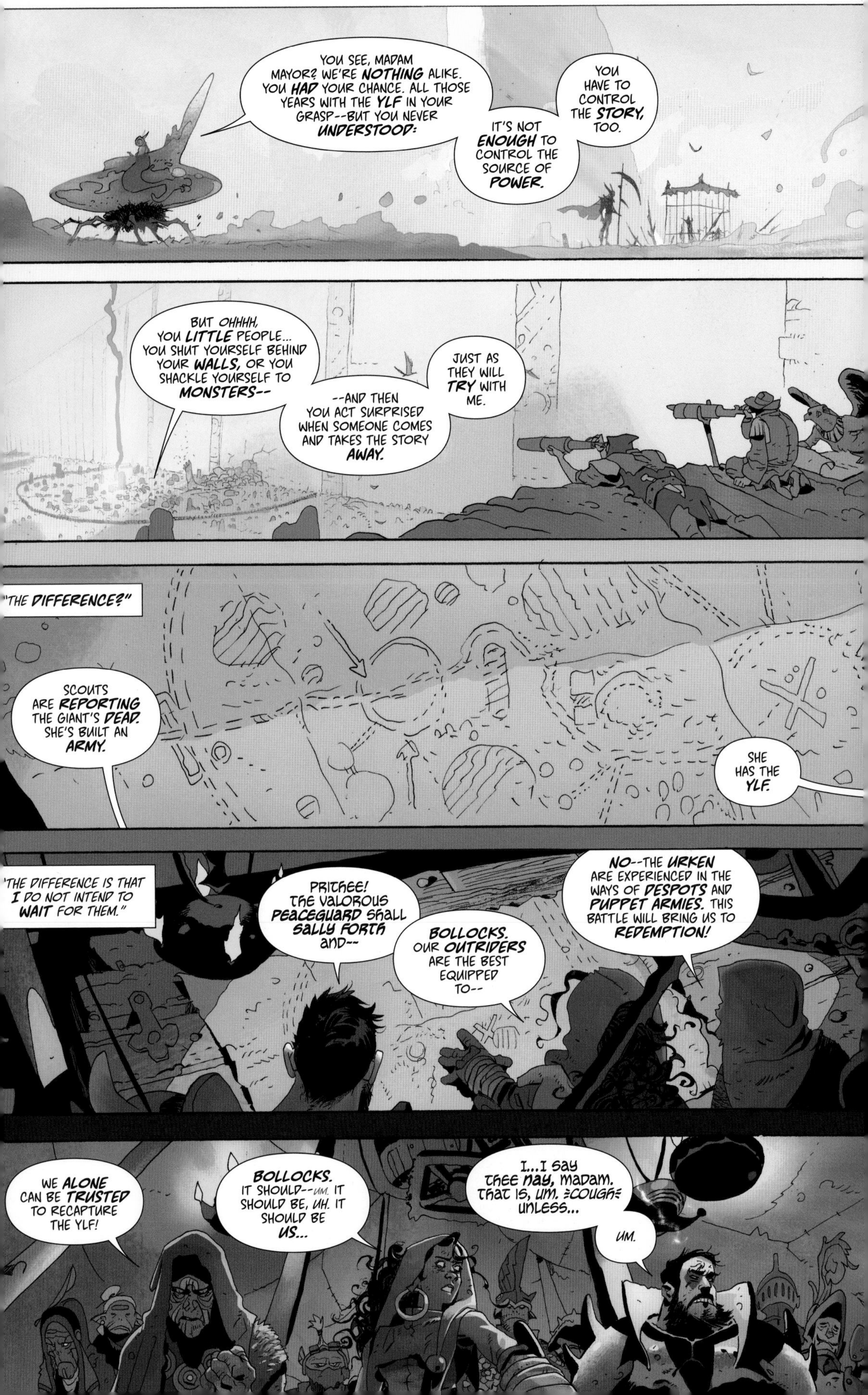
YOU SEE, MADAM MAYOR? WE'RE NOTHING ALIKE. YOU HAD YOUR CHANCE. ALL THOSE YEARS WITH THE YLF IN YOUR GRASP--BUT YOU NEVER UNDERSTOOD:
IT'S NOT ENOUGH TO CONTROL THE SOURCE OF POWER.
YOU HAVE TO CONTROL THE STORY, TOO.
BUT OHHHH, YOU LITTLE PEOPLE... YOU SHUT YOURSELF BEHIND YOUR WALLS, OR YOU SHACKLE YOURSELF TO MONSTERS--
--AND THEN YOU ACT SURPRISED WHEN SOMEONE COMES AND TAKES THE STORY AWAY.
JUST AS THEY WILL TRY WITH ME.
"THE DIFFERENCE?"
SCOUTS ARE REPORTING THE GIANT'S DEAD. SHE'S BUILT AN ARMY.
SHE HAS THE YLF.
"THE DIFFERENCE IS THAT I DO NOT INTEND TO WAIT FOR THEM."
PRITHEE! THE VALOROUS PEACEGUARD SHALL SALLY FORTH AND--
BOLLOCKS. OUR OUTRIDERS ARE THE BEST EQUIPPED TO--
NO--THE URKEN ARE EXPERIENCED IN THE WAYS OF DESPOTS AND PUPPET ARMIES. THIS BATTLE WILL BRING US TO REDEMPTION!
WE ALONE CAN BE TRUSTED TO RECAPTURE THE YLF!
BOLLOCKS. IT SHOULD--UM. IT SHOULD BE, UH. IT SHOULD BE US...
I...I SAY THEE NAY, MADAM. THAT IS, UM. *COUGH* UNLESS...
UM.

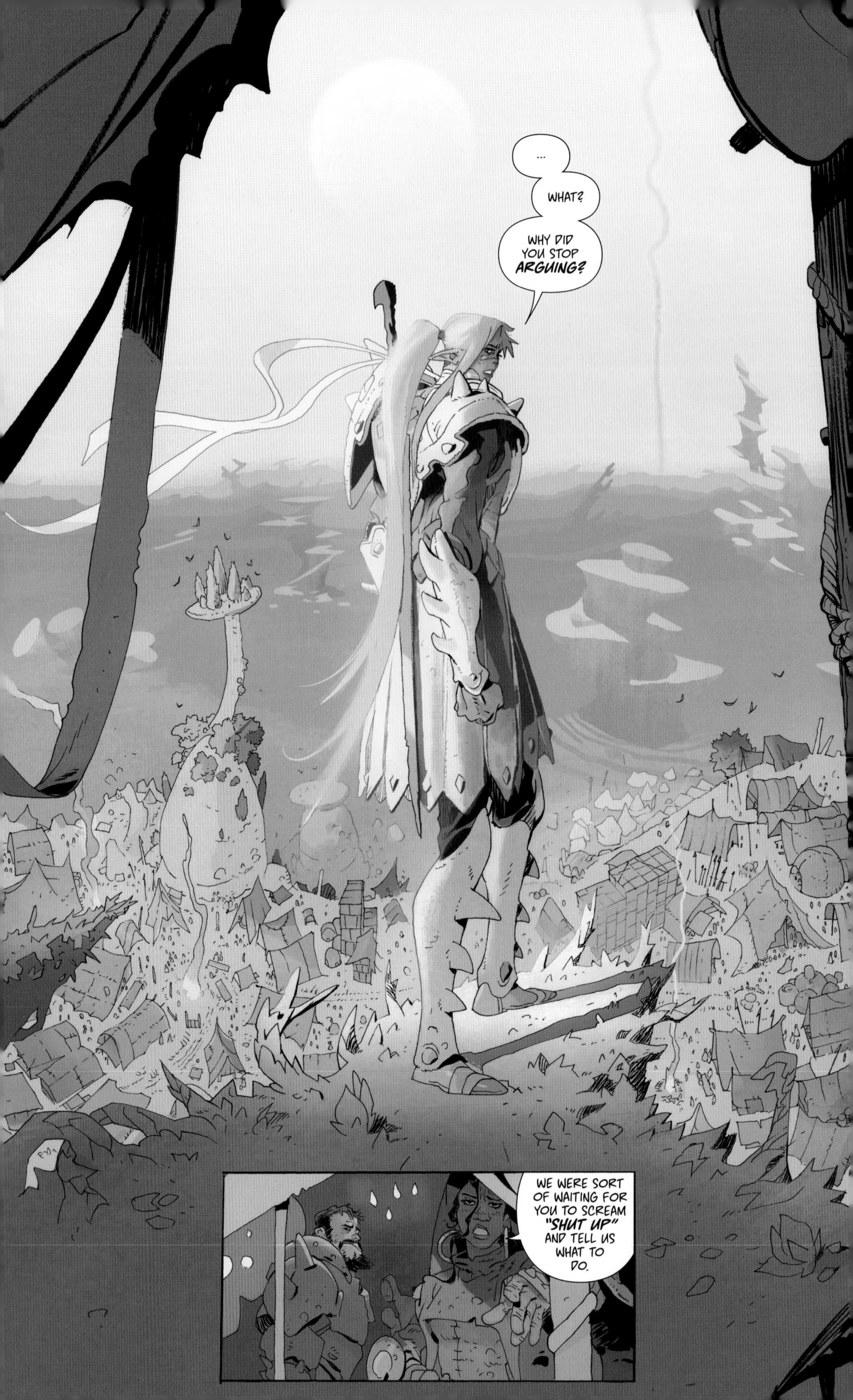
...
WHAT?
WHY DID YOU STOP **ARGUING?**
WE WERE SORT OF WAITING FOR YOU TO SCREAM **"SHUT UP"** AND TELL US WHAT TO DO.

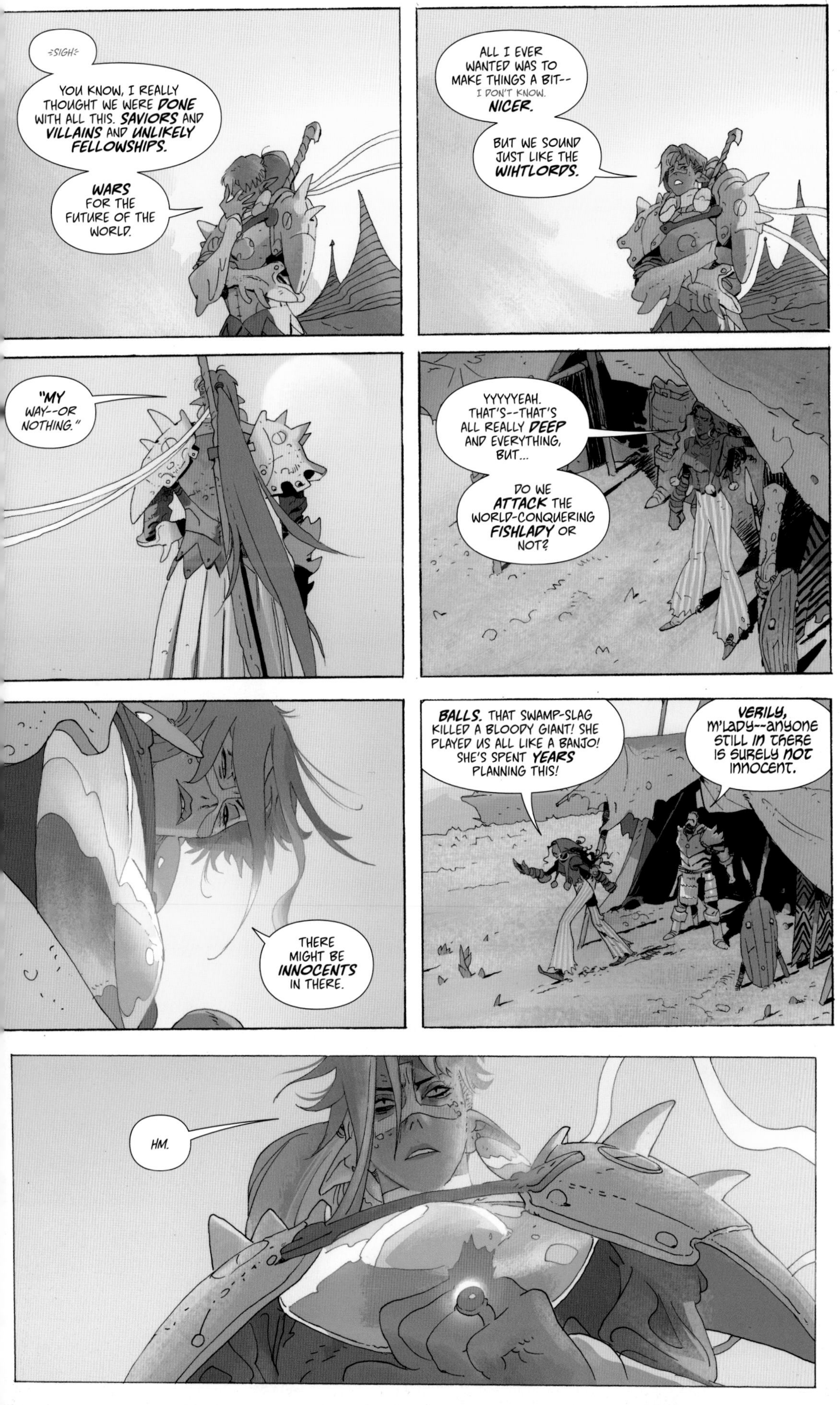

=SIGH=
YOU KNOW, I REALLY THOUGHT WE WERE DONE WITH ALL THIS. SAVIORS AND VILLAINS AND UNLIKELY FELLOWSHIPS.
WARS FOR THE FUTURE OF THE WORLD.
ALL I EVER WANTED WAS TO MAKE THINGS A BIT-- I DON'T KNOW. NICER.
BUT WE SOUND JUST LIKE THE WIHTLORDS.
"MY WAY--OR NOTHING."
YYYYYEAH. THAT'S--THAT'S ALL REALLY DEEP AND EVERYTHING, BUT...
DO WE ATTACK THE WORLD-CONQUERING FISHLADY OR NOT?
THERE MIGHT BE INNOCENTS IN THERE.
BALLS. THAT SWAMP-SLAG KILLED A BLOODY GIANT! SHE PLAYED US ALL LIKE A BANJO! SHE'S SPENT YEARS PLANNING THIS!
VERILY, M'LADY--ANYONE STILL IN THERE IS SURELY NOT INNOCENT.
HM.

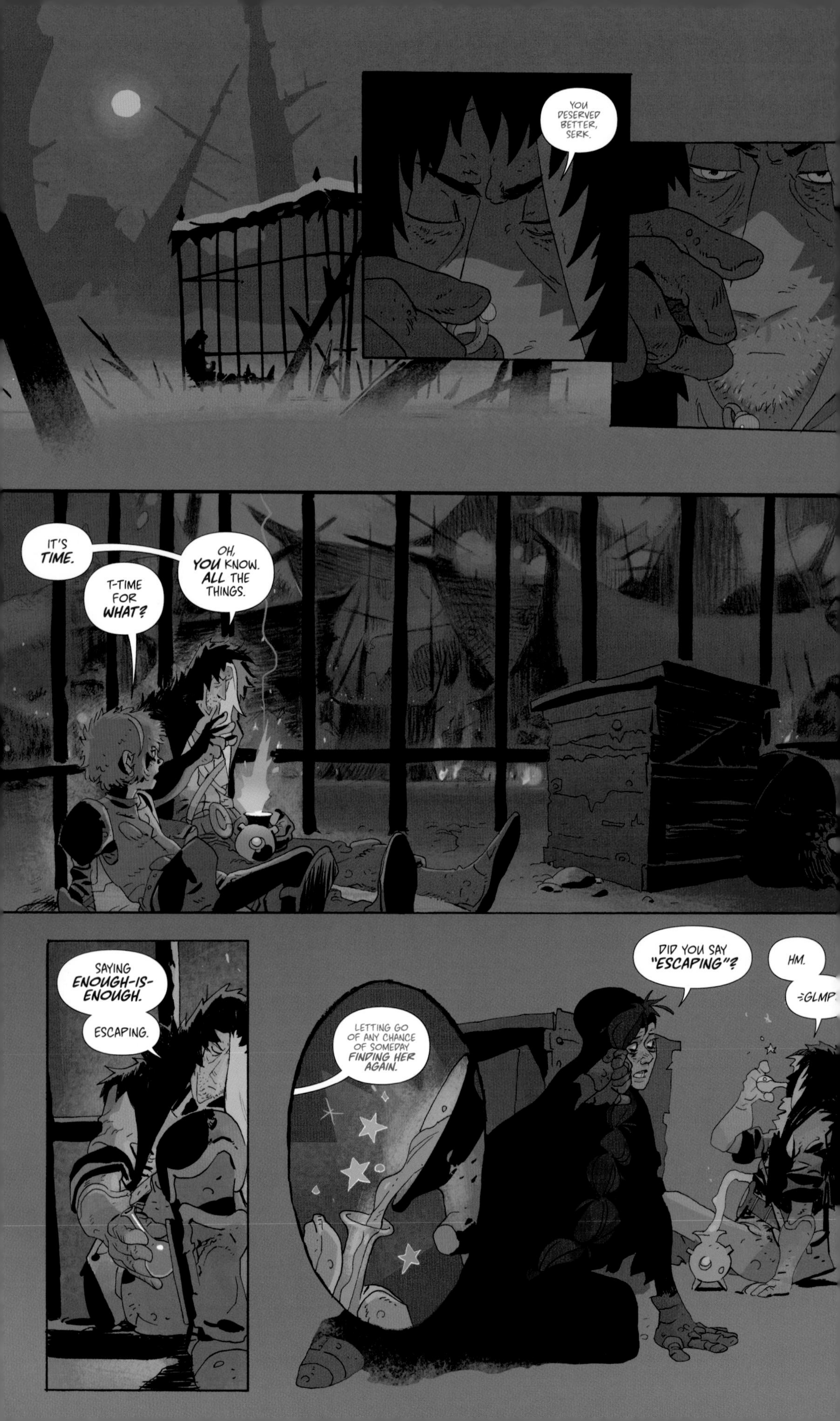
YOU DESERVED BETTER, SERK.
IT'S TIME.
T-TIME FOR WHAT?
OH, YOU KNOW. ALL THE THINGS.
SAYING ENOUGH-IS-ENOUGH.
ESCAPING.
LETTING GO OF ANY CHANCE OF SOMEDAY FINDING HER AGAIN.
DID YOU SAY "ESCAPING"?
HM.
=GLMP

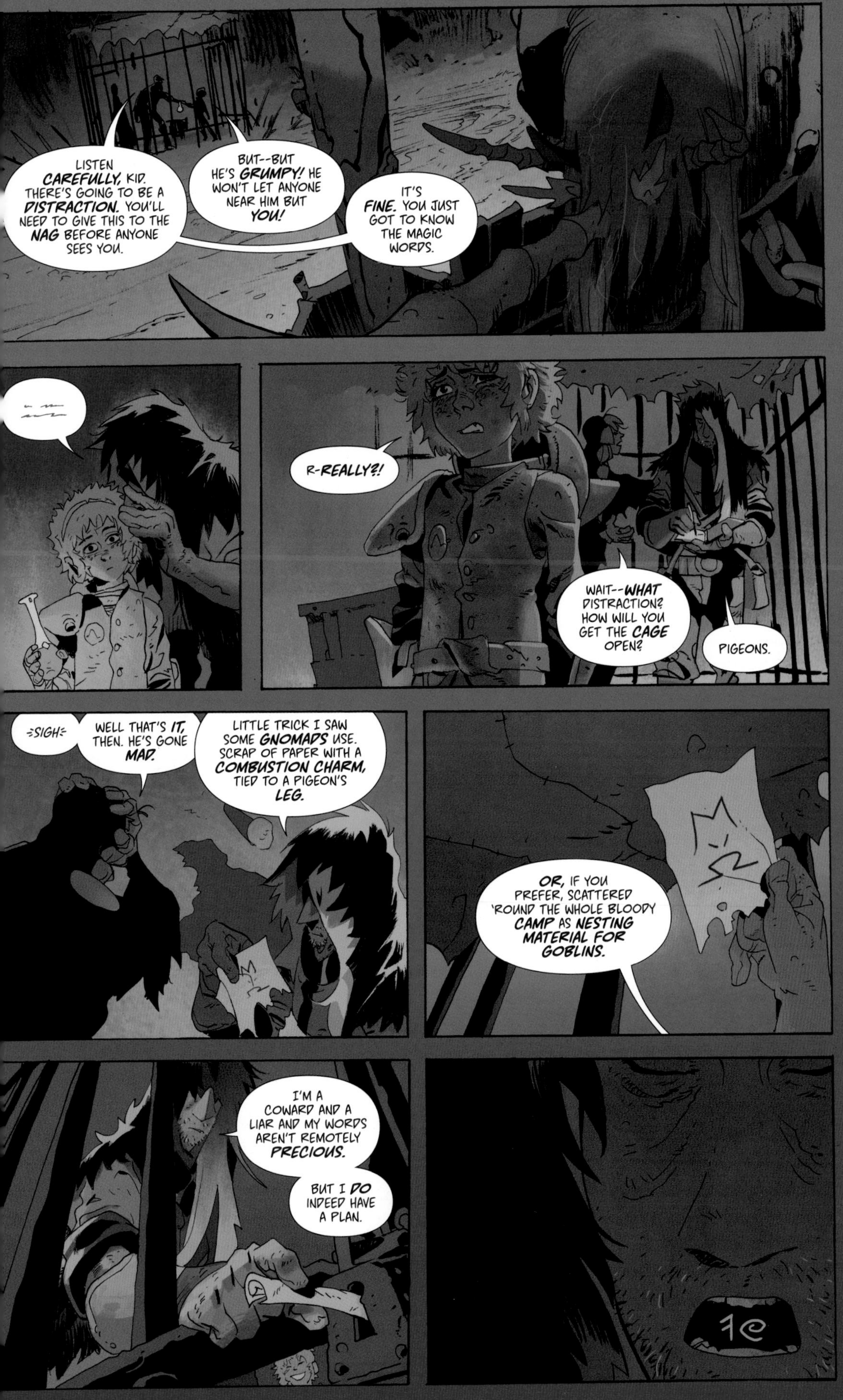
LISTEN CAREFULLY, KID. THERE'S GOING TO BE A DISTRACTION. YOU'LL NEED TO GIVE THIS TO THE NAG BEFORE ANYONE SEES YOU.
BUT--BUT HE'S GRUMPY! HE WON'T LET ANYONE NEAR HIM BUT YOU!
IT'S FINE. YOU JUST GOT TO KNOW THE MAGIC WORDS.
R-REALLY?!
WAIT--WHAT DISTRACTION? HOW WILL YOU GET THE CAGE OPEN?
PIGEONS.
=SIGH=
WELL THAT'S IT, THEN. HE'S GONE MAD.
LITTLE TRICK I SAW SOME GNOMADS USE. SCRAP OF PAPER WITH A COMBUSTION CHARM, TIED TO A PIGEON'S LEG.
OR, IF YOU PREFER, SCATTERED 'ROUND THE WHOLE BLOODY CAMP AS NESTING MATERIAL FOR GOBLINS.
I'M A COWARD AND A LIAR AND MY WORDS AREN'T REMOTELY PRECIOUS.
BUT I DO INDEED HAVE A PLAN.

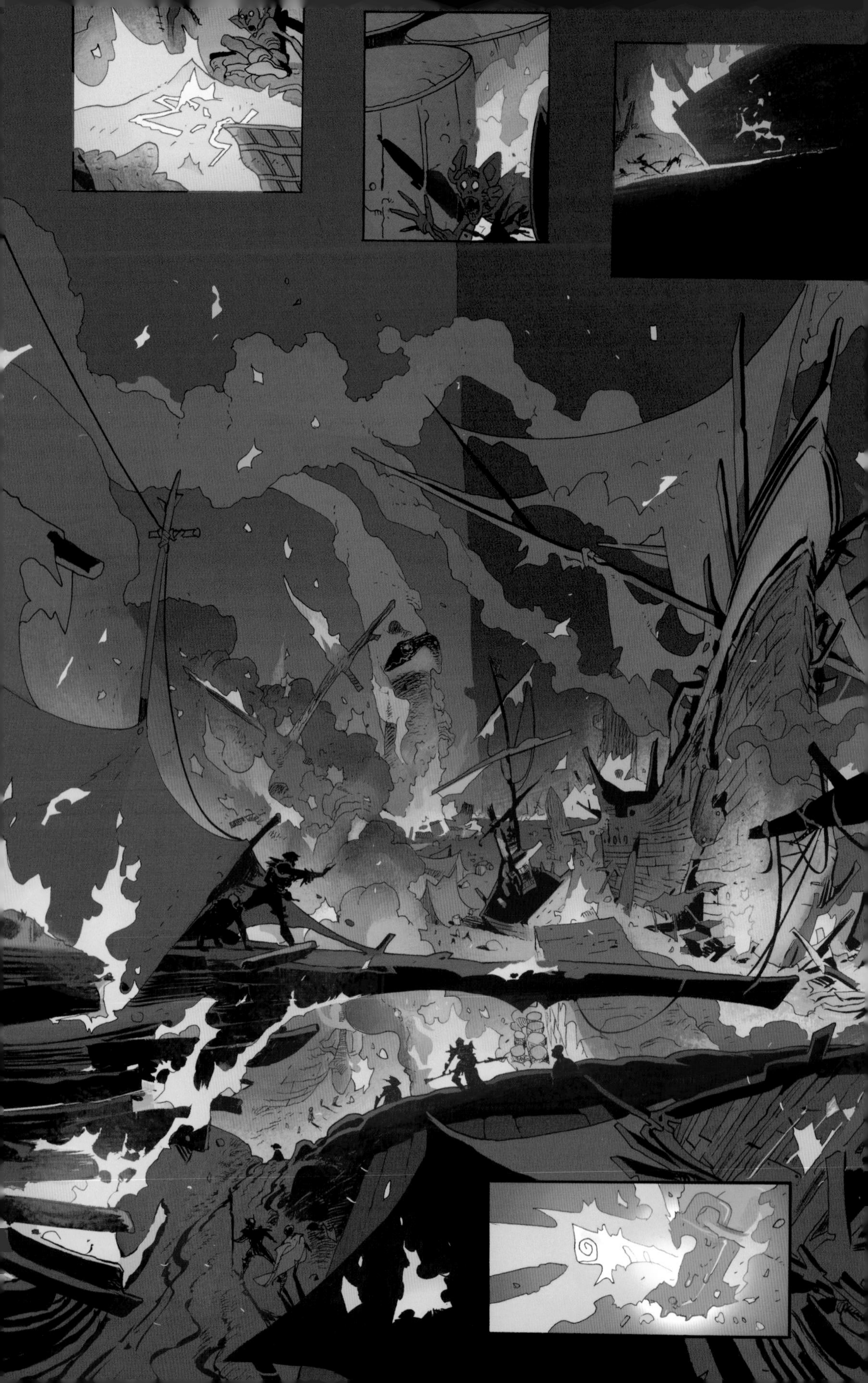

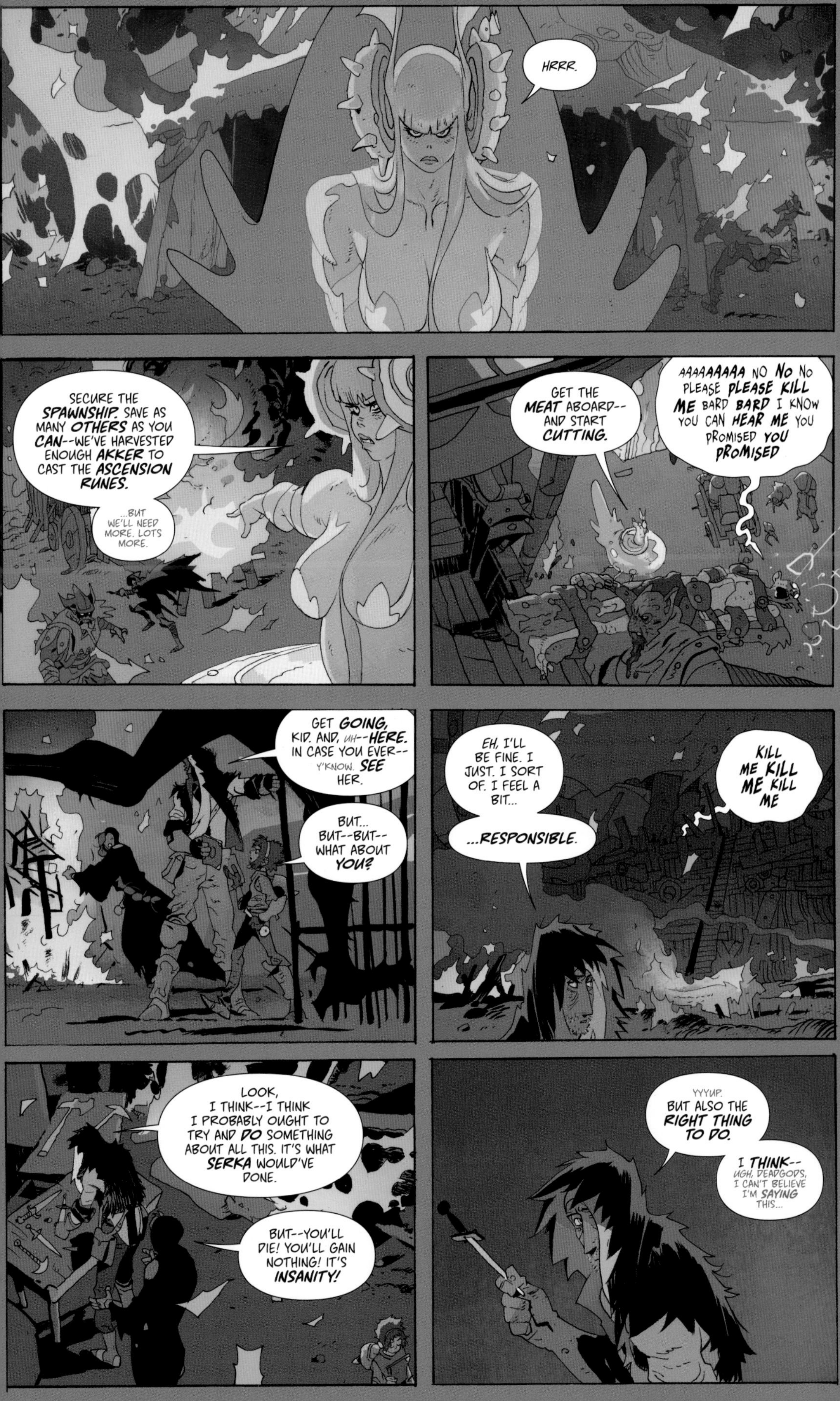
HRRR.
SECURE THE SPAWNSHIP. SAVE AS MANY OTHERS AS YOU CAN--WE'VE HARVESTED ENOUGH AKKER TO CAST THE ASCENSION RUNES.
...BUT WE'LL NEED MORE. LOTS MORE.
GET THE MEAT ABOARD-- AND START CUTTING.
AAAAAAAAA NO NO NO PLEASE PLEASE KILL ME BARD BARD I KNOW YOU CAN HEAR ME YOU PROMISED YOU PROMISED
GET GOING, KID. AND, UH--HERE. IN CASE YOU EVER-- Y'KNOW. SEE HER.
BUT... BUT--BUT-- WHAT ABOUT YOU?
EH, I'LL BE FINE. I JUST. I SORT OF. I FEEL A BIT...
...RESPONSIBLE.
KILL ME KILL ME KILL ME
LOOK, I THINK--I THINK I PROBABLY OUGHT TO TRY AND DO SOMETHING ABOUT ALL THIS. IT'S WHAT SERKA WOULD'VE DONE.
BUT--YOU'LL DIE! YOU'LL GAIN NOTHING! IT'S INSANITY!
YYYUP. BUT ALSO THE RIGHT THING TO DO.
I THINK-- UGH, DEADGODS, I CAN'T BELIEVE I'M SAYING THIS...

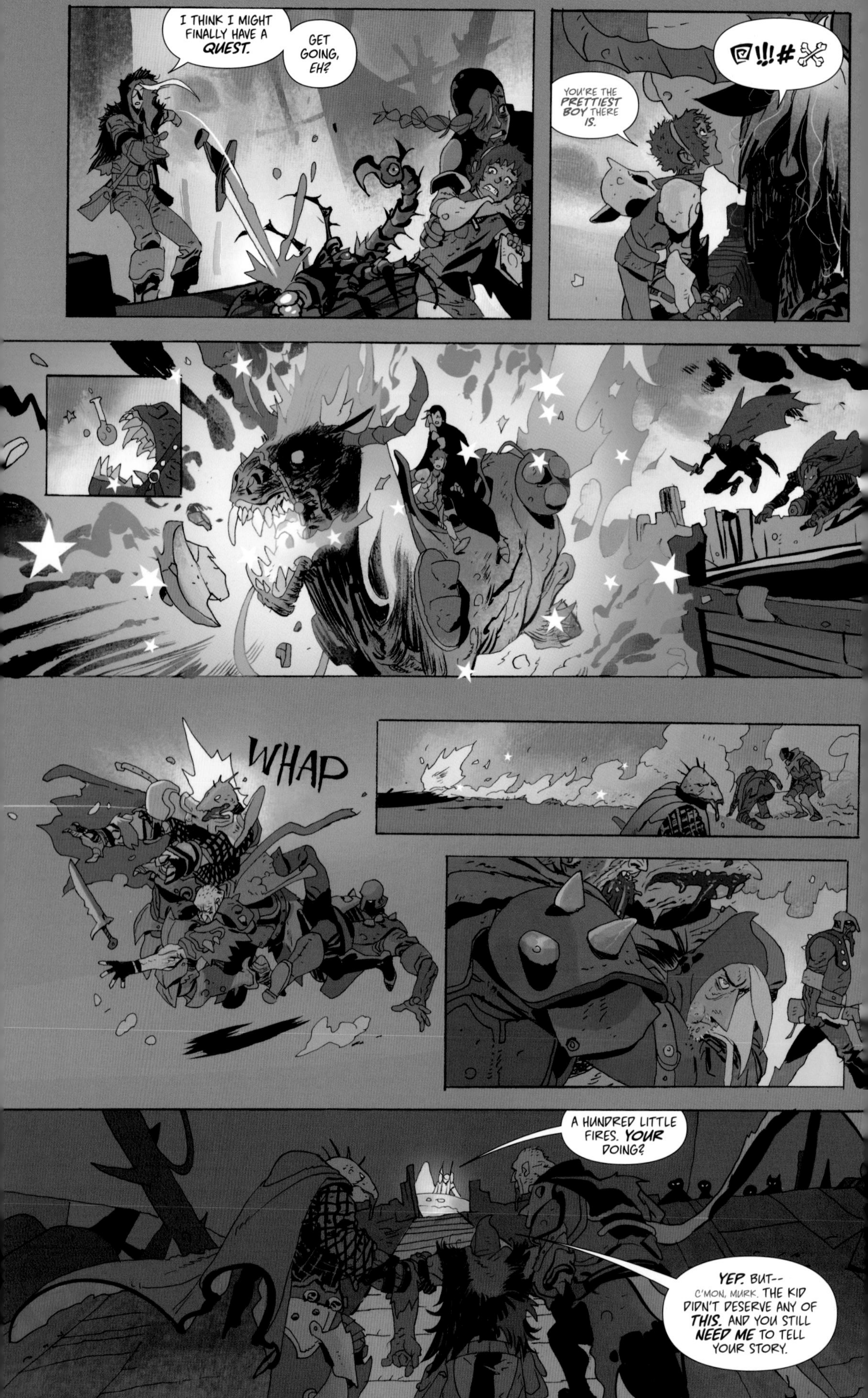
I THINK I MIGHT FINALLY HAVE A QUEST.
GET GOING, EH?
YOU'RE THE PRETTIEST BOY THERE IS.
@!!!#
WHAP
A HUNDRED LITTLE FIRES. YOUR DOING?
YEP. BUT-- C'MON, MURK. THE KID DIDN'T DESERVE ANY OF THIS. AND YOU STILL NEED ME TO TELL YOUR STORY.

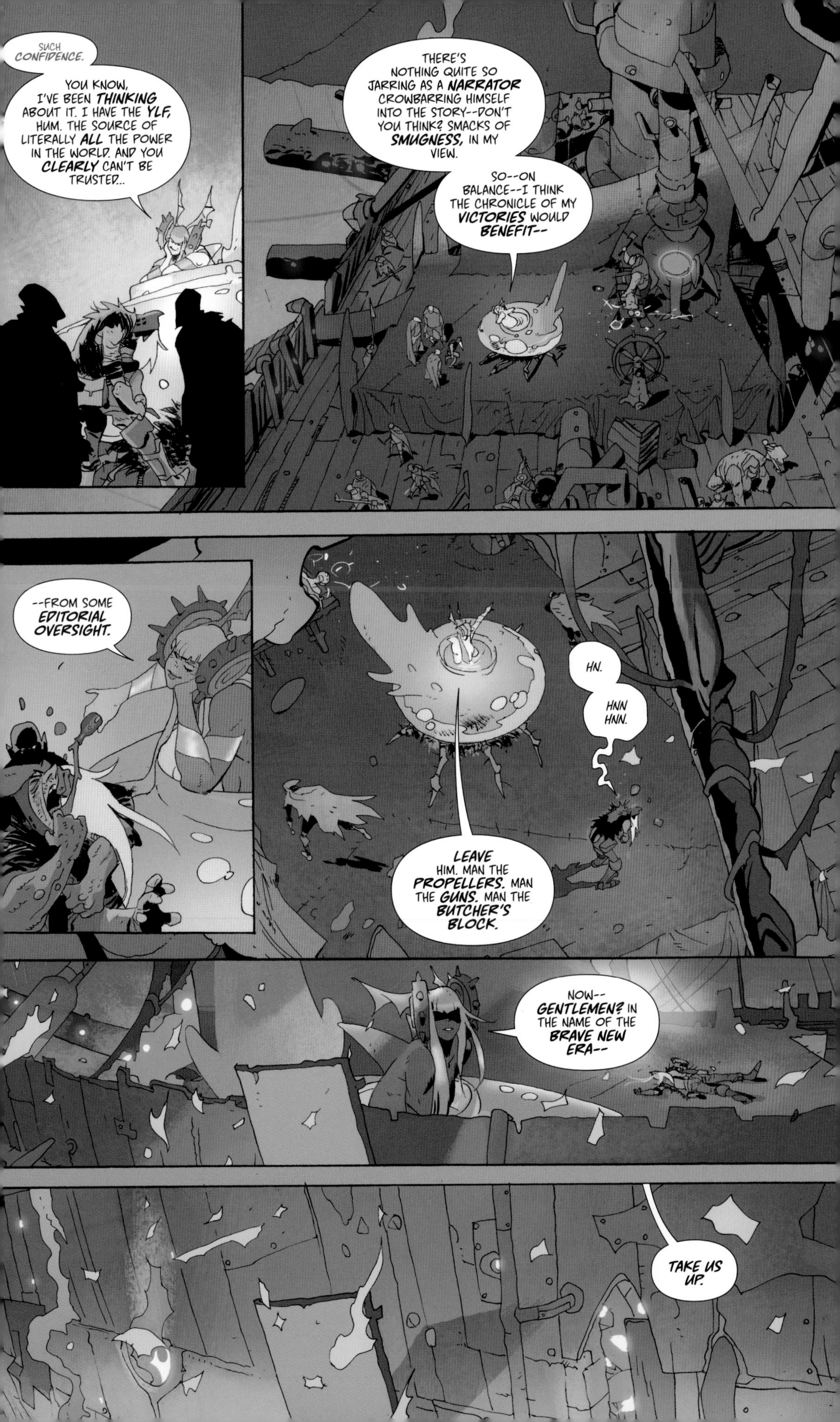
SUCH CONFIDENCE.
YOU KNOW, I'VE BEEN THINKING ABOUT IT. I HAVE THE YLF, HUM. THE SOURCE OF LITERALLY ALL THE POWER IN THE WORLD. AND YOU CLEARLY CAN'T BE TRUSTED...
THERE'S NOTHING QUITE SO JARRING AS A NARRATOR CROWBARRING HIMSELF INTO THE STORY--DON'T YOU THINK? SMACKS OF SMUGNESS, IN MY VIEW.
SO--ON BALANCE--I THINK THE CHRONICLE OF MY VICTORIES WOULD BENEFIT--
--FROM SOME EDITORIAL OVERSIGHT.
HN.
HNN HNN.
LEAVE HIM. MAN THE PROPELLERS. MAN THE GUNS. MAN THE BUTCHER'S BLOCK.
NOW--GENTLEMEN? IN THE NAME OF THE BRAVE NEW ERA--
TAKE US UP.

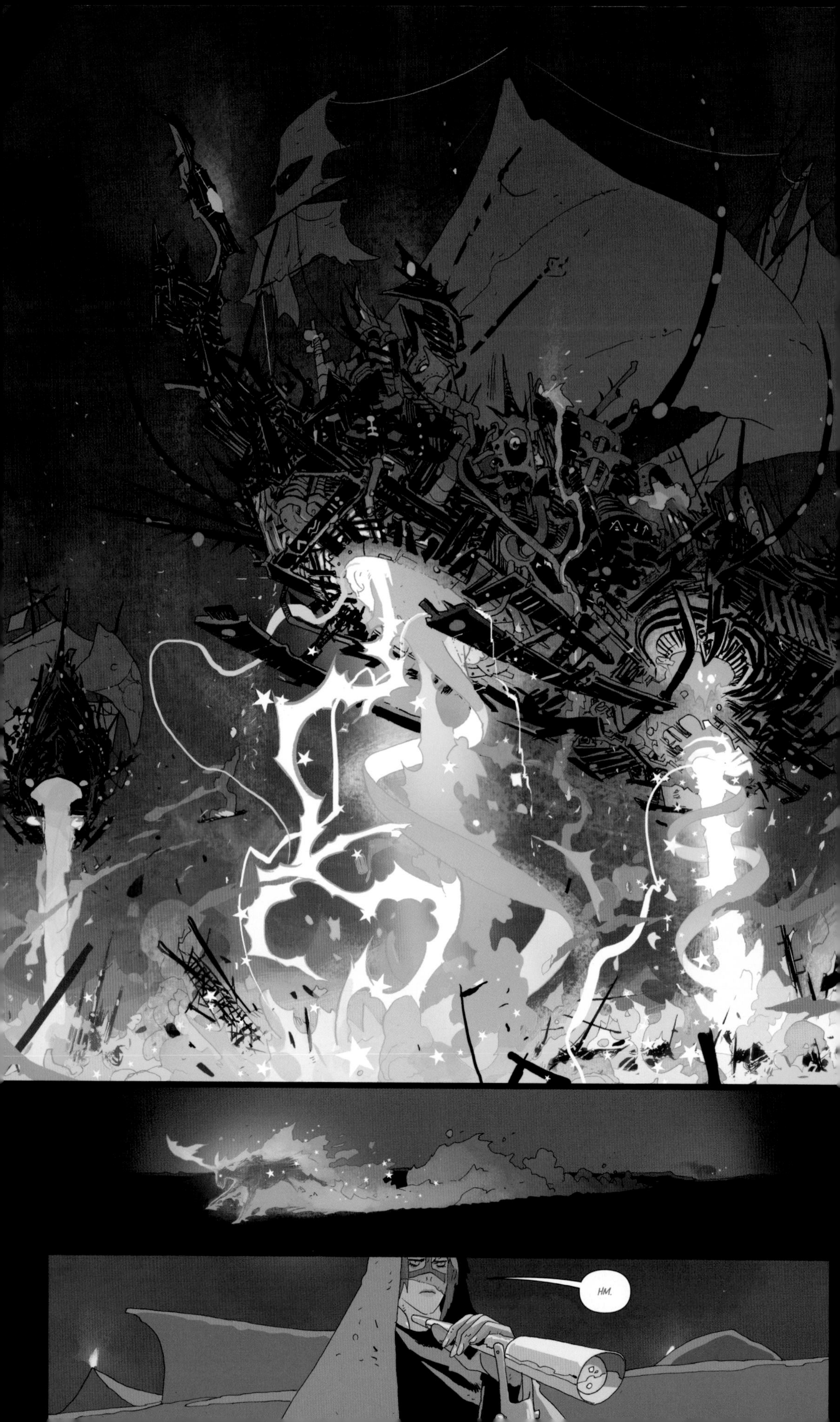
HM.

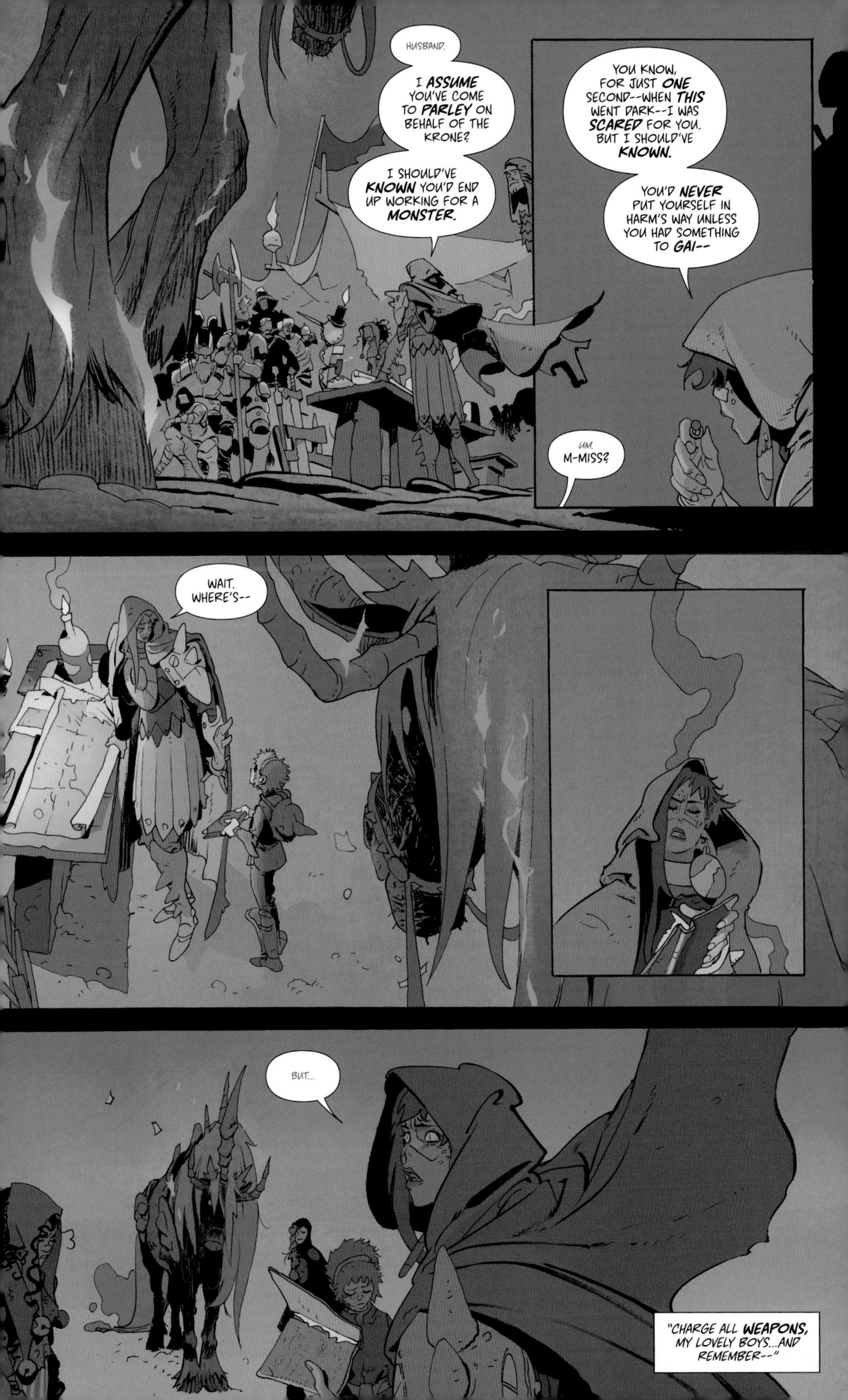
HUSBAND.
I ASSUME YOU'VE COME TO PARLEY ON BEHALF OF THE KRONE?
I SHOULD'VE KNOWN YOU'D END UP WORKING FOR A MONSTER.
YOU KNOW, FOR JUST ONE SECOND--WHEN THIS WENT DARK--I WAS SCARED FOR YOU. BUT I SHOULD'VE KNOWN.
YOU'D NEVER PUT YOURSELF IN HARM'S WAY UNLESS YOU HAD SOMETHING TO GAI--
UM. M-MISS?
WAIT. WHERE'S--
BUT...
"CHARGE ALL WEAPONS, MY LOVELY BOYS...AND REMEMBER--"

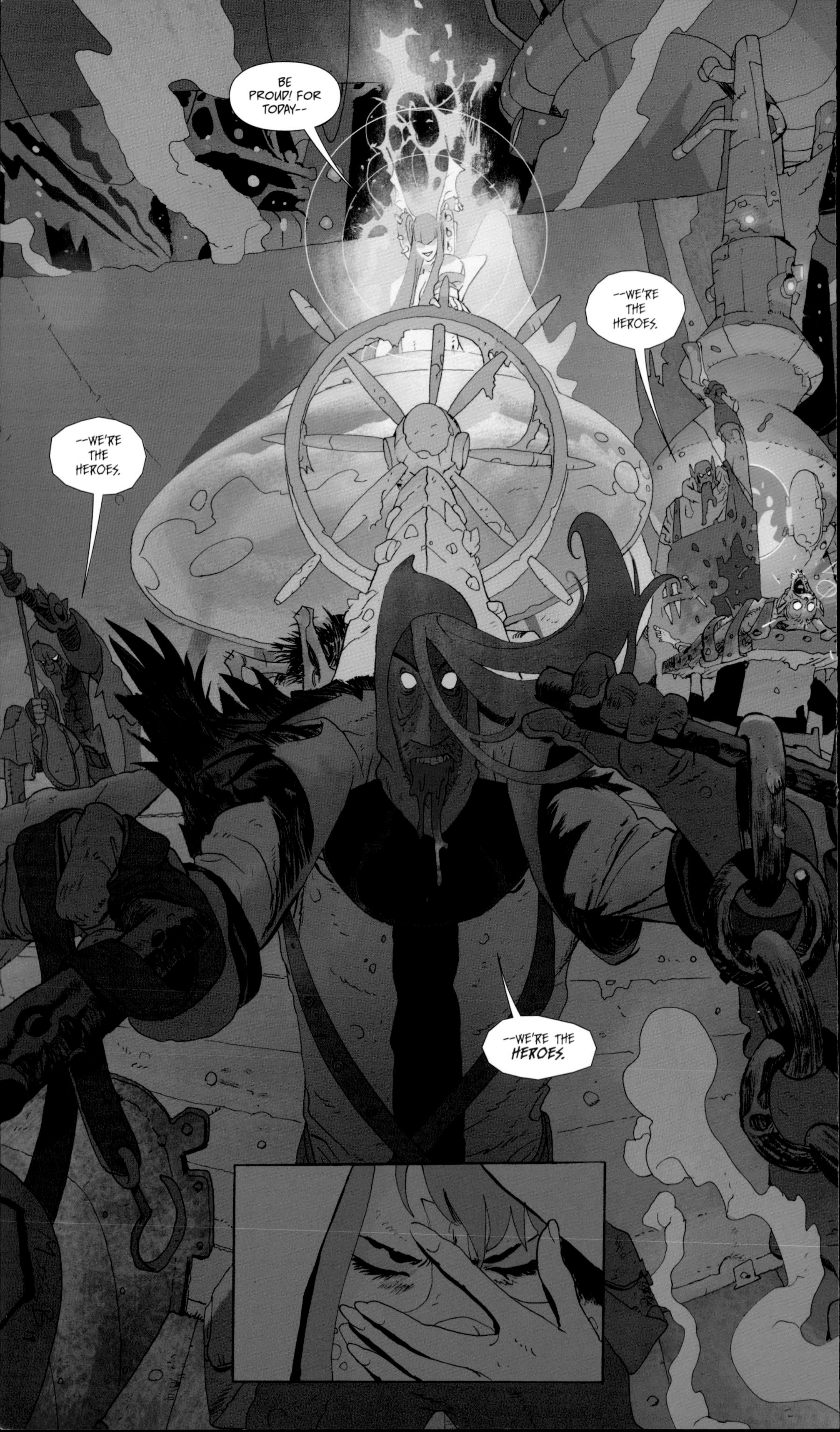
BE PROUD! FOR TODAY--
--WE'RE THE HEROES.
--WE'RE THE HEROES.
--WE'RE THE HEROES.

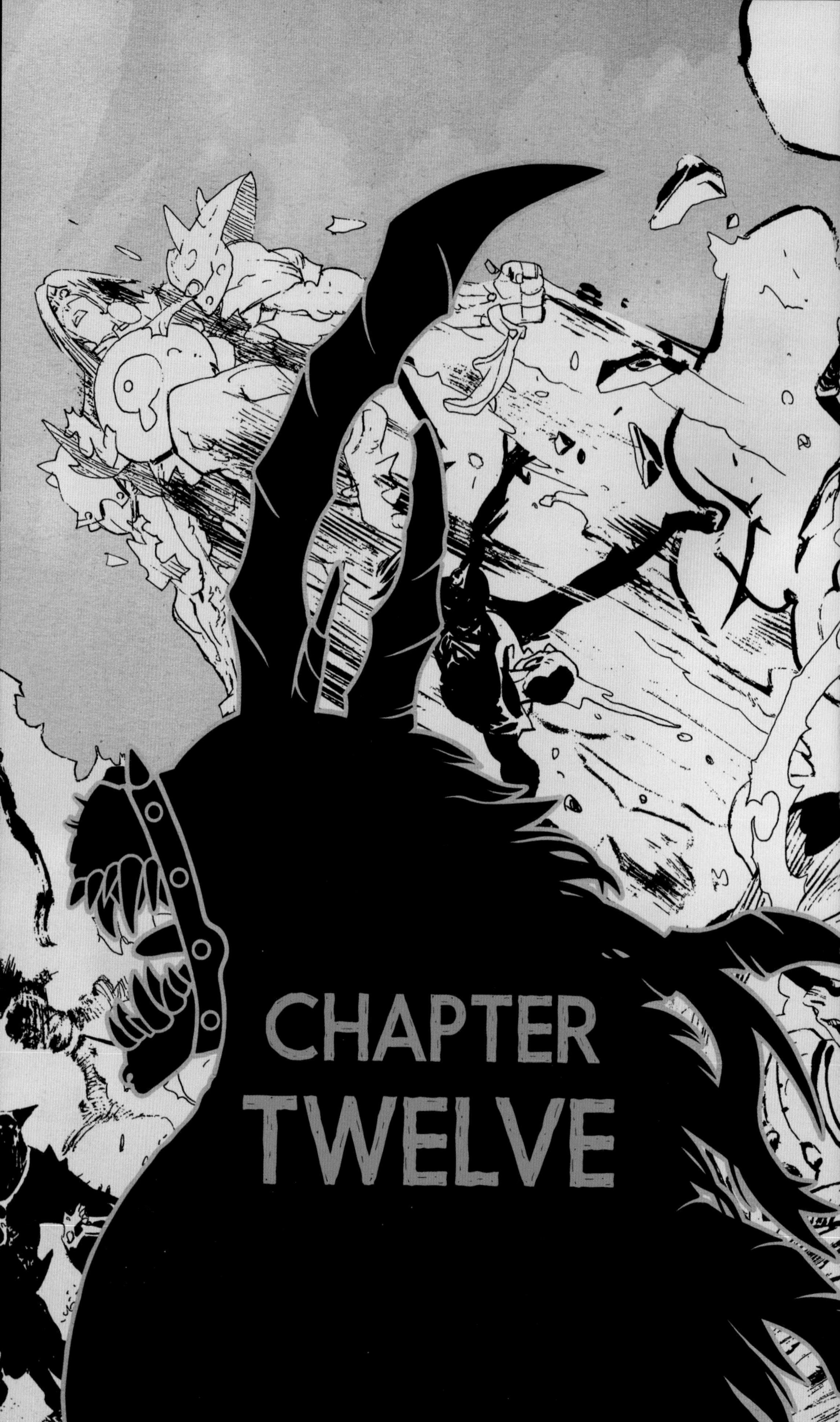
CHAPTER
TWELVE

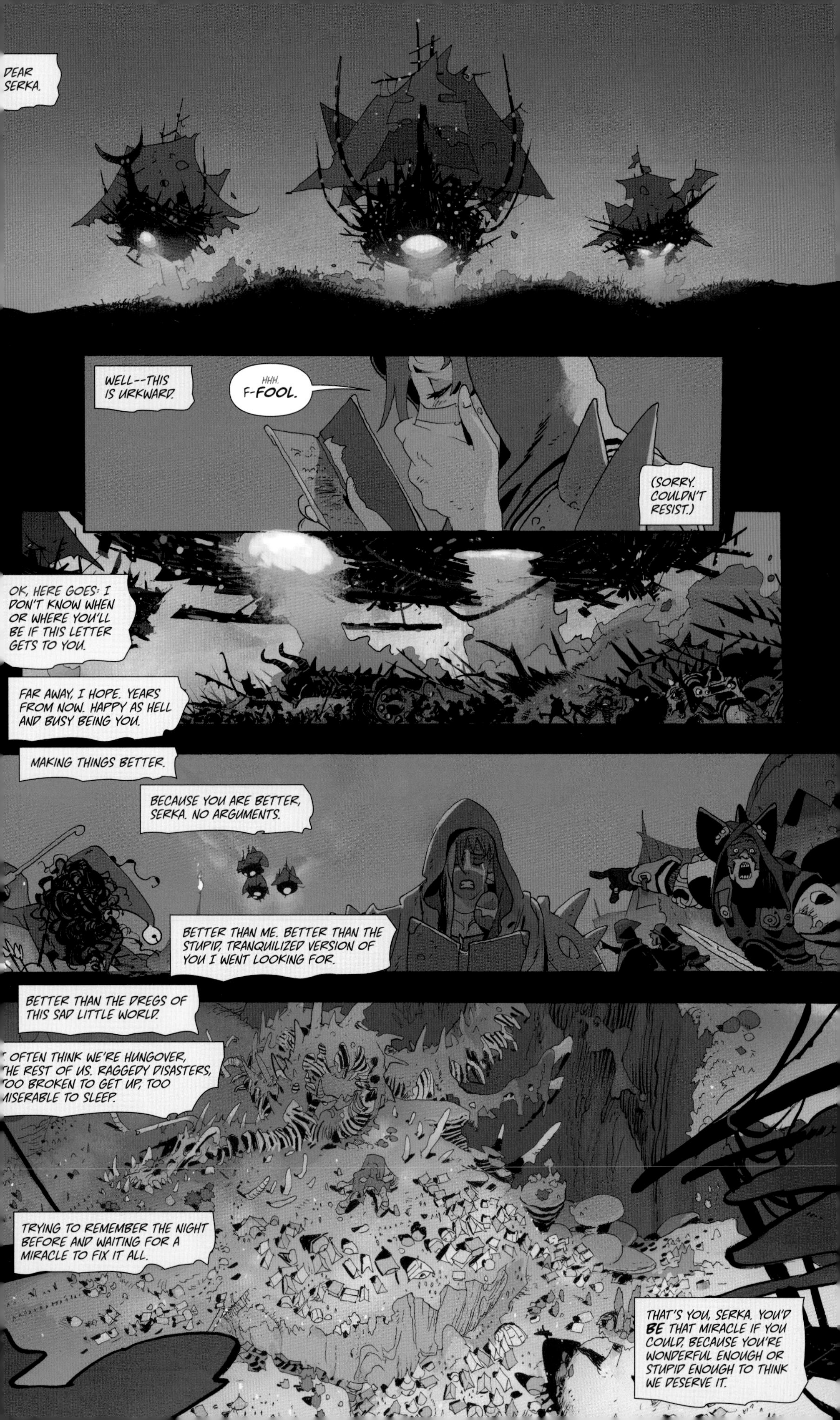
DEAR SERKA.
WELL--THIS IS URKWARD.
HHH. F-FOOL.
(SORRY. COULDN'T RESIST.)
OK, HERE GOES: I DON'T KNOW WHEN OR WHERE YOU'LL BE IF THIS LETTER GETS TO YOU.
FAR AWAY, I HOPE. YEARS FROM NOW. HAPPY AS HELL AND BUSY BEING YOU.
MAKING THINGS BETTER.
BECAUSE YOU ARE BETTER, SERKA. NO ARGUMENTS.
BETTER THAN ME. BETTER THAN THE STUPID, TRANQUILIZED VERSION OF YOU I WENT LOOKING FOR.
BETTER THAN THE DREGS OF THIS SAD LITTLE WORLD.
I OFTEN THINK WE'RE HUNGOVER, THE REST OF US. RAGGEDY DISASTERS, TOO BROKEN TO GET UP, TOO MISERABLE TO SLEEP.
TRYING TO REMEMBER THE NIGHT BEFORE AND WAITING FOR A MIRACLE TO FIX IT ALL.
THAT'S YOU, SERKA. YOU'D BE THAT MIRACLE IF YOU COULD, BECAUSE YOU'RE WONDERFUL ENOUGH OR STUPID ENOUGH TO THINK WE DESERVE IT.

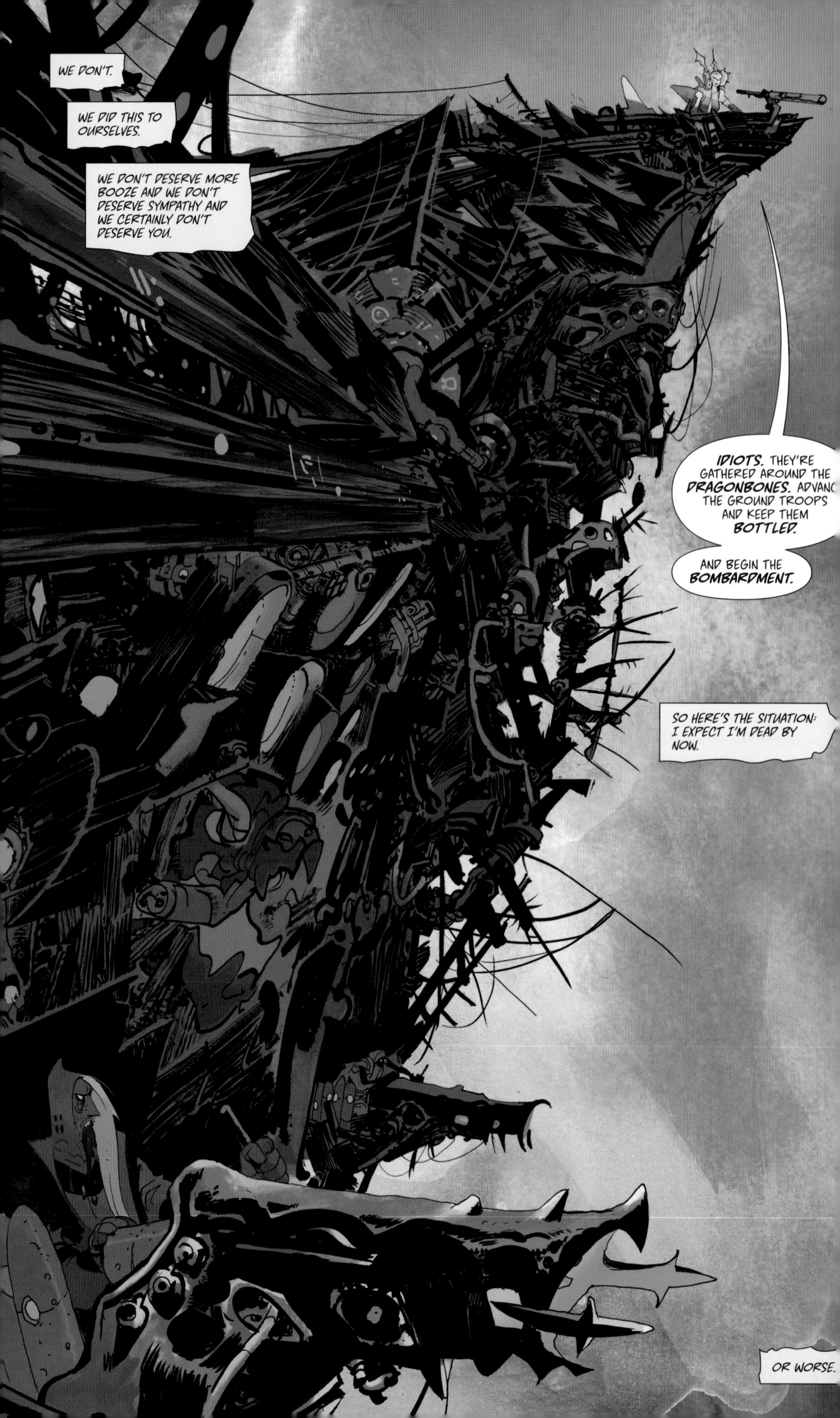

WE DON'T.
WE DID THIS TO OURSELVES.
WE DON'T DESERVE MORE BOOZE AND WE DON'T DESERVE SYMPATHY AND WE CERTAINLY DON'T DESERVE YOU.
IDIOTS. THEY'RE GATHERED AROUND THE DRAGONBONES. ADVANC THE GROUND TROOPS AND KEEP THEM BOTTLED.
AND BEGIN THE BOMBARDMENT.
SO HERE'S THE SITUATION: I EXPECT I'M DEAD BY NOW.
OR WORSE.

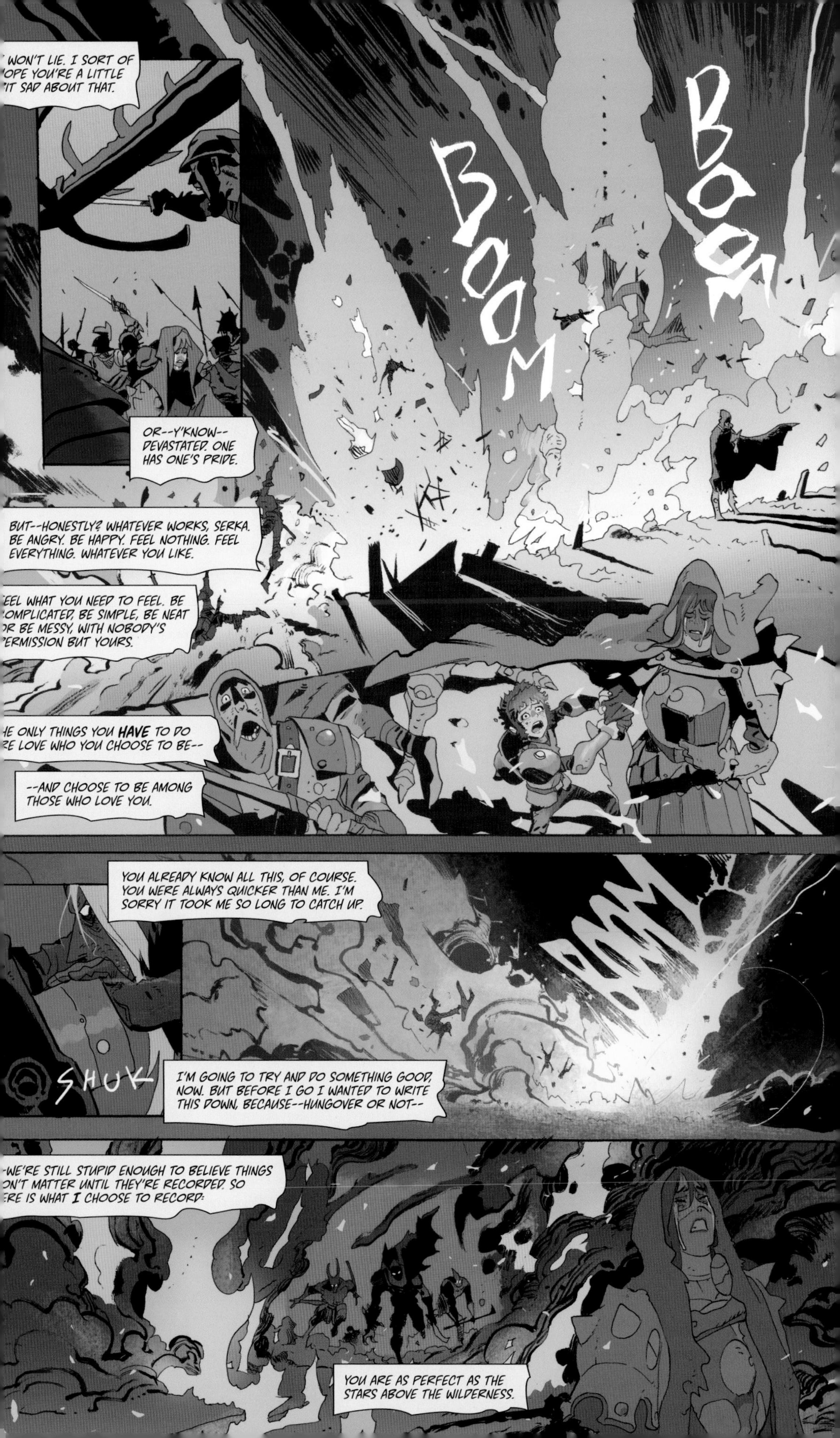
I WON'T LIE. I SORT OF HOPE YOU'RE A LITTLE BIT SAD ABOUT THAT.
BOOM
BOOM
OR--Y'KNOW--DEVASTATED. ONE HAS ONE'S PRIDE.
BUT--HONESTLY? WHATEVER WORKS, SERKA. BE ANGRY. BE HAPPY. FEEL NOTHING. FEEL EVERYTHING. WHATEVER YOU LIKE.
FEEL WHAT YOU NEED TO FEEL. BE COMPLICATED, BE SIMPLE, BE NEAT OR BE MESSY, WITH NOBODY'S PERMISSION BUT YOURS.
THE ONLY THINGS YOU **HAVE** TO DO ARE LOVE WHO YOU CHOOSE TO BE--
--AND CHOOSE TO BE AMONG THOSE WHO LOVE YOU.
YOU ALREADY KNOW ALL THIS, OF COURSE. YOU WERE ALWAYS QUICKER THAN ME. I'M SORRY IT TOOK ME SO LONG TO CATCH UP.
BOOM
SHUK
I'M GOING TO TRY AND DO SOMETHING GOOD, NOW. BUT BEFORE I GO I WANTED TO WRITE THIS DOWN, BECAUSE--HUNGOVER OR NOT--
--WE'RE STILL STUPID ENOUGH TO BELIEVE THINGS DON'T MATTER UNTIL THEY'RE RECORDED. SO HERE IS WHAT **I** CHOOSE TO RECORD:
YOU ARE AS PERFECT AS THE STARS ABOVE THE WILDERNESS.

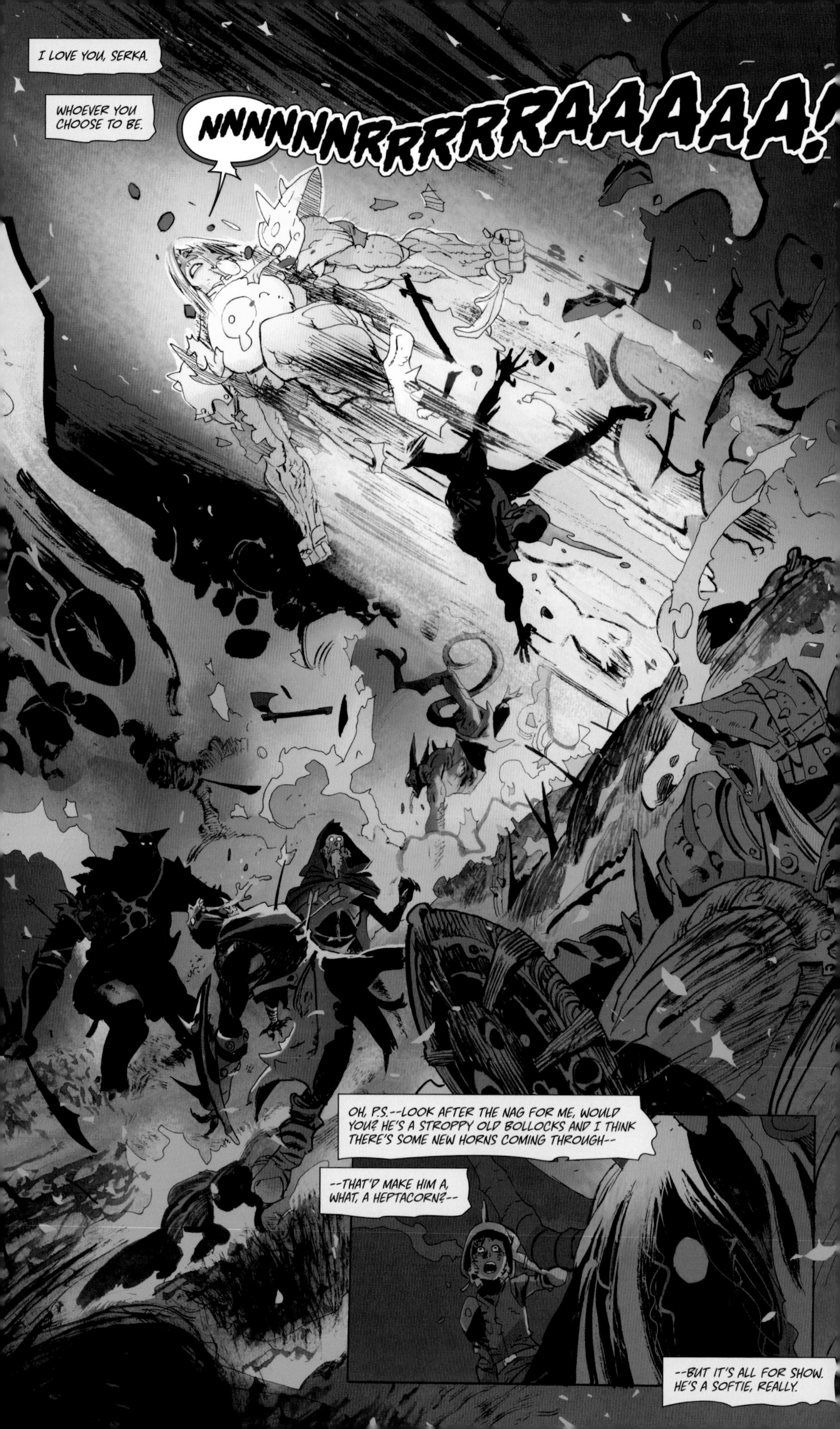
I LOVE YOU, SERKA.
WHOEVER YOU CHOOSE TO BE.
NNNNNNRRRRRAAAAAA!
OH, P.S.--LOOK AFTER THE NAG FOR ME, WOULD YOU? HE'S A STROPPY OLD BOLLOCKS AND I THINK THERE'S SOME NEW HORNS COMING THROUGH--
--THAT'D MAKE HIM A, WHAT, A HEPTACORN?--
--BUT IT'S ALL FOR SHOW. HE'S A SOFTIE, REALLY.

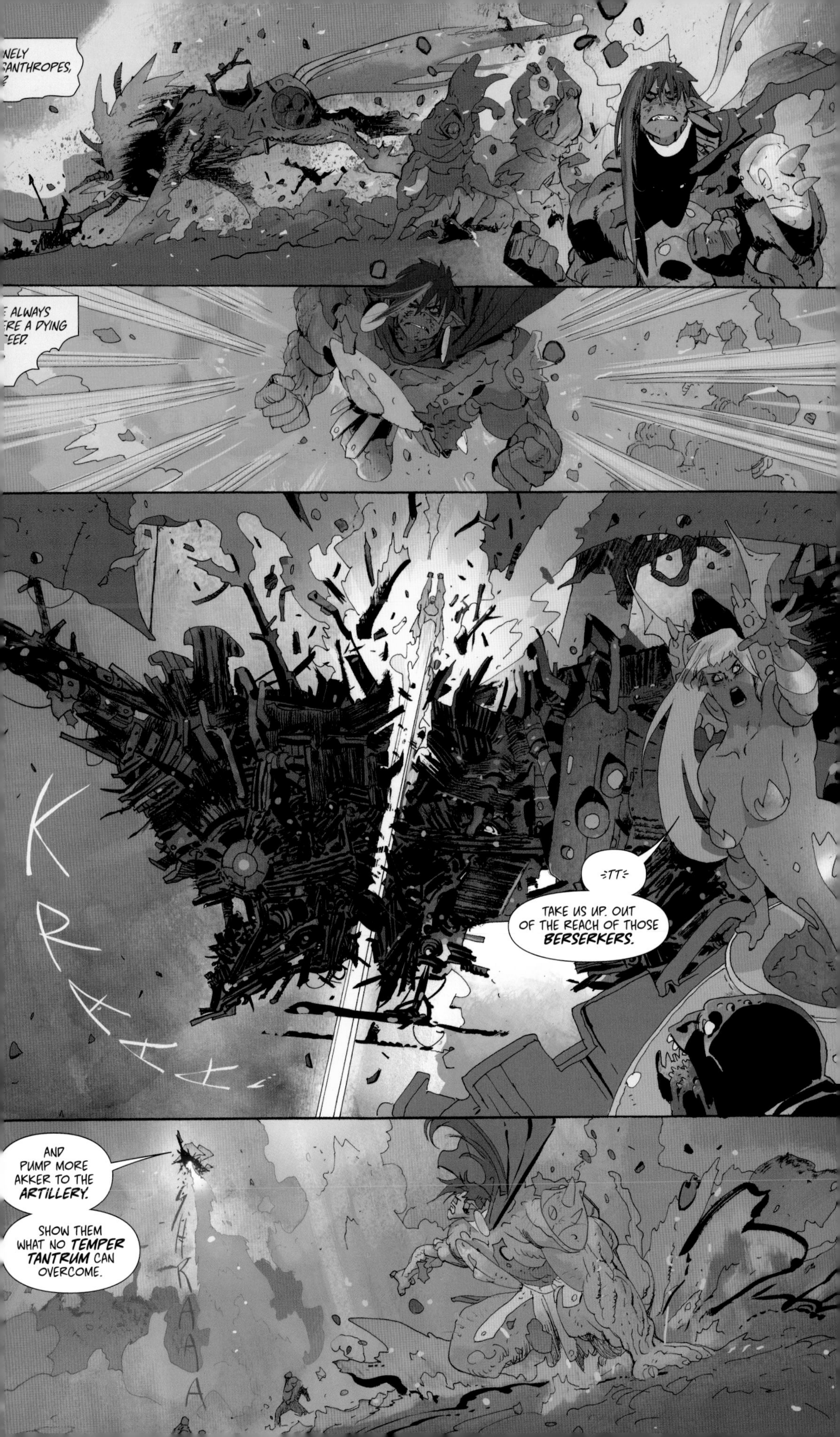
NELY
SANTHROPES,
E ALWAYS
ERE A DYING
EED.
KRAAAA
TT
TAKE US UP. OUT OF THE REACH OF THOSE **BERSERKERS.**
AND PUMP MORE AKKER TO THE **ARTILLERY.**
SHOW THEM WHAT NO **TEMPER TANTRUM** CAN OVERCOME.

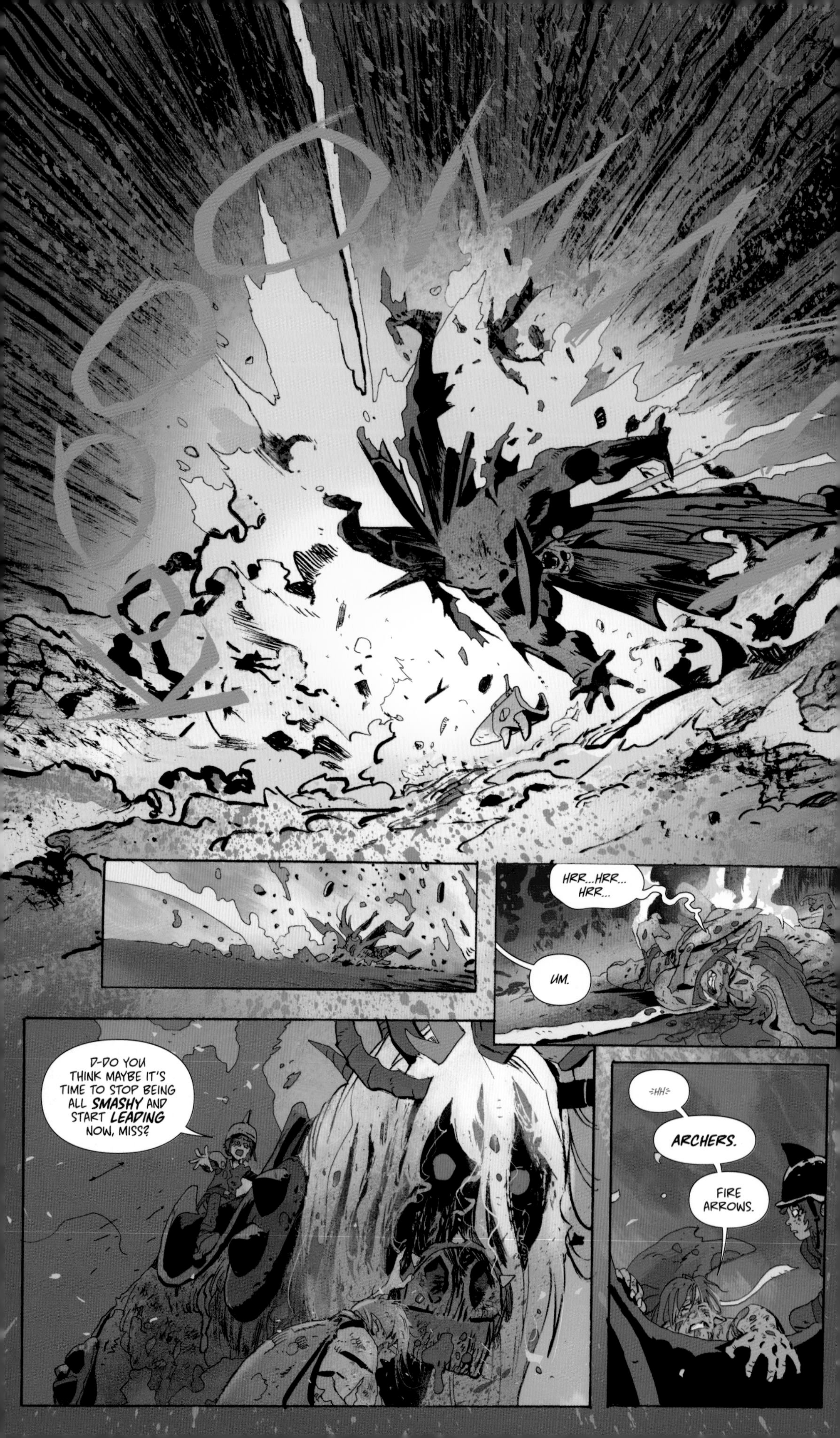
BOOOOM
HRR...HRR...
HRR...
UM.
D-DO YOU THINK MAYBE IT'S TIME TO STOP BEING ALL SMASHY AND START LEADING NOW, MISS?
HH
ARCHERS.
FIRE ARROWS.

"TELL THEM TO AIM OR THE **BOMBS**."

THWOT

THWIP

THWISH

BLAARGG

M...

M-MUTANT **SCORPION**...

MAKES YOU PUKE WHATEVER'S IN YOU...

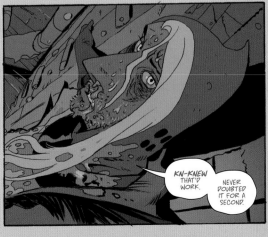

KN-KNEW THAT'D WORK.

NEVER DOUBTED IT FOR A SECOND.

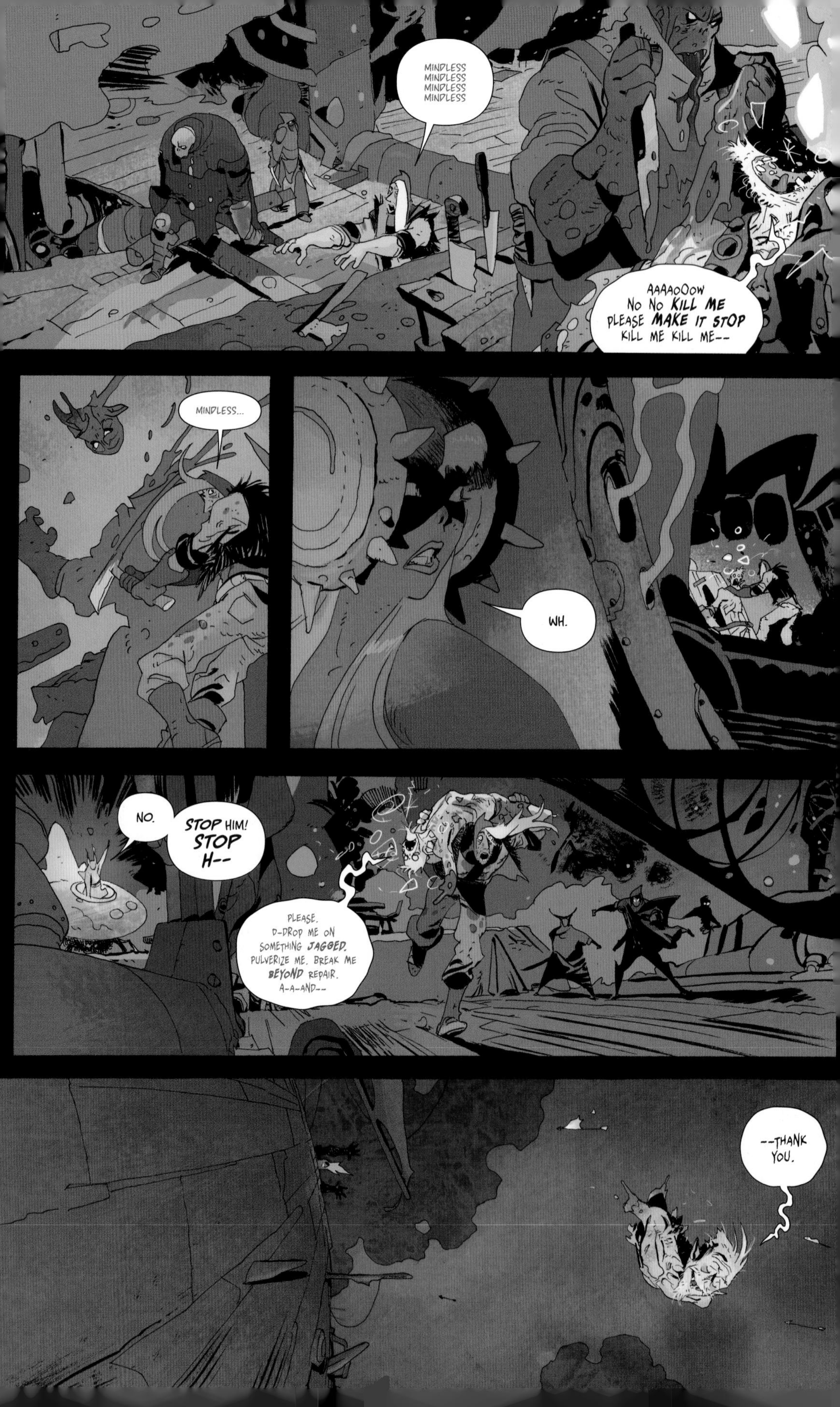
MINDLESS MINDLESS MINDLESS MINDLESS
AAAAOOOW No No KILL ME PLEASE MAKE IT STOP KILL ME KILL ME--
MINDLESS...
WH.
NO.
STOP HIM! STOP H--
PLEASE. D-DROP ME ON SOMETHING JAGGED. PULVERIZE ME. BREAK ME BEYOND REPAIR. A-A-AND--
--THANK YOU.

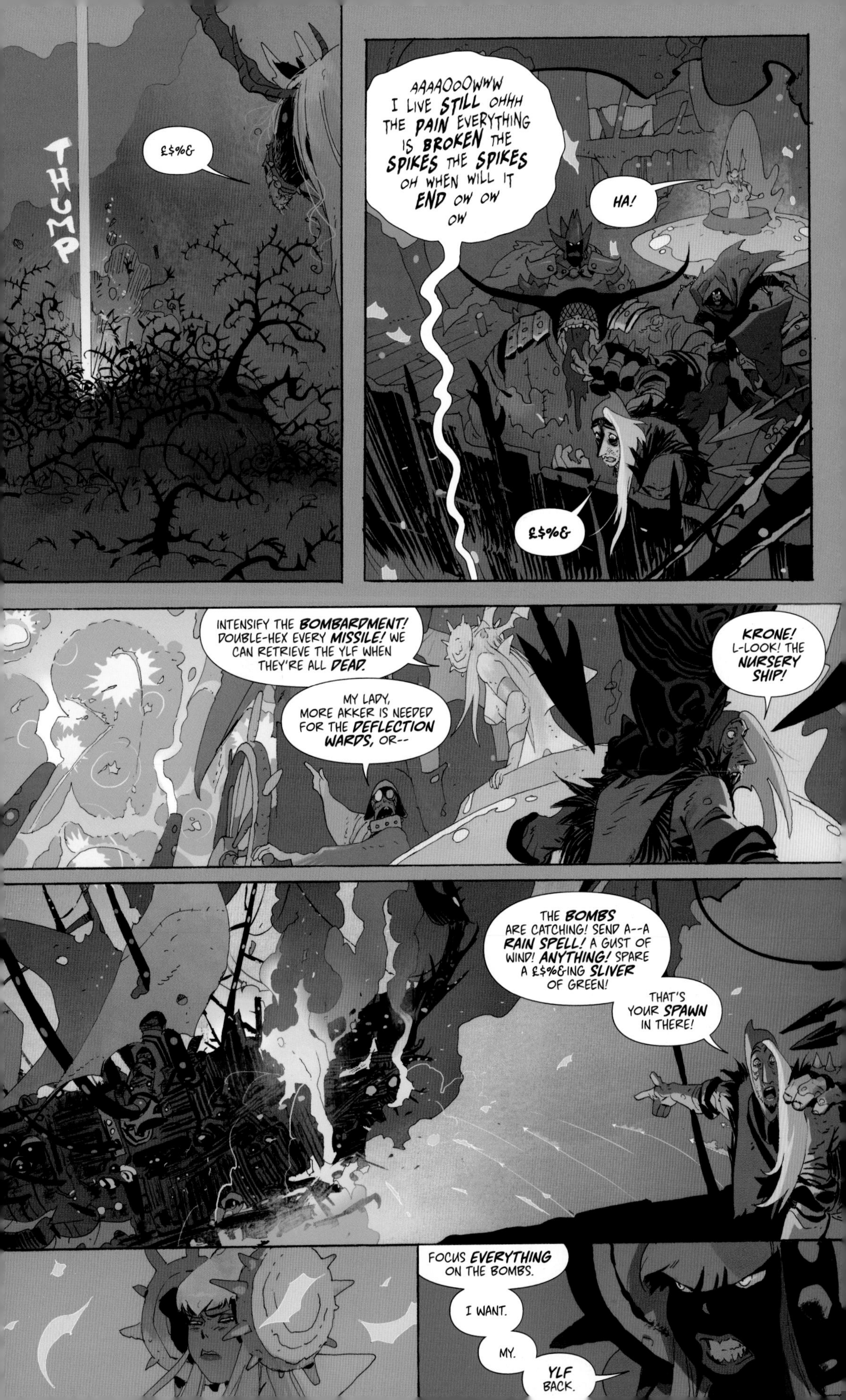
THUMP
£$%&
AAAAOOOWWW I LIVE STILL OHHH THE PAIN EVERYTHING IS BROKEN THE SPIKES THE SPIKES OH WHEN WILL IT END OW OW OW
HA!
£$%&
INTENSIFY THE BOMBARDMENT! DOUBLE-HEX EVERY MISSILE! WE CAN RETRIEVE THE YLF WHEN THEY'RE ALL DEAD.
MY LADY, MORE AKKER IS NEEDED FOR THE DEFLECTION WARDS, OR--
KRONE! L-LOOK! THE NURSERY SHIP!
THE BOMBS ARE CATCHING! SEND A--A RAIN SPELL! A GUST OF WIND! ANYTHING! SPARE A £$%&ING SLIVER OF GREEN!
THAT'S YOUR SPAWN IN THERE!
FOCUS EVERYTHING ON THE BOMBS.
I WANT.
MY.
YLF BACK.

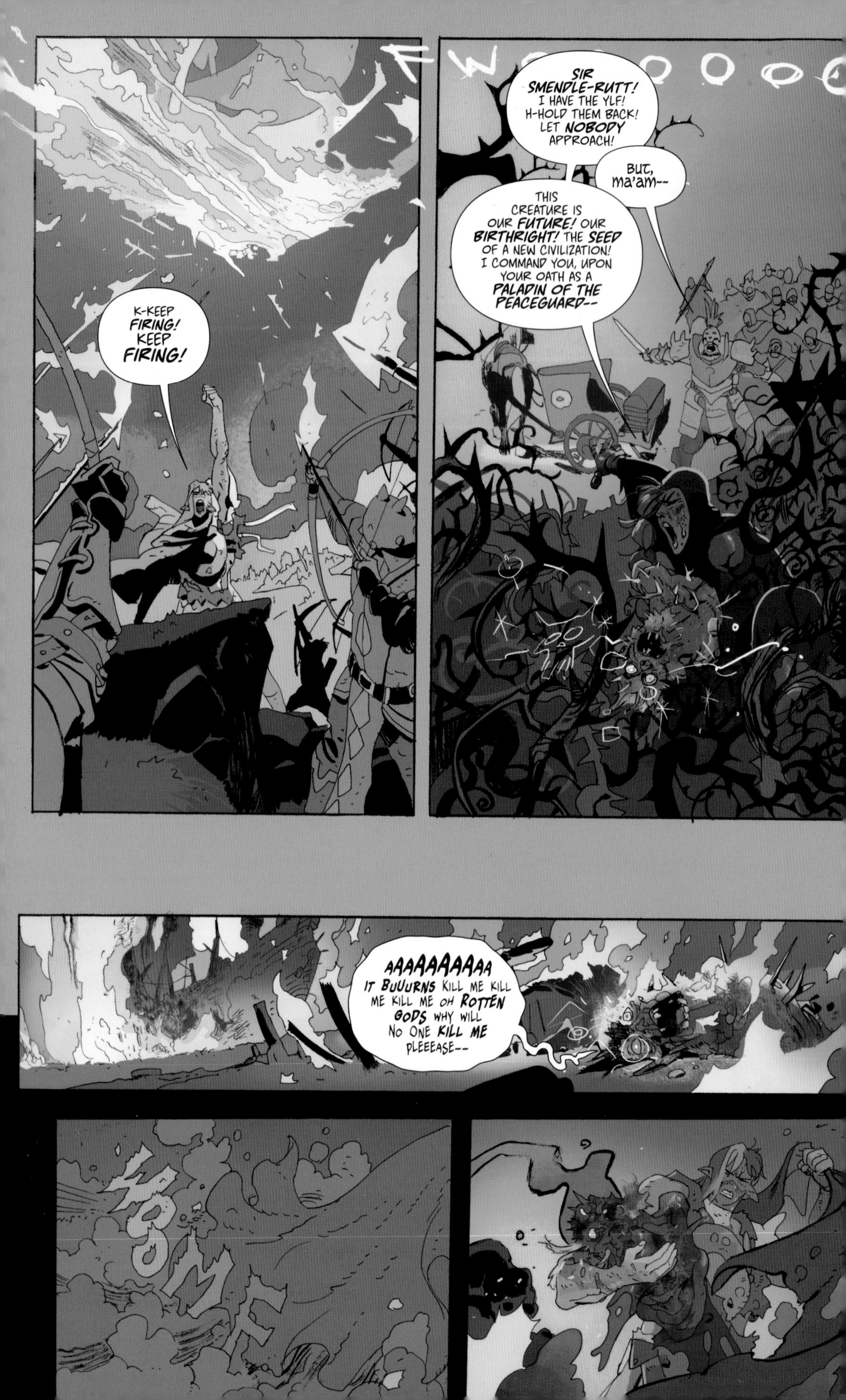
K-KEEP FIRING! KEEP FIRING!
FWOOOOOOO
SIR SMENDLE-RUTT! I HAVE THE YLF! H-HOLD THEM BACK! LET NOBODY APPROACH!
BUT, MA'AM--
THIS CREATURE IS OUR FUTURE! OUR BIRTHRIGHT! THE SEED OF A NEW CIVILIZATION! I COMMAND YOU, UPON YOUR OATH AS A PALADIN OF THE PEACEGUARD--
AAAAAAAAAA IT BUUURNS KILL ME KILL ME KILL ME OH ROTTEN GODS WHY WILL NO ONE KILL ME PLEEEASE--

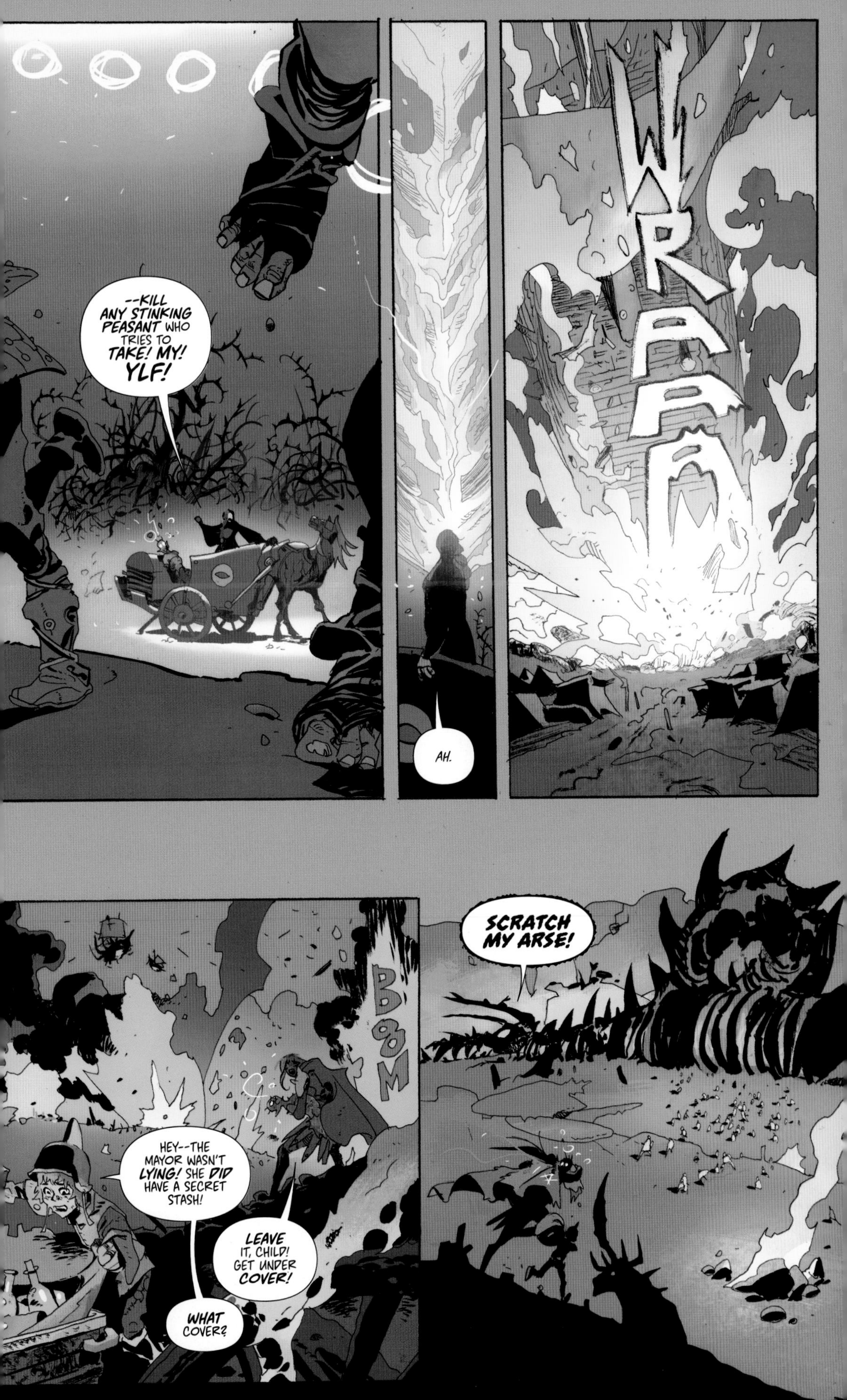
--KILL ANY STINKING PEASANT WHO TRIES TO TAKE! MY! YLF!
AH.
WRAAAA
BOOM
HEY--THE MAYOR WASN'T LYING! SHE DID HAVE A SECRET STASH!
LEAVE IT, CHILD! GET UNDER COVER!
WHAT COVER?
SCRATCH MY ARSE!

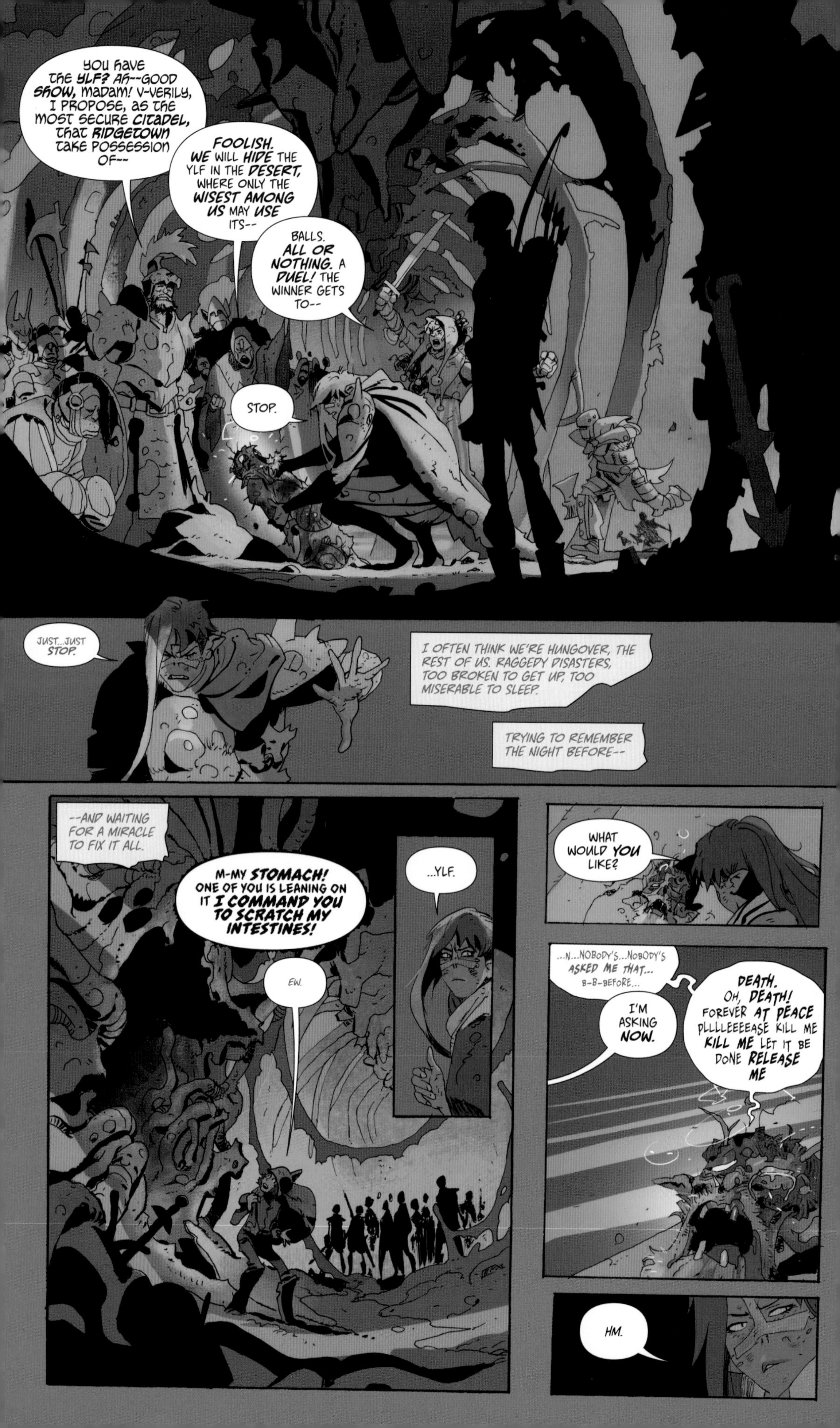

YOU HAVE THE YLF? AH--GOOD SHOW, MADAM! V-VERILY, I PROPOSE, AS THE MOST SECURE CITADEL, THAT RIDGETOWN TAKE POSSESSION OF--
FOOLISH. WE WILL HIDE THE YLF IN THE DESERT, WHERE ONLY THE WISEST AMONG US MAY USE ITS--
BALLS. ALL OR NOTHING. A DUEL! THE WINNER GETS TO--
STOP.
JUST...JUST STOP.
I OFTEN THINK WE'RE HUNGOVER, THE REST OF US. RAGGEDY DISASTERS, TOO BROKEN TO GET UP, TOO MISERABLE TO SLEEP.
TRYING TO REMEMBER THE NIGHT BEFORE--
--AND WAITING FOR A MIRACLE TO FIX IT ALL.
M-MY STOMACH! ONE OF YOU IS LEANING ON IT I COMMAND YOU TO SCRATCH MY INTESTINES!
EW.
...YLF.
WHAT WOULD YOU LIKE?
...N...NOBODY'S...NOBODY'S ASKED ME THAT... B-B-BEFORE...
I'M ASKING NOW.
DEATH. OH, DEATH! FOREVER AT PEACE PLLLLEEEEASE KILL ME KILL ME LET IT BE DONE RELEASE ME
HM.

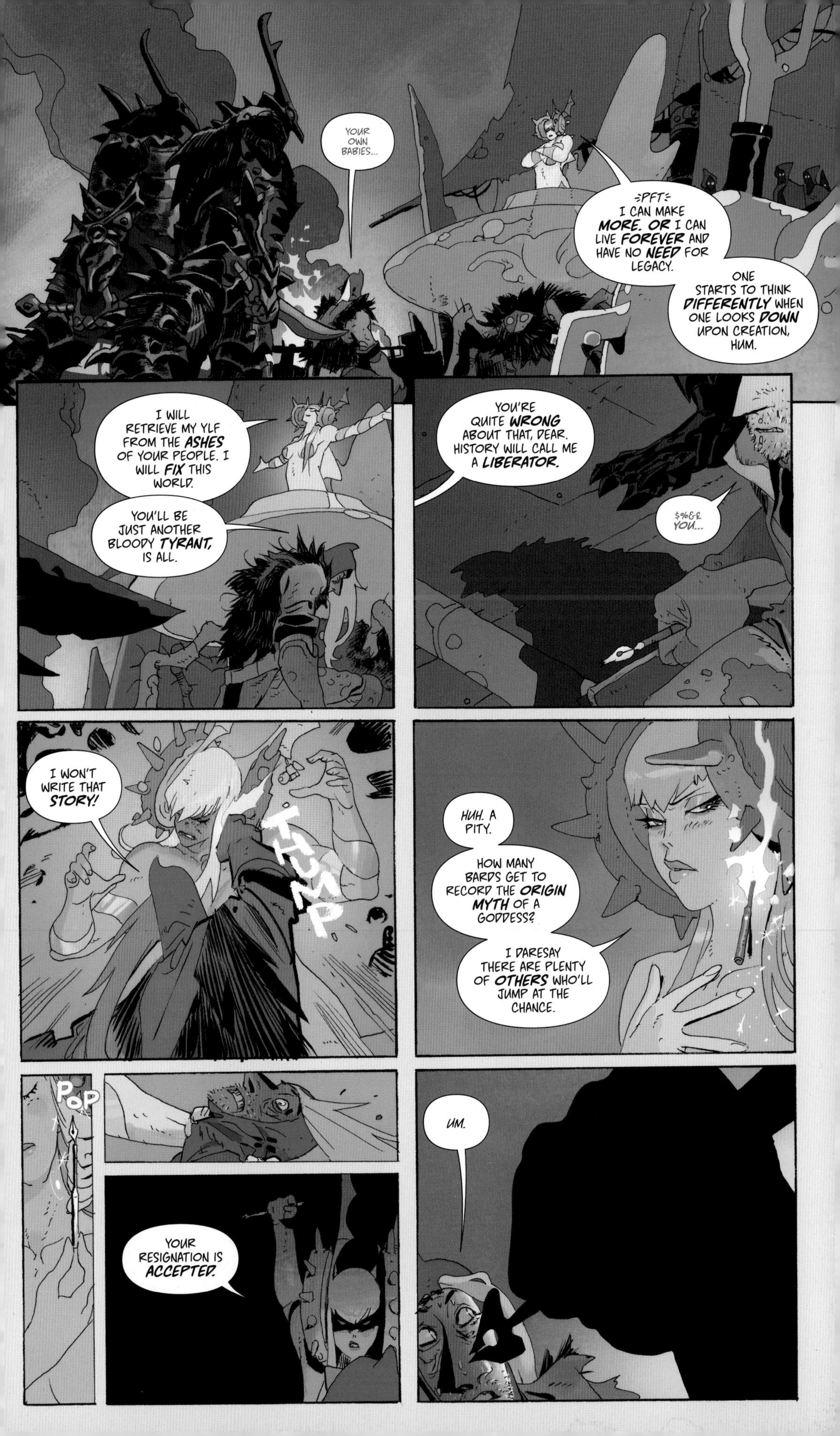
YOUR OWN BABIES...
=PFT= I CAN MAKE MORE. OR I CAN LIVE FOREVER AND HAVE NO NEED FOR LEGACY.
ONE STARTS TO THINK DIFFERENTLY WHEN ONE LOOKS DOWN UPON CREATION, HUM.
I WILL RETRIEVE MY YLF FROM THE ASHES OF YOUR PEOPLE. I WILL FIX THIS WORLD.
YOU'LL BE JUST ANOTHER BLOODY TYRANT, IS ALL.
YOU'RE QUITE WRONG ABOUT THAT, DEAR. HISTORY WILL CALL ME A LIBERATOR.
$%&£ YOU...
I WON'T WRITE THAT STORY!
THUMP
HUH. A PITY.
HOW MANY BARDS GET TO RECORD THE ORIGIN MYTH OF A GODDESS?
I DARESAY THERE ARE PLENTY OF OTHERS WHO'LL JUMP AT THE CHANCE.
POP
YOUR RESIGNATION IS ACCEPTED.
UM.

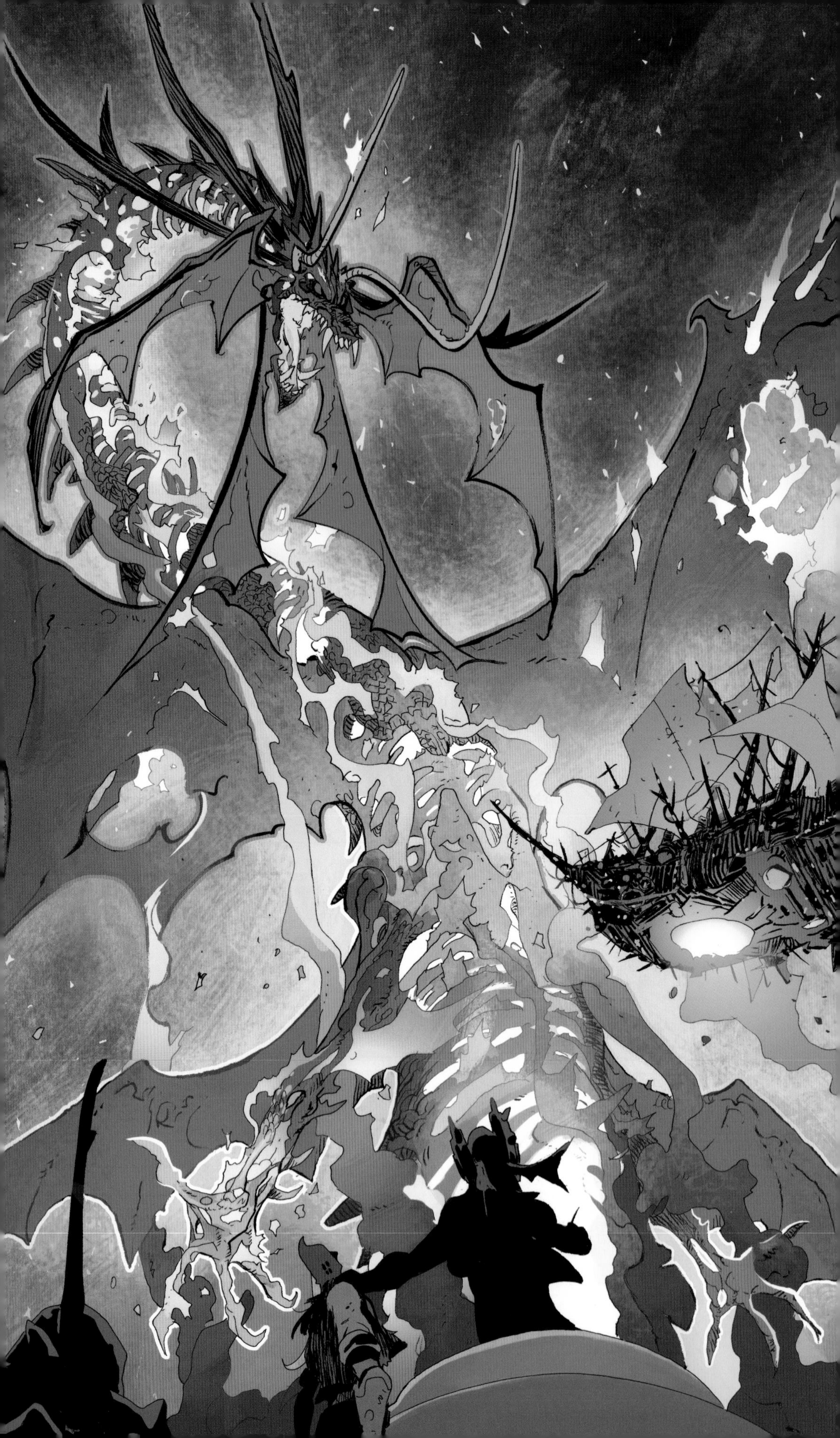

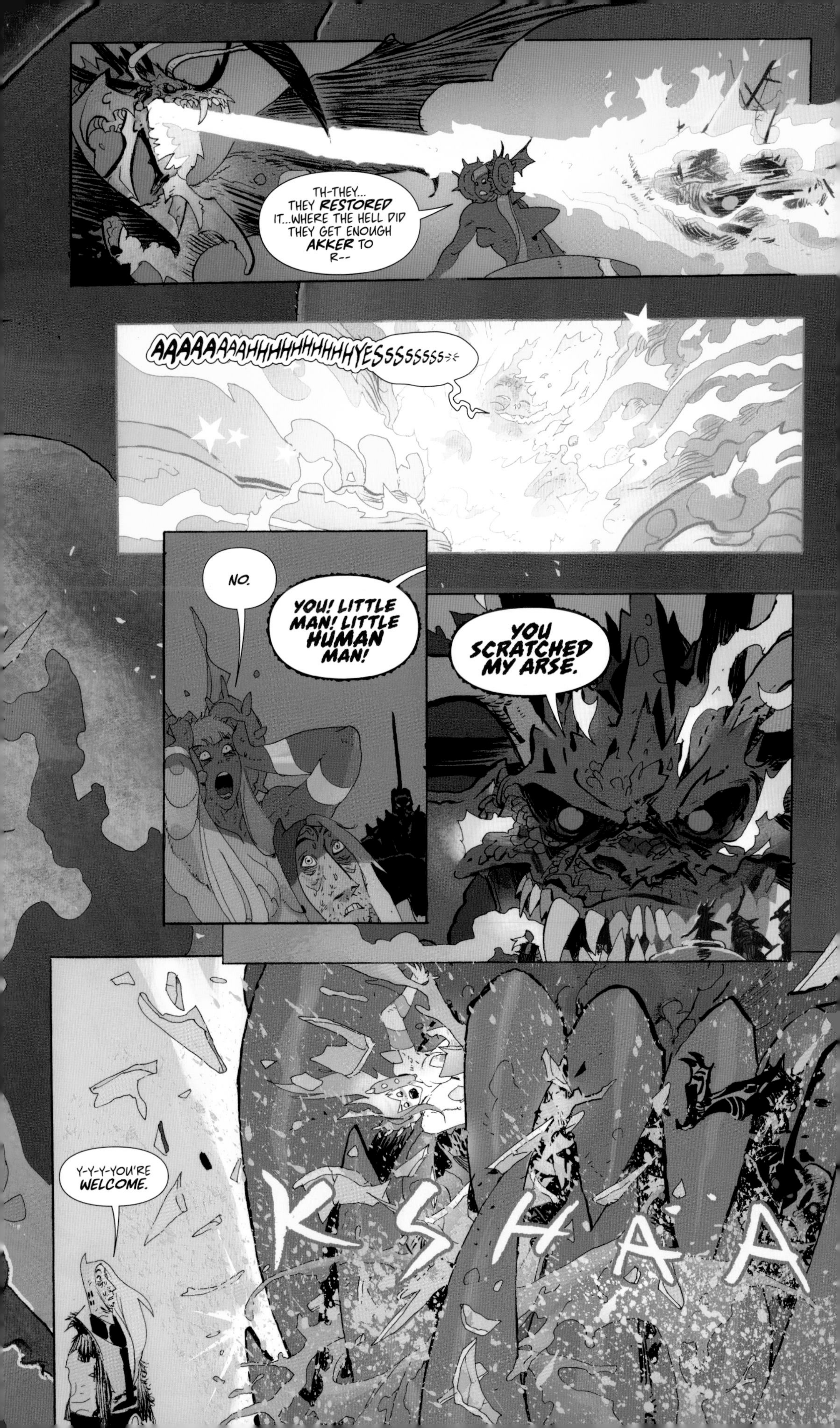

TH-THEY... THEY **RESTORED** IT...WHERE THE HELL DID THEY GET ENOUGH **AKKER** TO R--
AAAAAAAAHHHHHHHHHHYESSSSSSSS
NO.
YOU! LITTLE MAN! LITTLE HUMAN MAN!
YOU SCRATCHED MY ARSE.
Y-Y-Y-YOU'RE **WELCOME.**
KSHAA

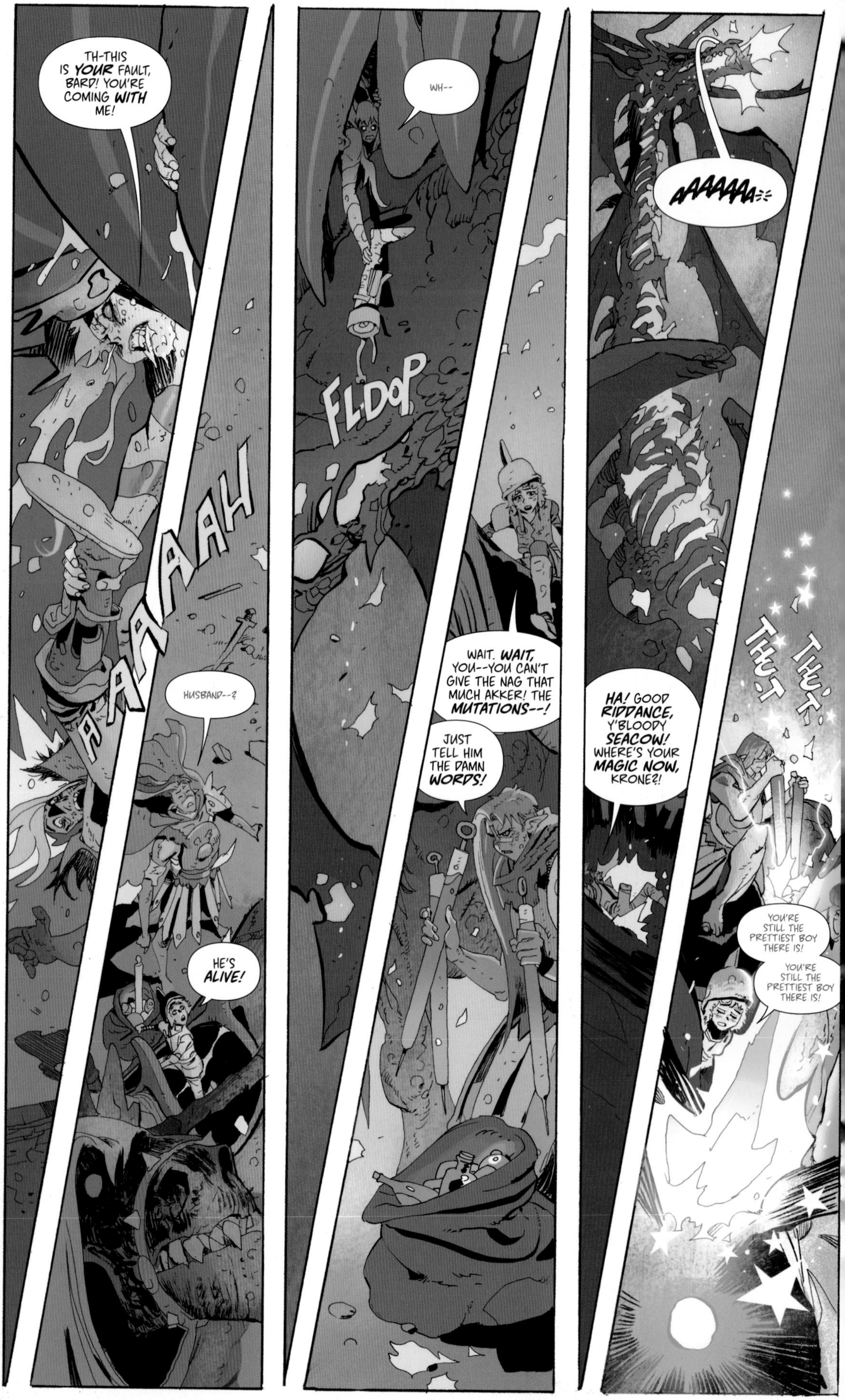

TH-THIS IS YOUR FAULT, BARD! YOU'RE COMING WITH ME!
AAAAAH
HUSBAND--?
HE'S ALIVE!
WH--
FL-DOP
WAIT. WAIT, YOU--YOU CAN'T GIVE THE NAG THAT MUCH AKKER! THE MUTATIONS--!
JUST TELL HIM THE DAMN WORDS!
AAAAAA
HA! GOOD RIDDANCE, Y'BLOODY SEACOW! WHERE'S YOUR MAGIC NOW, KRONE?!
THUT
THUT
YOU'RE STILL THE PRETTIEST BOY THERE IS!
YOU'RE STILL THE PRETTIEST BOY THERE IS!

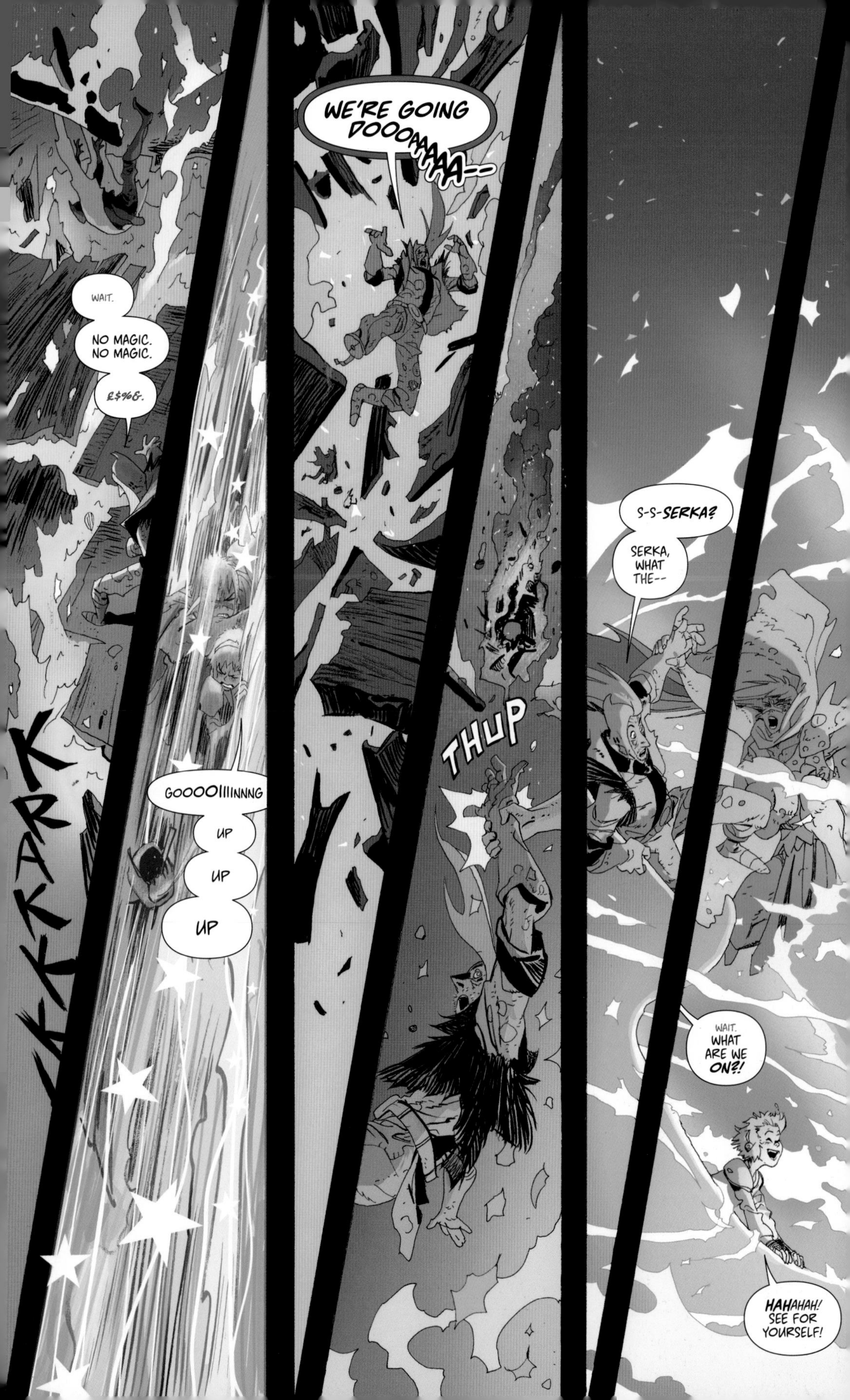
WAIT.
NO MAGIC. NO MAGIC.
£$%&.
KRAKRAKRAK
GOOOOIIIINNNG
UP
UP
UP
WE'RE GOING DOOOAAAAAA--
THUP
S-S-SERKA?
SERKA, WHAT THE--
WAIT. WHAT ARE WE ON?!
HAHAHAH! SEE FOR YOURSELF!

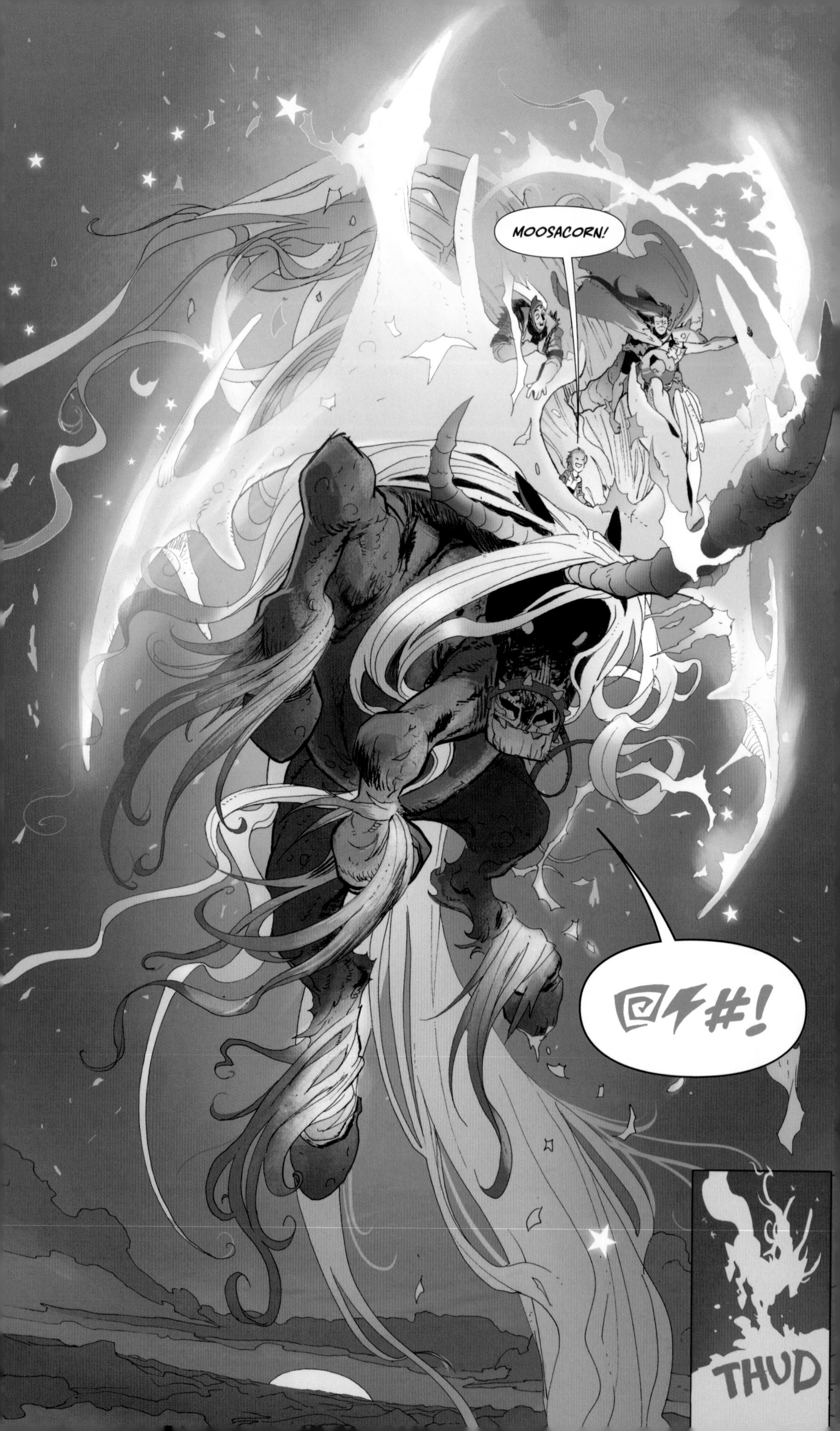
MOOSACORN!
THUD

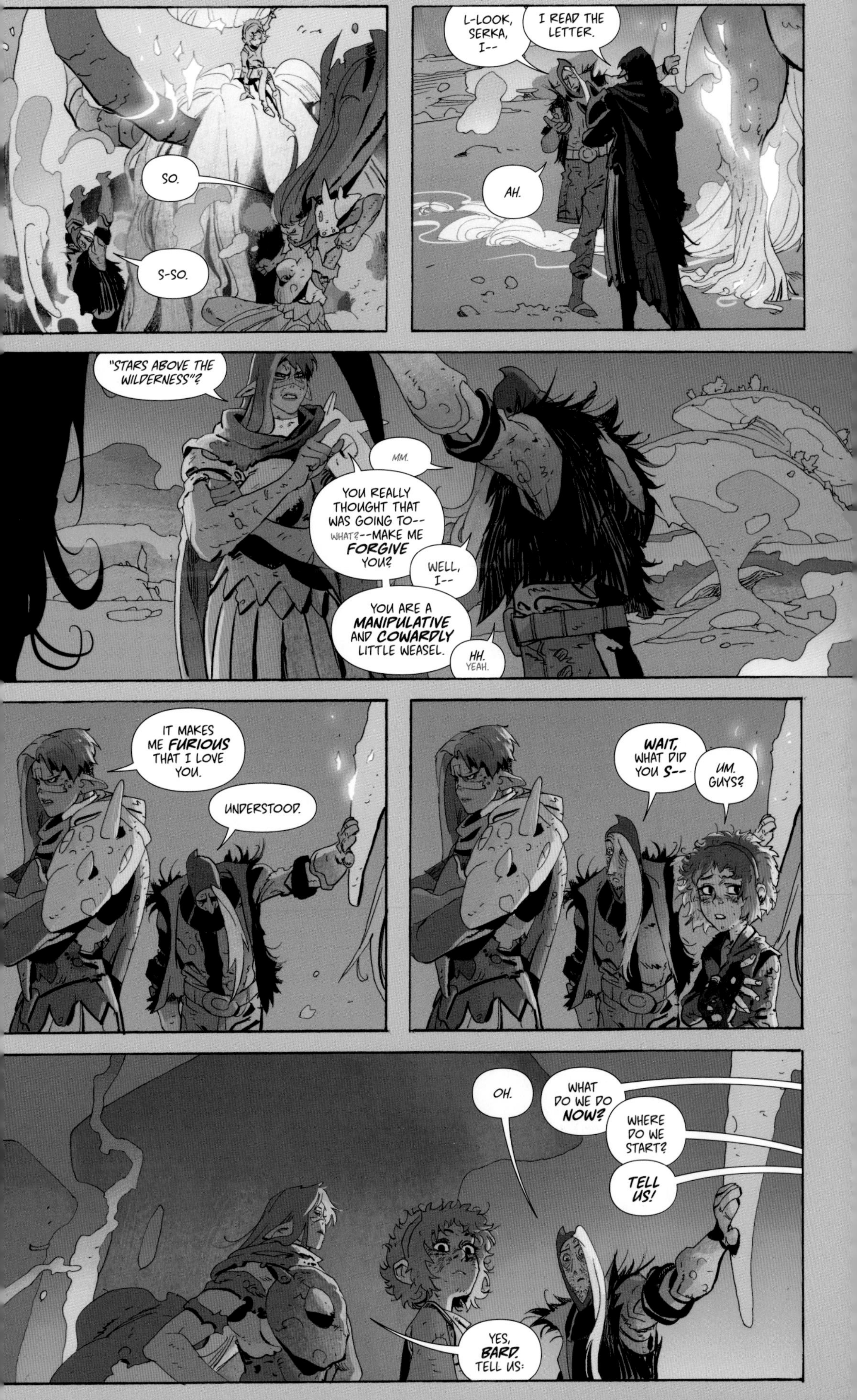
SO.
S-SO.
L-LOOK, SERKA, I--
I READ THE LETTER.
AH.
"STARS ABOVE THE WILDERNESS"?
MM.
YOU REALLY THOUGHT THAT WAS GOING TO-- WHAT?--MAKE ME FORGIVE YOU?
WELL, I--
YOU ARE A MANIPULATIVE AND COWARDLY LITTLE WEASEL.
HH. YEAH.
IT MAKES ME FURIOUS THAT I LOVE YOU.
UNDERSTOOD.
WAIT, WHAT DID YOU S--
UM. GUYS?
OH.
WHAT DO WE DO NOW?
WHERE DO WE START?
TELL US!
YES, BARD. TELL US:

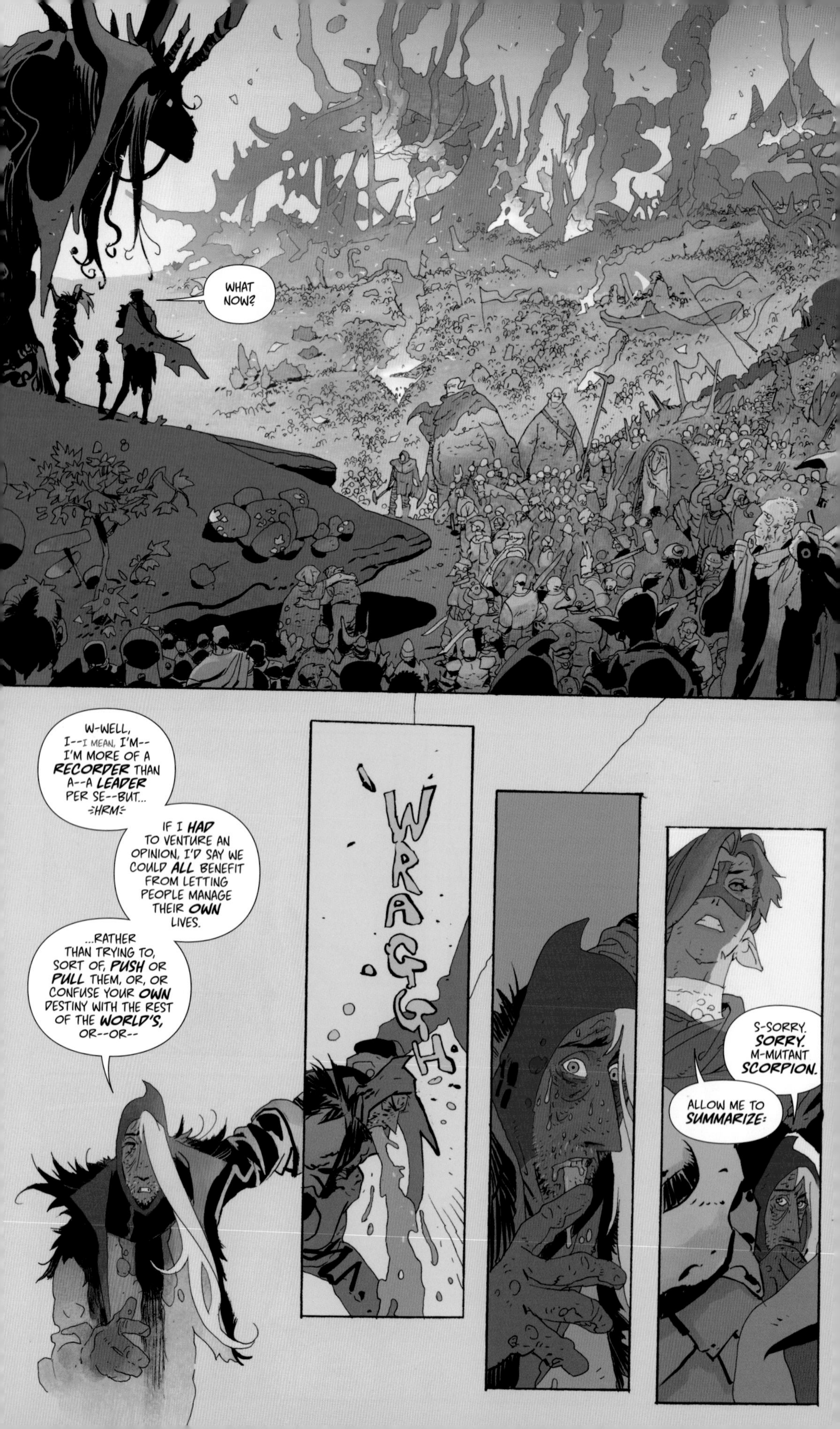
WHAT NOW?
W-WELL, I--I MEAN, I'M--I'M MORE OF A RECORDER THAN A--A LEADER PER SE--BUT... HRM
IF I HAD TO VENTURE AN OPINION, I'D SAY WE COULD ALL BENEFIT FROM LETTING PEOPLE MANAGE THEIR OWN LIVES.
...RATHER THAN TRYING TO, SORT OF, PUSH OR PULL THEM, OR, OR CONFUSE YOUR OWN DESTINY WITH THE REST OF THE WORLD'S, OR--OR--
WRAGGH
S-SORRY. SORRY. M-MUTANT SCORPION.
ALLOW ME TO SUMMARIZE:

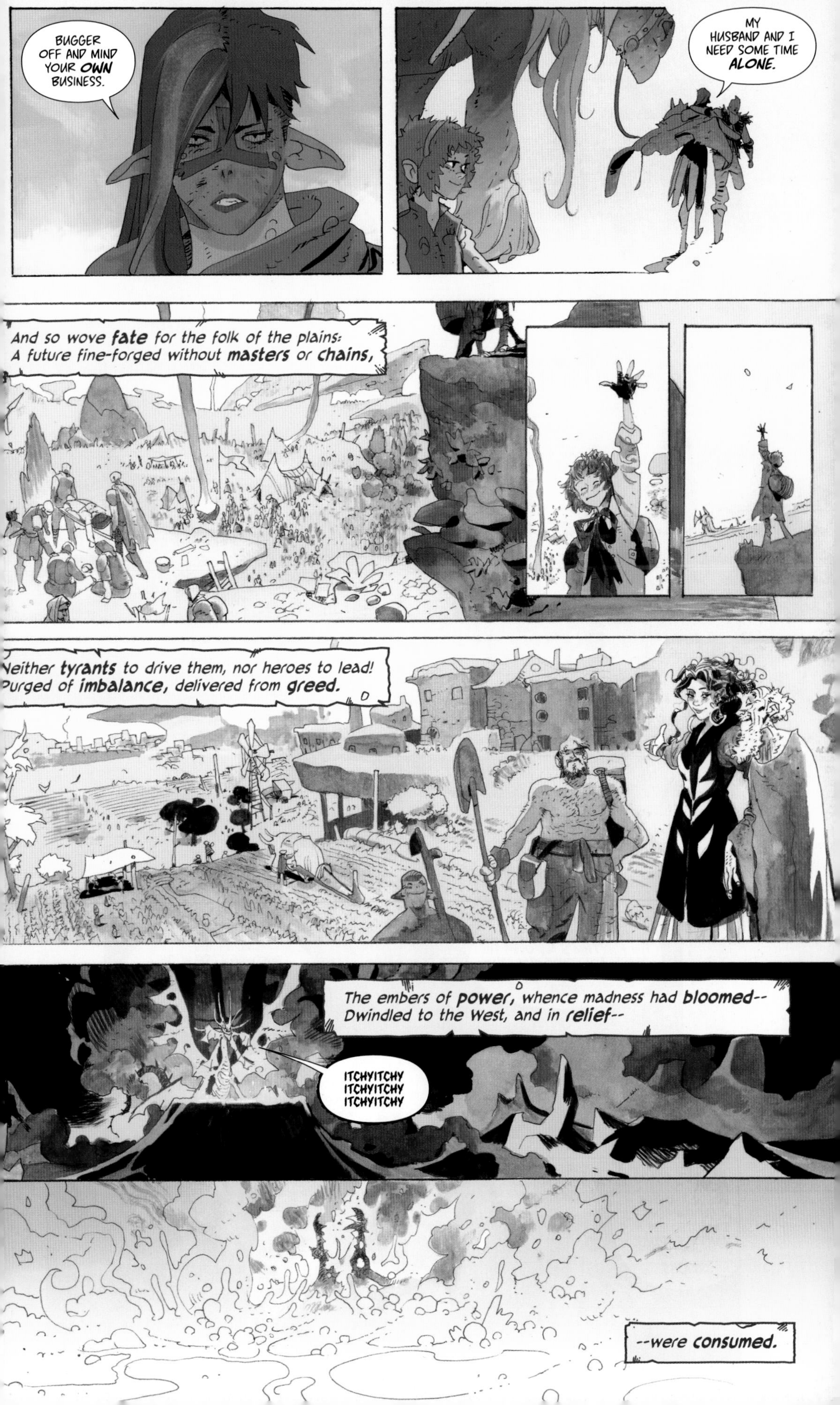
BUGGER OFF AND MIND YOUR OWN BUSINESS.
MY HUSBAND AND I NEED SOME TIME ALONE.
And so wove fate for the folk of the plains: A future fine-forged without masters or chains,
Neither tyrants to drive them, nor heroes to lead! Purged of imbalance, delivered from greed.
The embers of power, whence madness had bloomed-- Dwindled to the West, and in relief--
ITCHYITCHY ITCHYITCHY ITCHYITCHY
--were consumed.

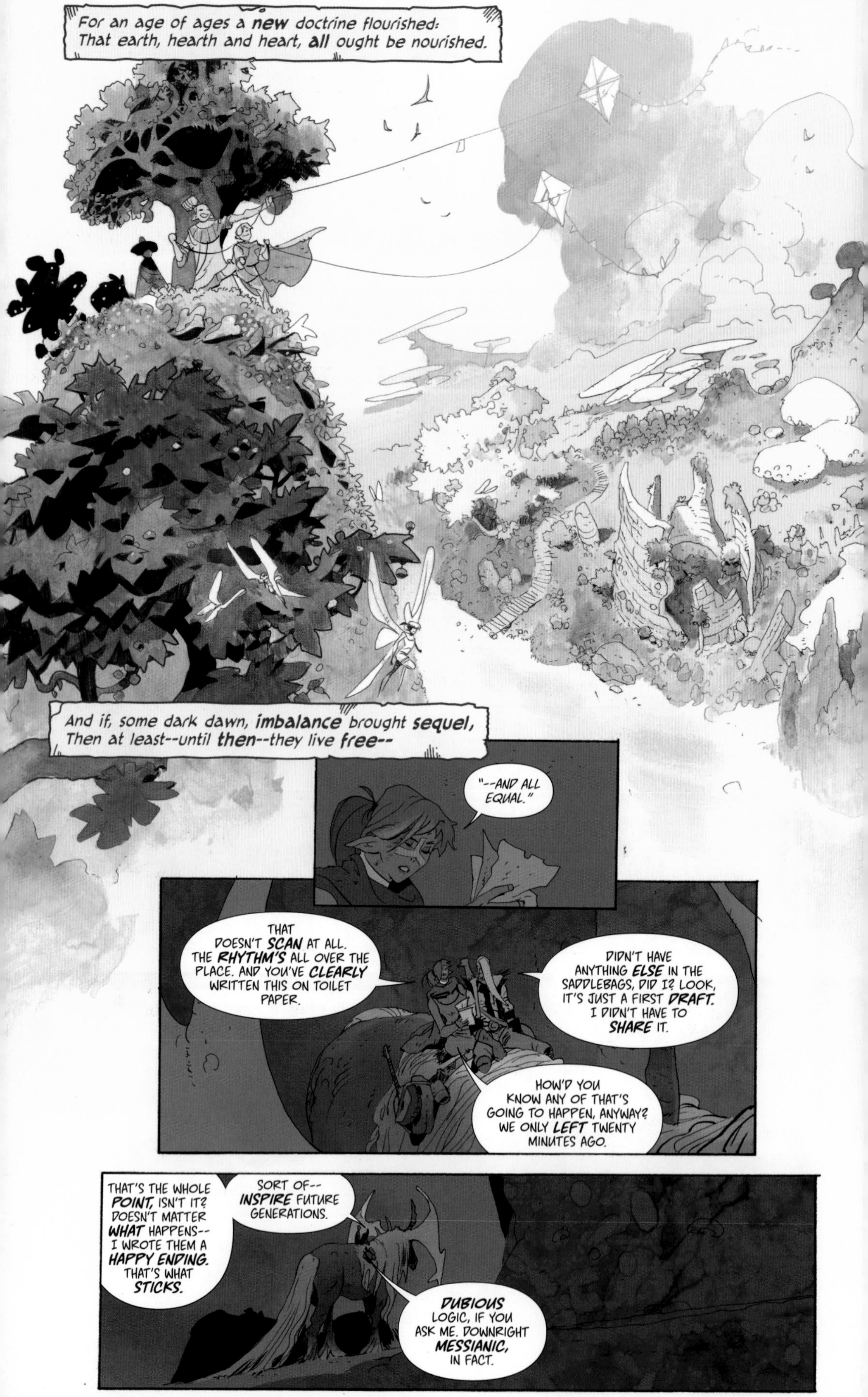
For an age of ages a **new** doctrine flourished:
That earth, hearth and heart, **all** ought be nourished.
And if, some dark dawn, **imbalance** brought **sequel**,
Then at least--until **then**--they live **free**--
"--AND ALL EQUAL."
THAT DOESN'T **SCAN** AT ALL. THE **RHYTHM'S** ALL OVER THE PLACE. AND YOU'VE **CLEARLY** WRITTEN THIS ON TOILET PAPER.
DIDN'T HAVE ANYTHING **ELSE** IN THE SADDLEBAGS, DID I? LOOK, IT'S JUST A FIRST **DRAFT.** I DIDN'T HAVE TO **SHARE** IT.
HOW'D YOU KNOW ANY OF THAT'S GOING TO HAPPEN, ANYWAY? WE ONLY **LEFT** TWENTY MINUTES AGO.
THAT'S THE WHOLE **POINT,** ISN'T IT? DOESN'T MATTER **WHAT** HAPPENS-- I WROTE THEM A **HAPPY ENDING.** THAT'S WHAT **STICKS.**
SORT OF-- **INSPIRE** FUTURE GENERATIONS.
DUBIOUS LOGIC, IF YOU ASK ME. DOWNRIGHT **MESSIANIC,** IN FACT.

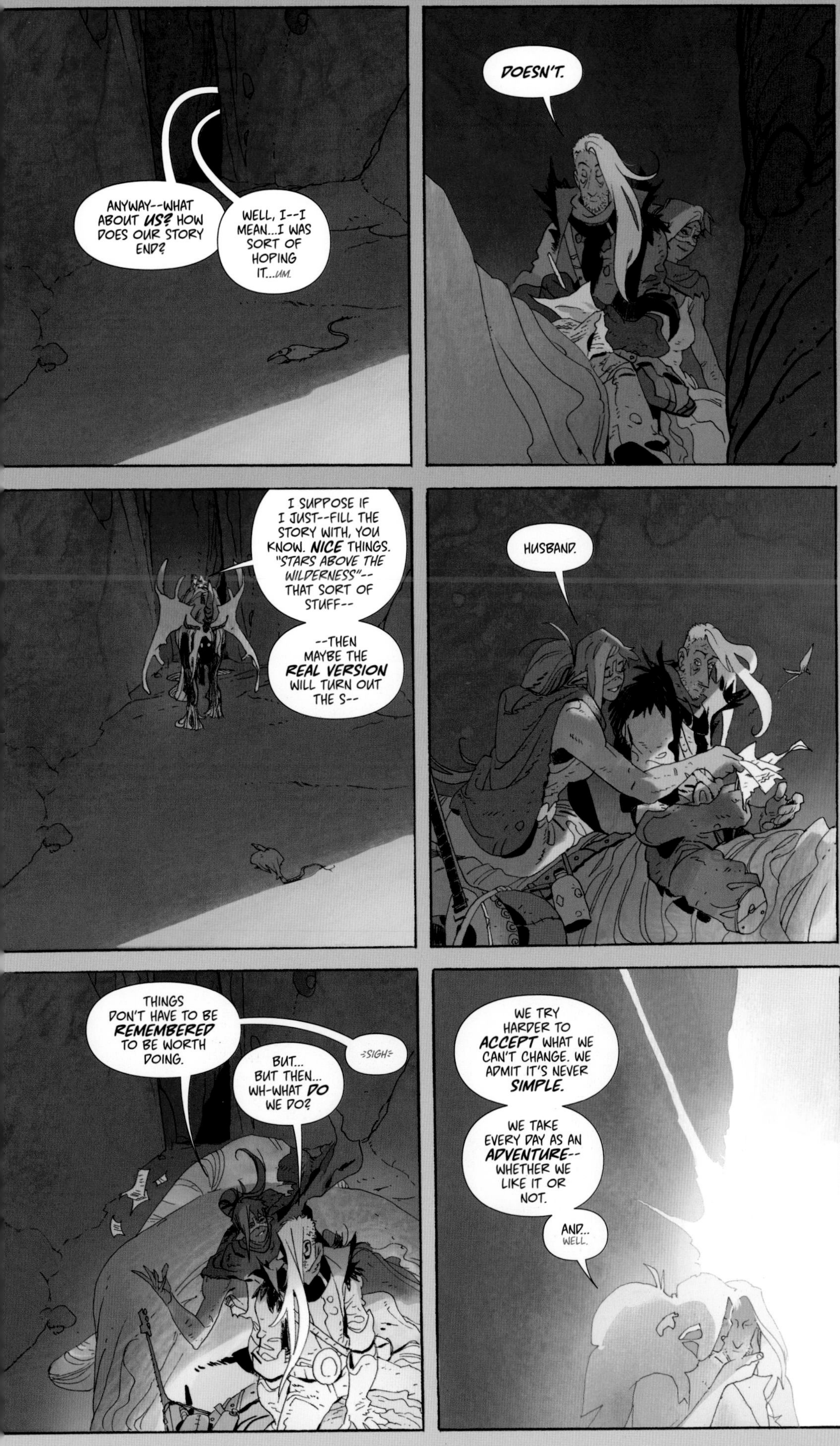

ANYWAY--WHAT ABOUT US? HOW DOES OUR STORY END?
WELL, I--I MEAN...I WAS SORT OF HOPING IT...UM.
DOESN'T.
I SUPPOSE IF I JUST--FILL THE STORY WITH, YOU KNOW. NICE THINGS. "STARS ABOVE THE WILDERNESS"-- THAT SORT OF STUFF--
--THEN MAYBE THE REAL VERSION WILL TURN OUT THE S--
HUSBAND.
THINGS DON'T HAVE TO BE REMEMBERED TO BE WORTH DOING.
BUT... BUT THEN... WH-WHAT DO WE DO?
SIGH
WE TRY HARDER TO ACCEPT WHAT WE CAN'T CHANGE. WE ADMIT IT'S NEVER SIMPLE.
WE TAKE EVERY DAY AS AN ADVENTURE-- WHETHER WE LIKE IT OR NOT.
AND... WELL.

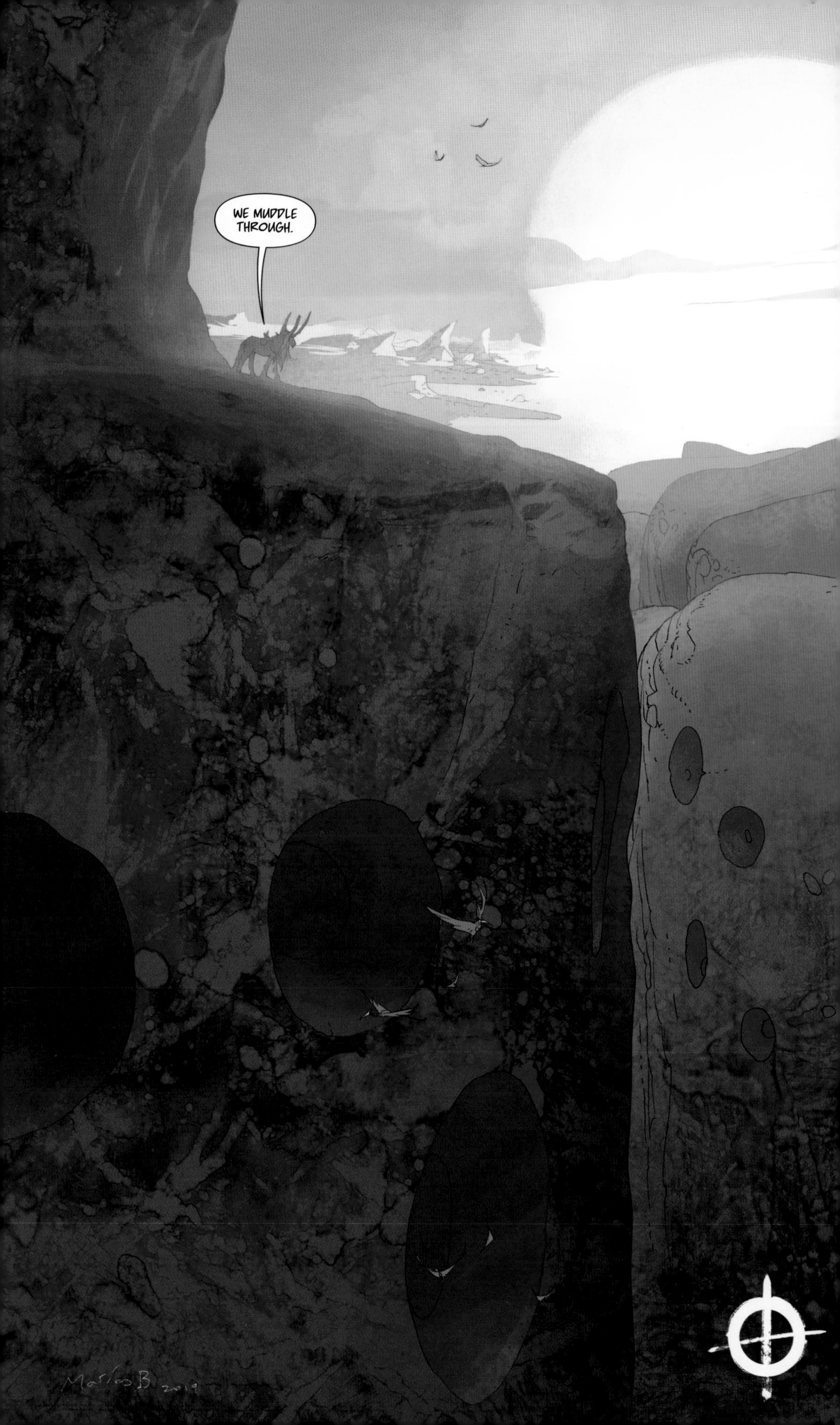
WE MUDDLE THROUGH.

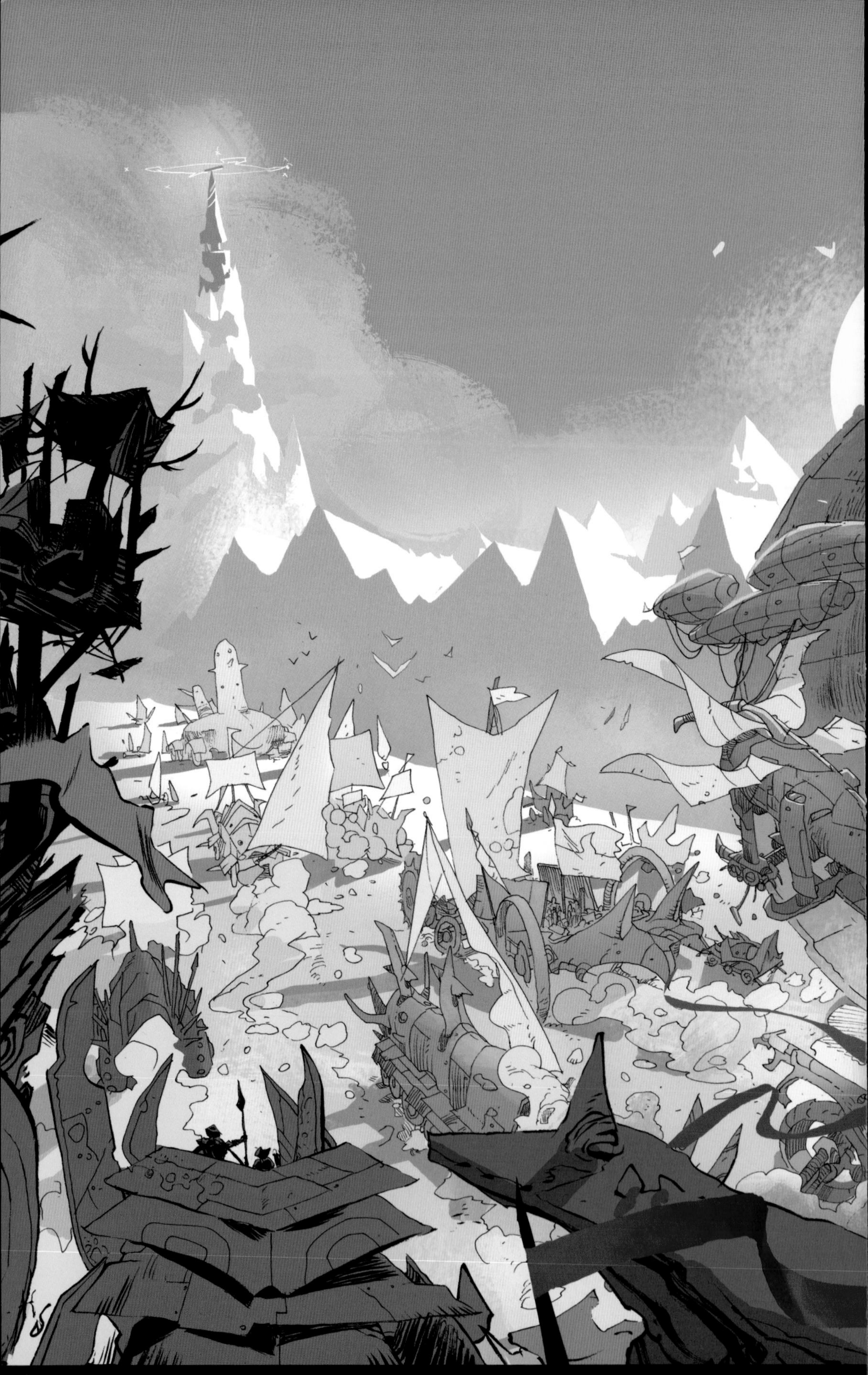

ISSUE NINE COVER BY **MATÍAS BERGARA**

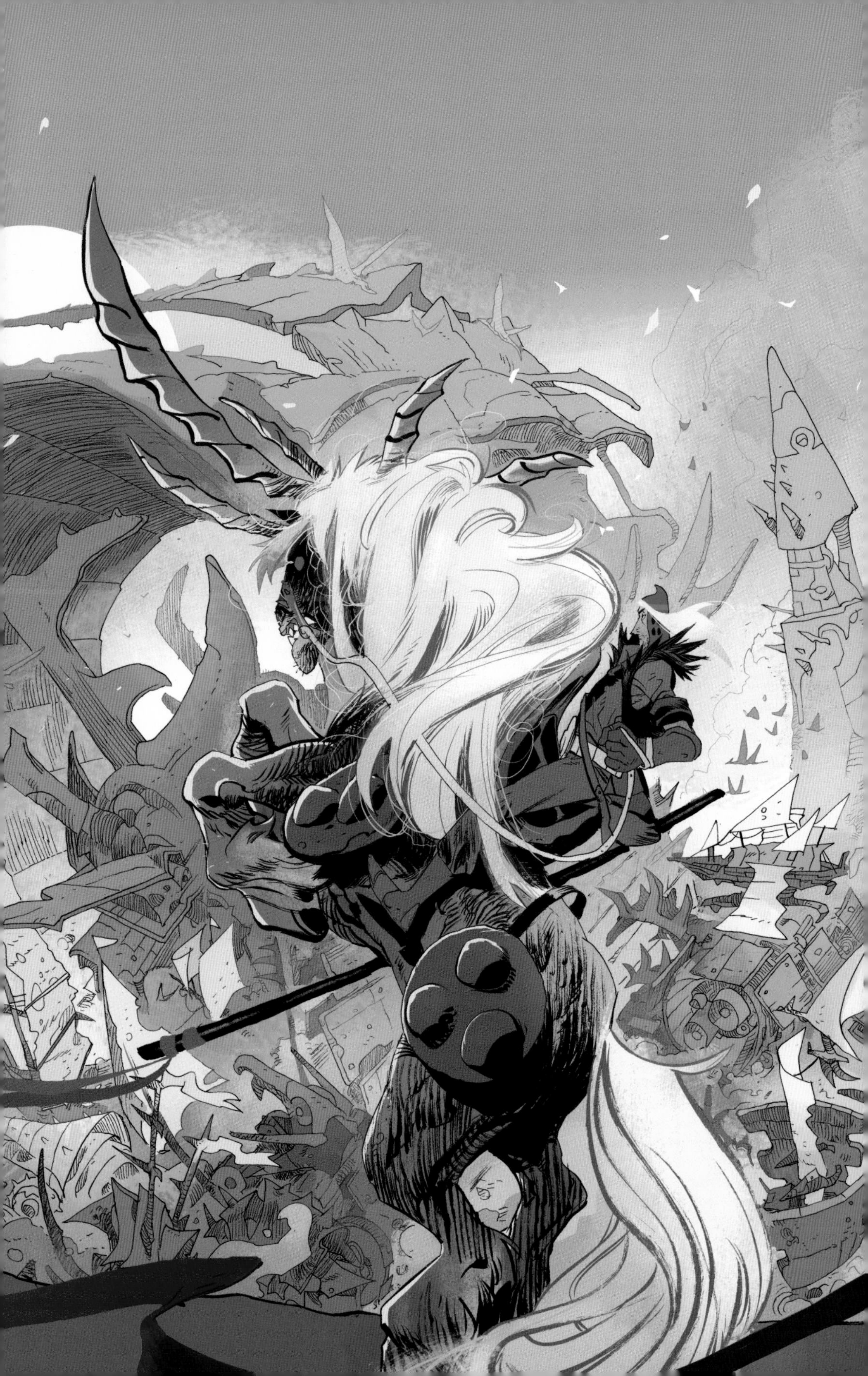

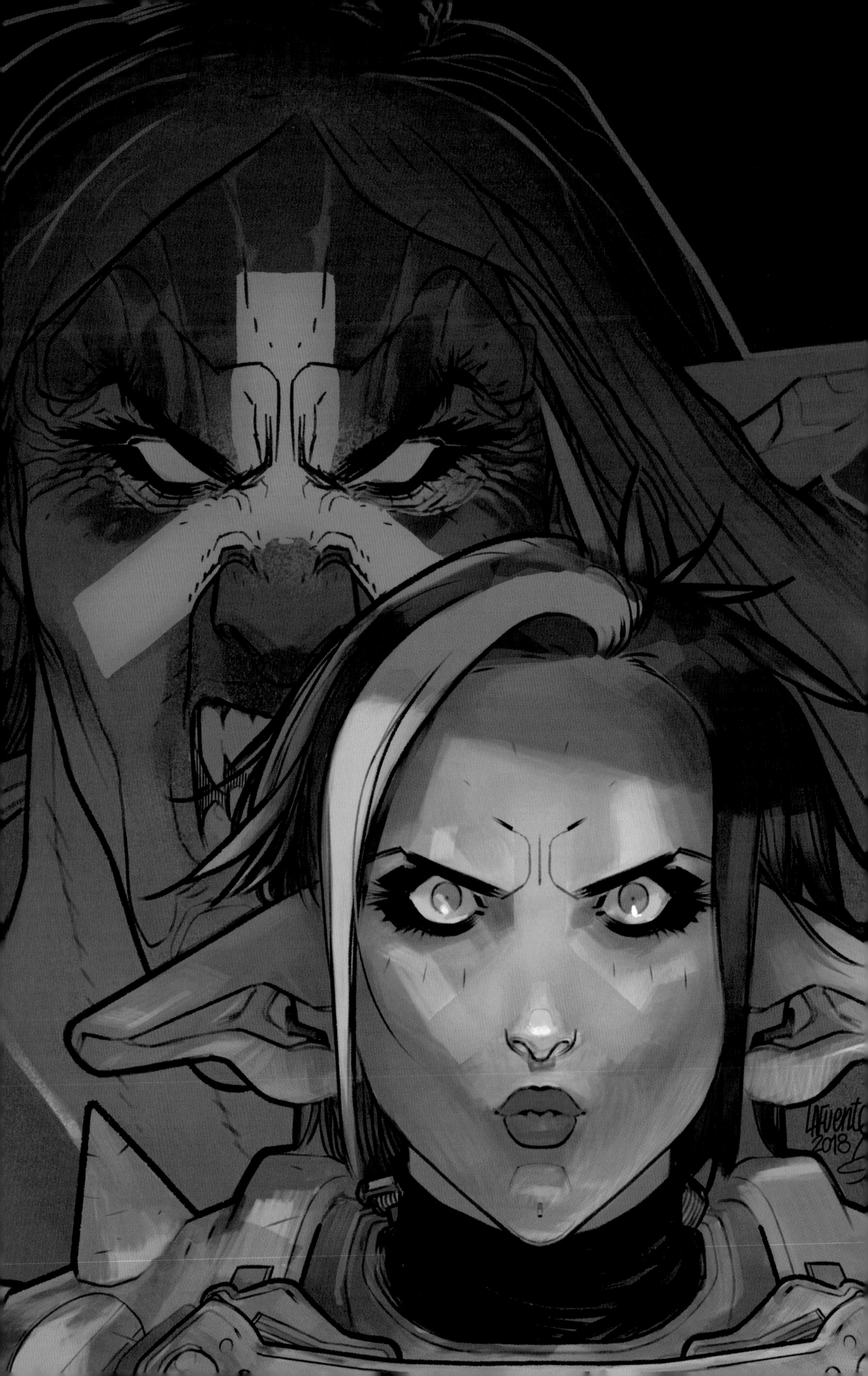

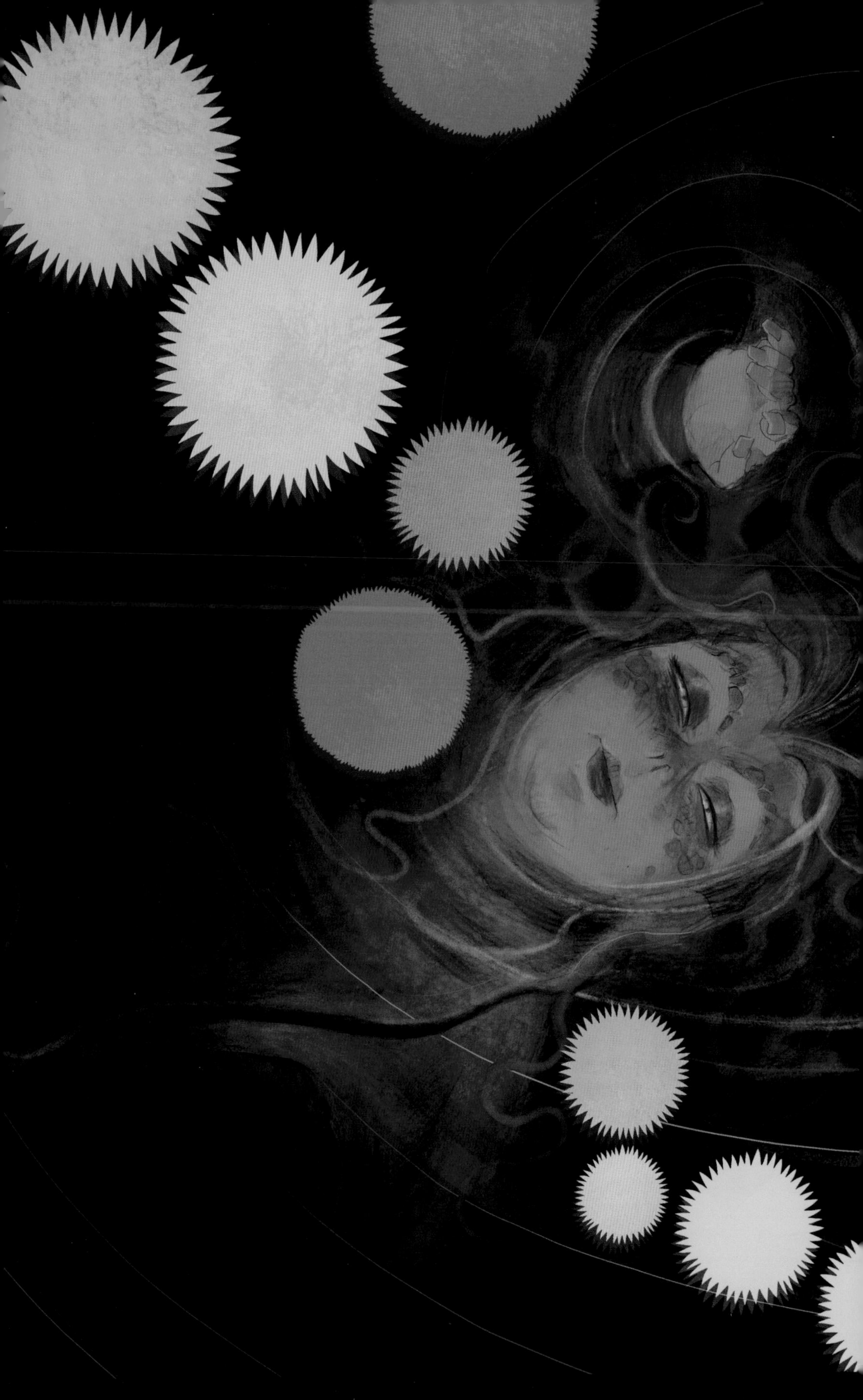

ISSUE TEN COVER BY **MATÍAS BERGARA**

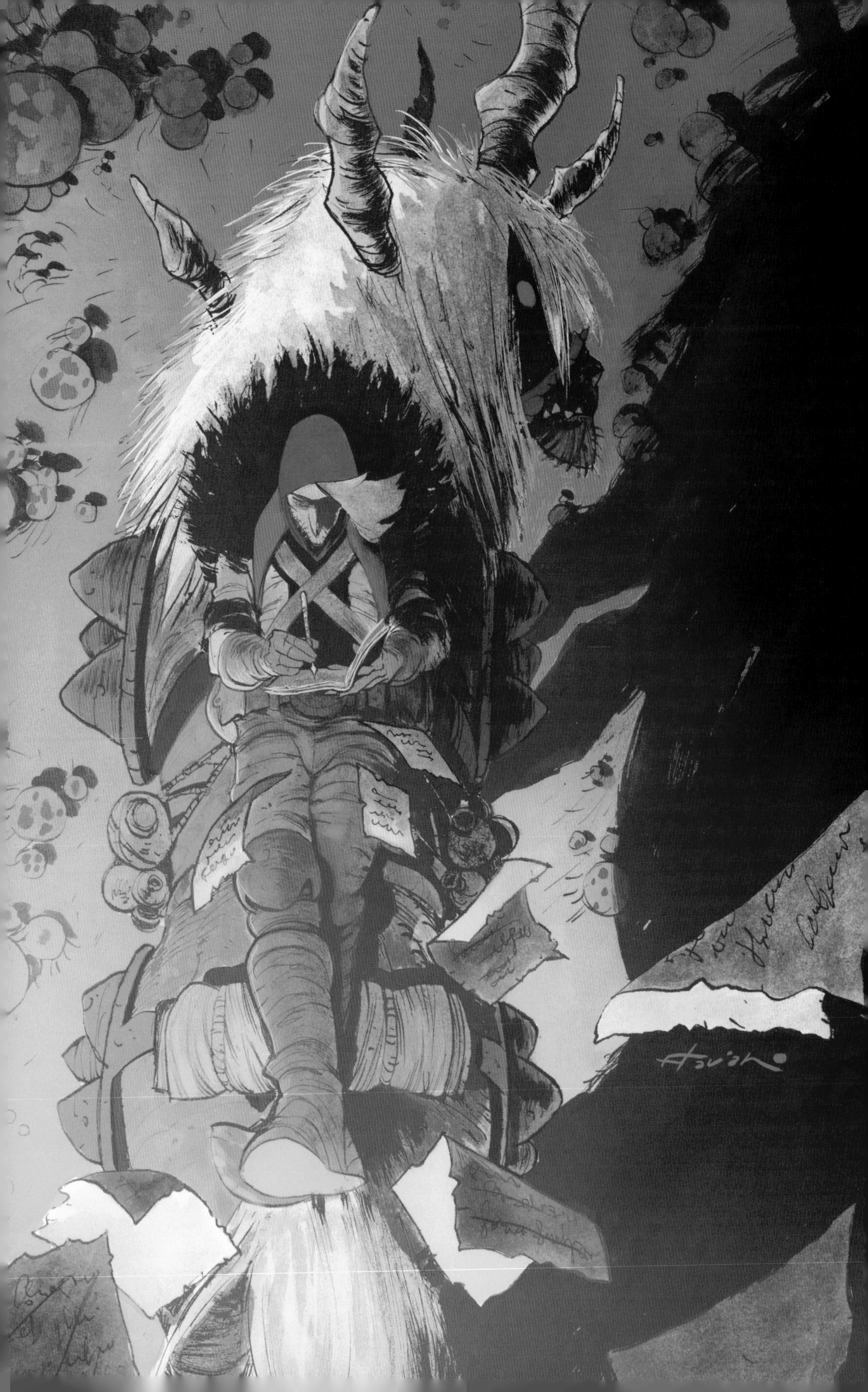

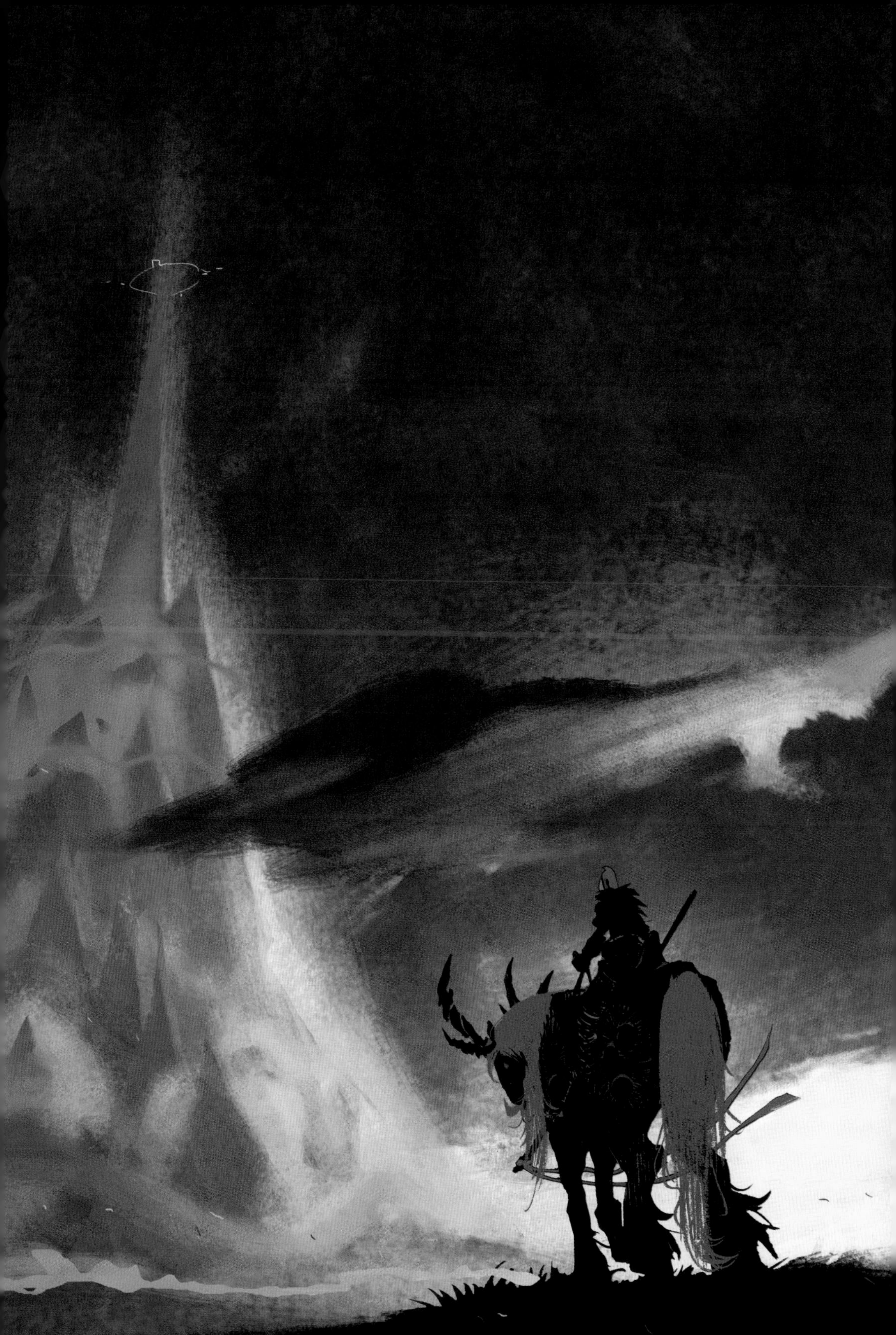

ISSUE ELEVEN COVER BY **MATÍAS BERGARA**

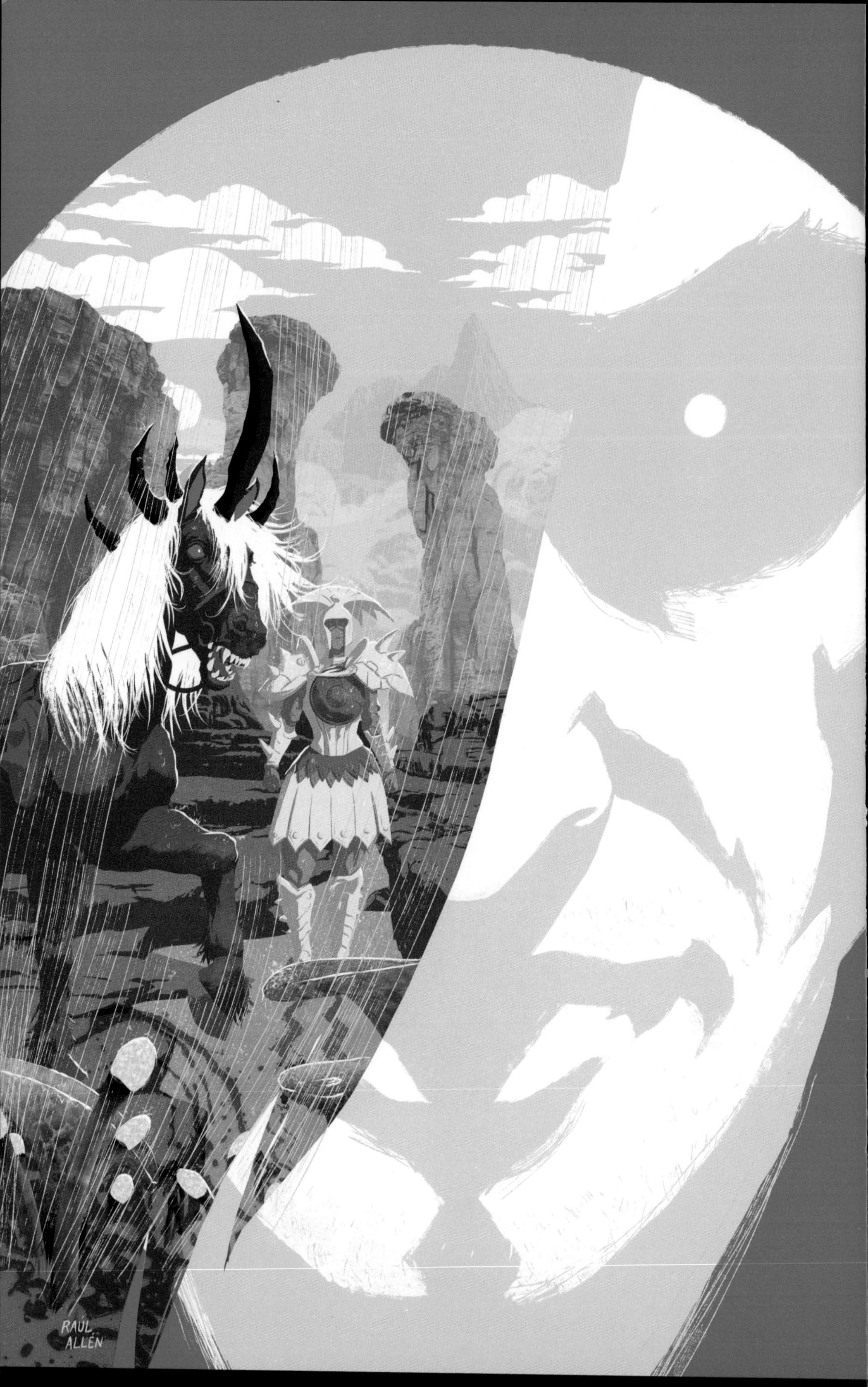

RAÚL
ALLÉN

ISSUE ELEVEN COVER BY **RAÚL ALLÉN** WITH COLORS BY **PATRICIA MARTÍN**

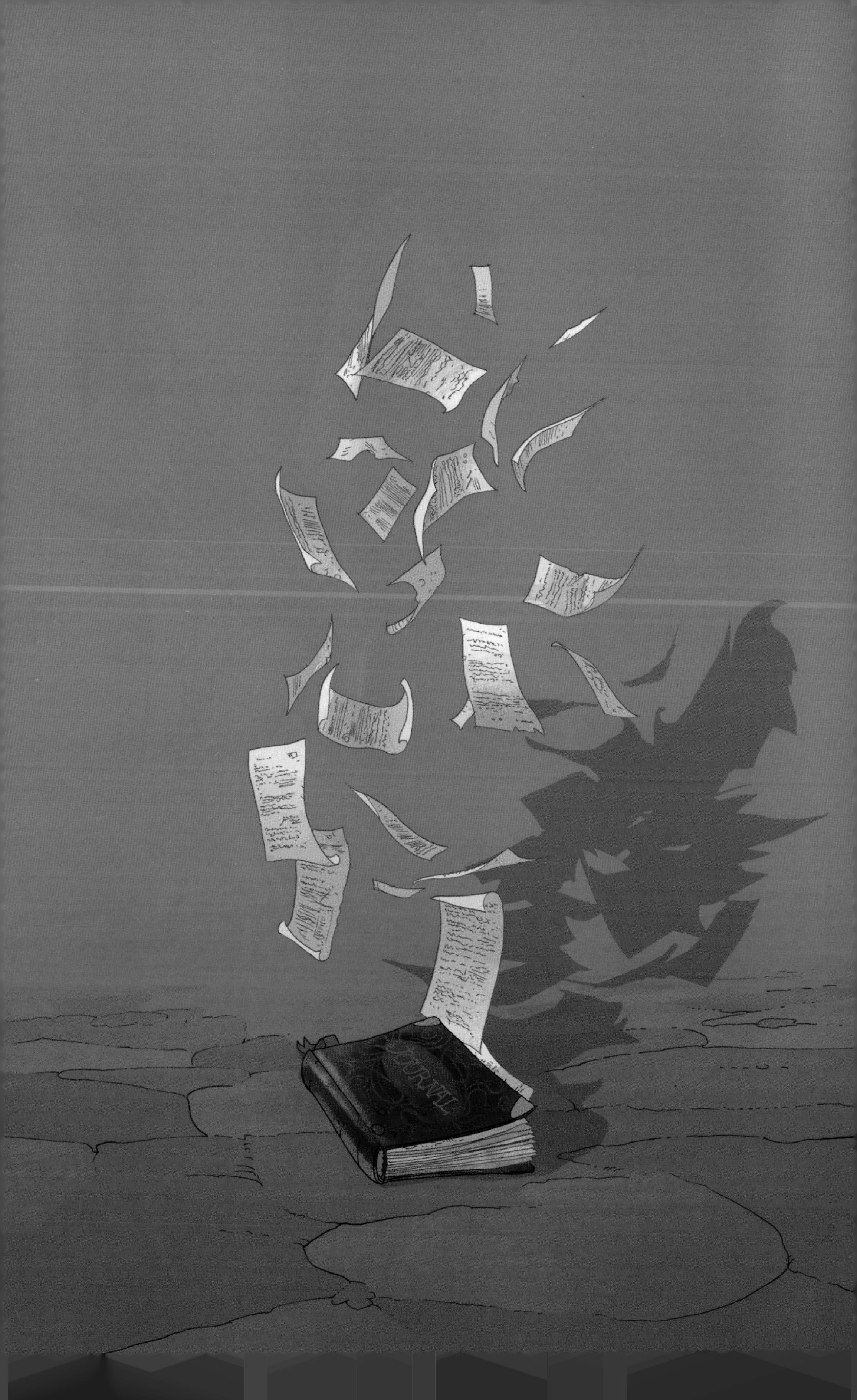
JOURNAL

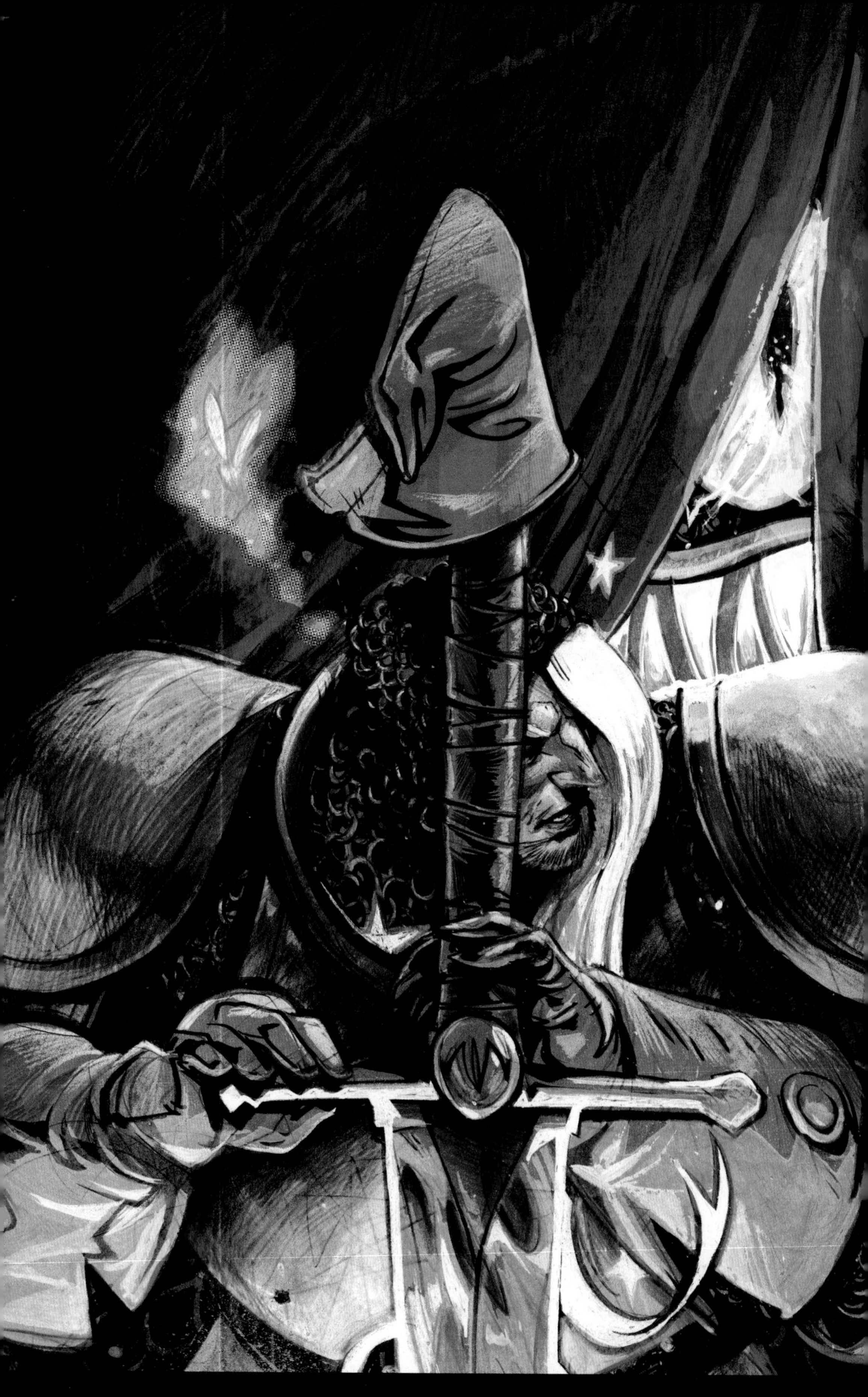

ISSUE TWELVE COVER BY **CHRIS VISIONS**

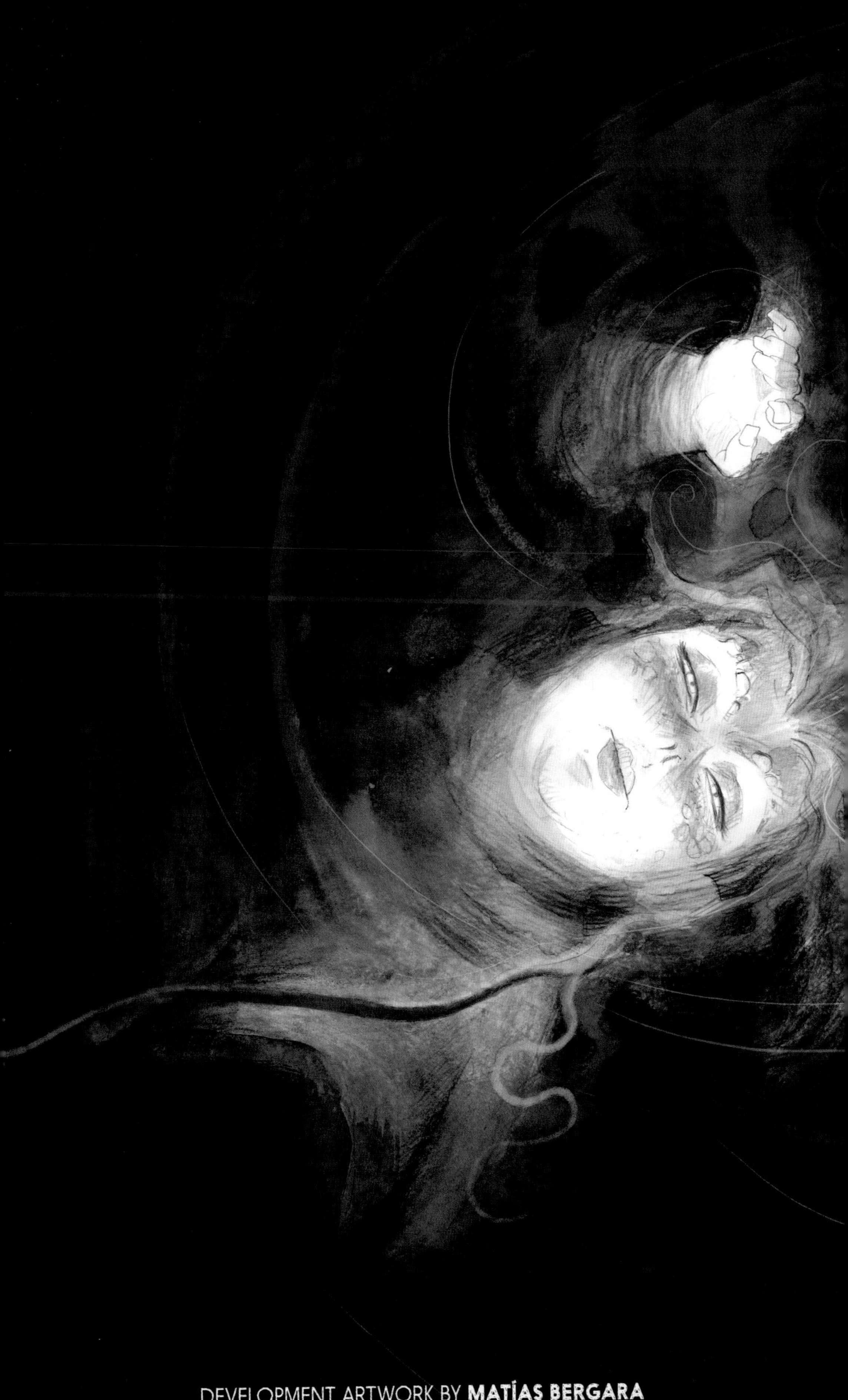

DEVELOPMENT ARTWORK BY **MATÍAS BERGARA**

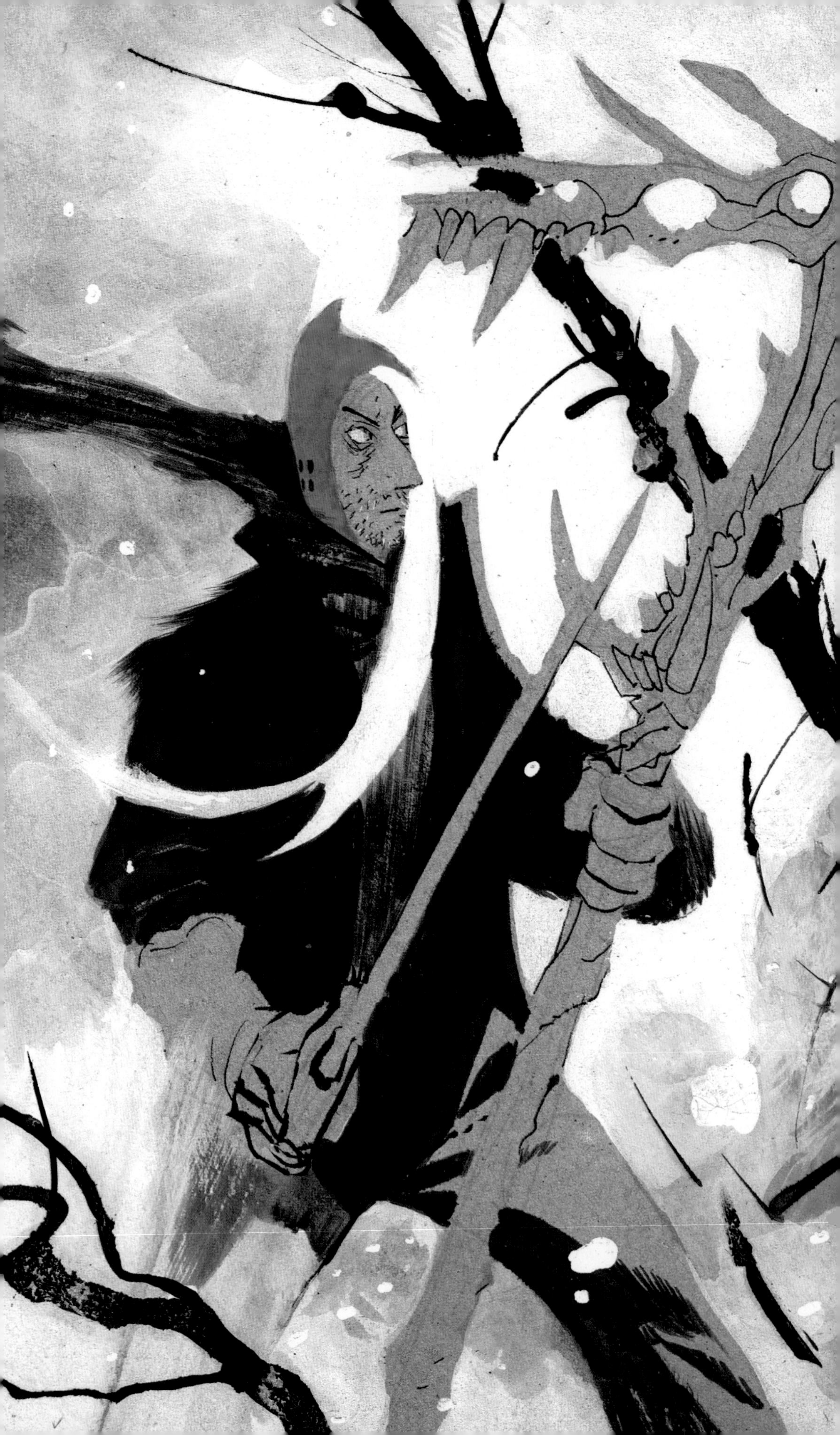

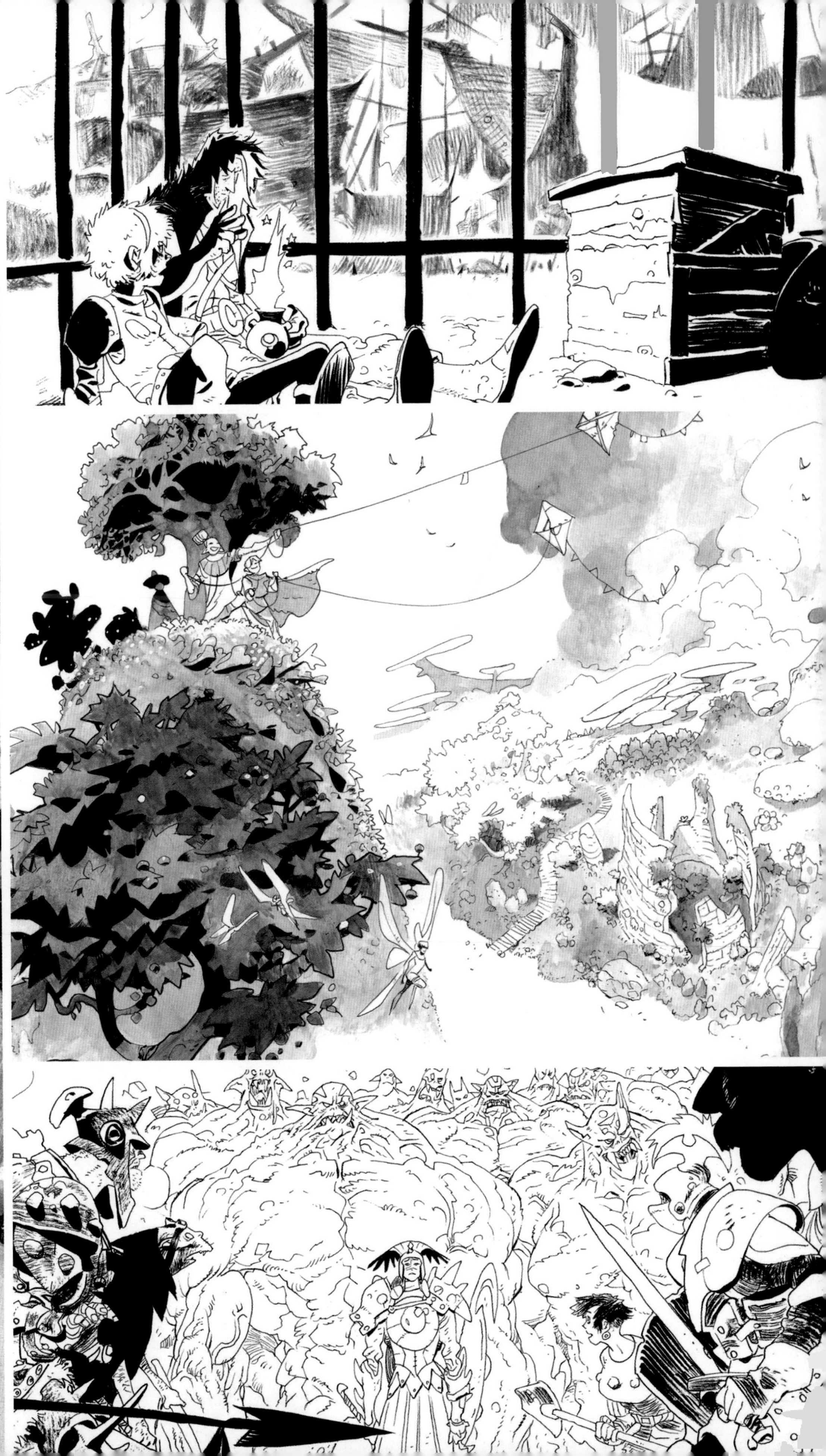

ABOUT THE AUTHORS

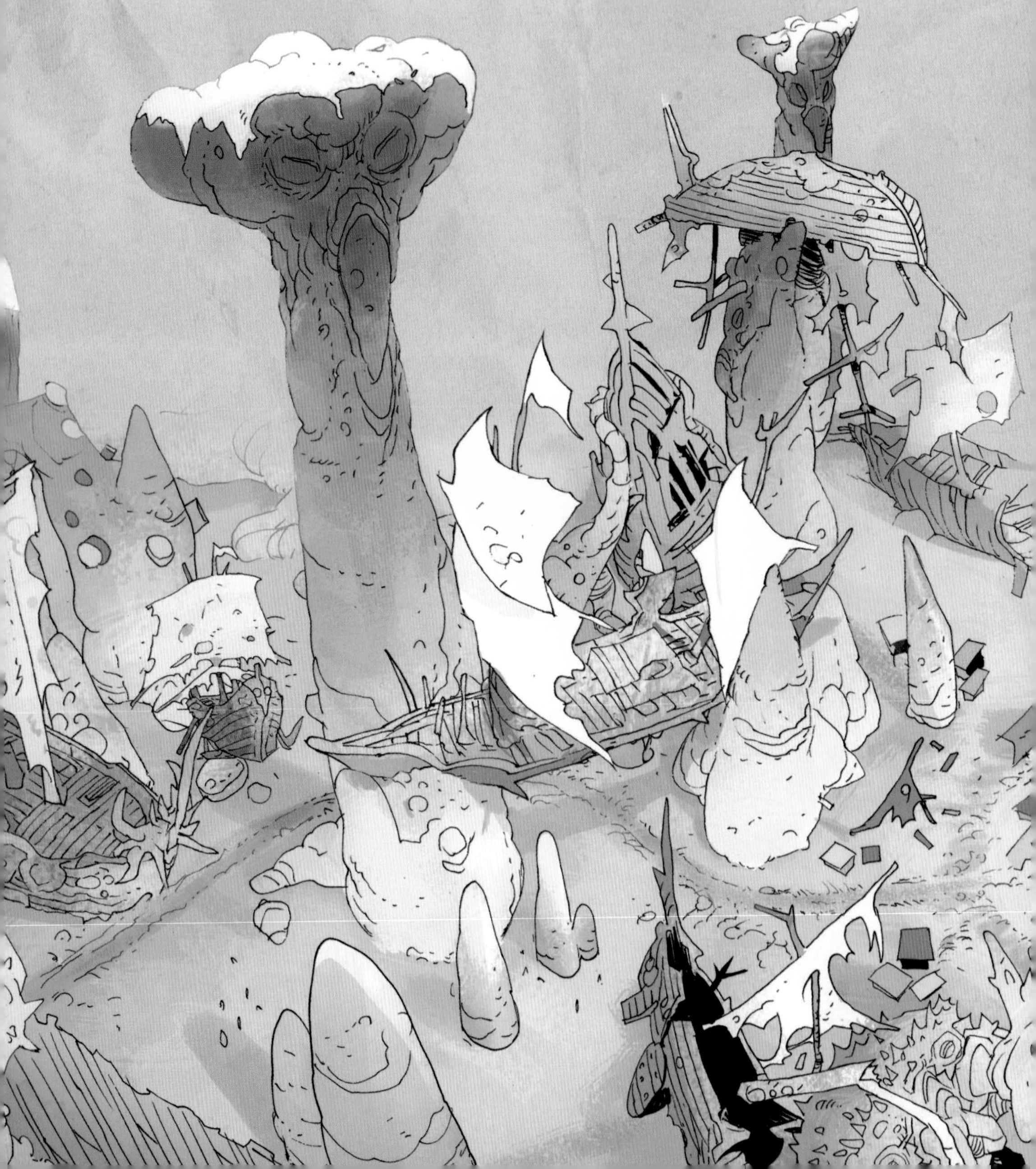

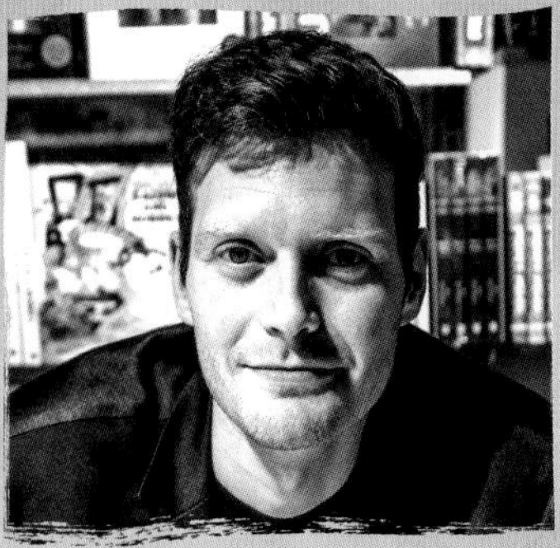

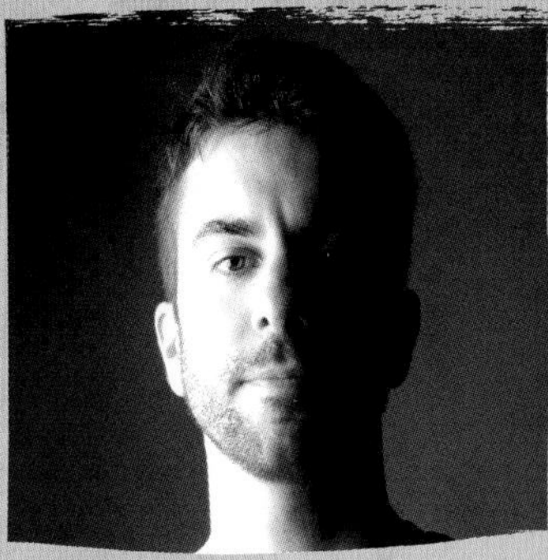

Simon Spurrier is a writer of actual words. His comic book credits stretch from *2000AD* and *Judge Dredd* to *X-Men Legacy*, *Sandman Universe*, and *Star Wars*. His creator-owned books include *Cry Havoc*, *Angelic*, and Eisner Nominee *The Spire*. He's published several prose novels, including *Contract* and *A Serpent Uncoiled*. His absurdist-noir novella *Unusual Concentrations* was shortlisted for the Shirley Jackson Award and is available online. He is currently working on new television and comic book projects. He lives in the south of Britain and normally isn't very good at writing about himself in the third person, but I think this time I'm actually doing pretty well.

Matías Bergara was born and still lives in the curious little country of Uruguay. He's been illustrating comics, book covers, and video game art ever since leaving a college career in literature. Most of his published work was created for Latin America and Europe, so he's a recent arrival on U.S. titles such as *Sons of Anarchy* (BOOM!, 2014) and *Cannibal* (Image, 2016). In 2019, he was nominated for the Eisner Award for Best Penciller/Inker for his work on *Coda*.

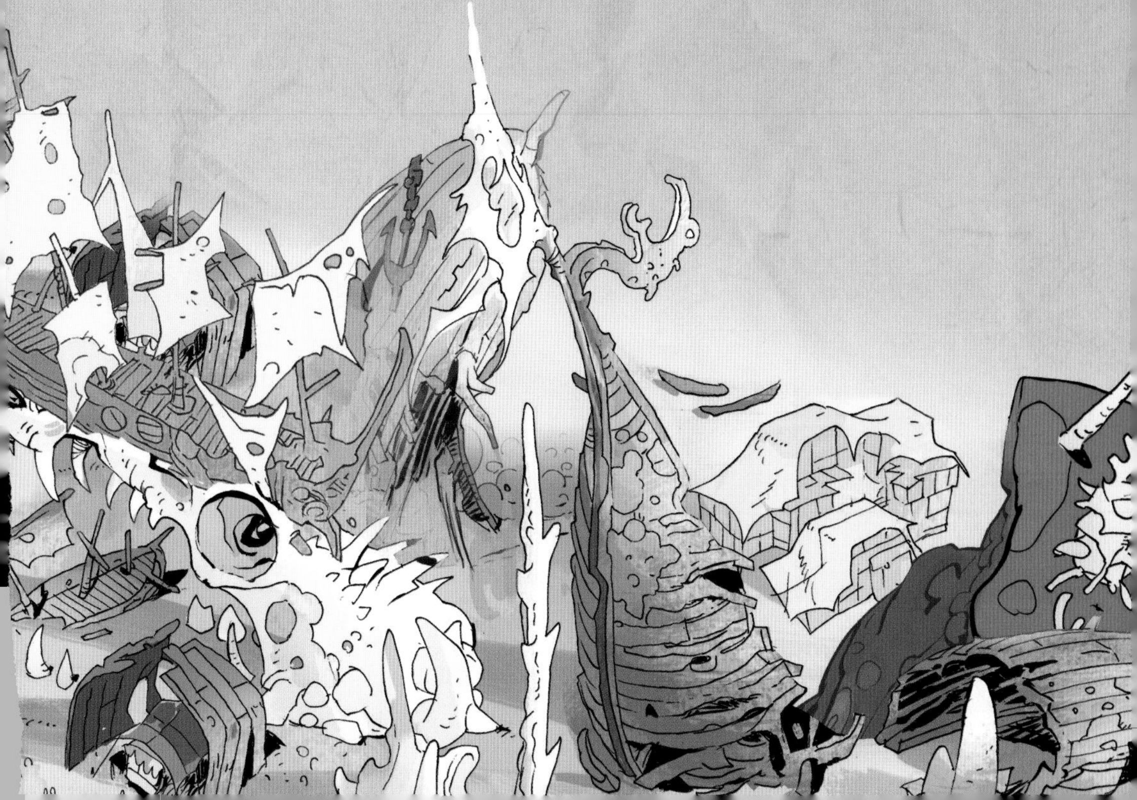

DISCOVER
EXCITING NEW WORLDS

SPURRIER
BURNETT
FARRELL
WEAVERS
—Comicosity

GODSHAPER
SIMON SPURRIER • JONAS GOONFACE

Jim Henson's
LABYRINTH
CORONATION
—IGN
VOLUME ONE
Simon Spurrier • Daniel Bayliss • Dan Jackson

Jim Henson's
THE POWER OF THE
DARK CRYSTAL
SIMON SPURRIER
KELLY AND NICHOLE MATTHEWS
"A bold leap forward for the franchise. 10/10"
—Newsarama

SIX-GUN
GORILLA
SIMON SPURRIER JEFF STOKELY
PLEASE
STAND BY

"The Spire is fantastic! My kind of genre free-for-all."
—BRIAN K. VAUGHAN (Saga)
THE
SPIRE
SIMON SPURRIER
JEFF STOKELY
ANDRÉ MAY
NOMINEE

Coda
Simon Spurrier, Matías Bergara
Volume 1
978-1-68415-321-3 | $9.99 US
Volume 2
978-1-68415-369-5 | $14.99 US

Extermination
Simon Spurrier, Jeffrey Edwards, V Ken Marion
Volume 1
978-1-60886-296-2 | $14.99 US
Volume 2
978-1-60886-315-0 | $14.99 US

Godshaper
Simon Spurrier, Jonas Goonface
978-1-60886-939-8 | $19.99 US

Jim Henson's Labyrinth: Coronation
Simon Spurrier, Ryan Ferrier, Daniel Bayliss
Volume 1
978-1-68415-266-7 | $24.99 US
Volume 2
I978-1-68415-358-9 | $24.99 US

Jim Henson's The Power of the Dark Crystal
Simon Spurrier, Phillip Kennedy Johnson, Kelly & Nichole Matthews
Volume 1
978-1-60886-992-3 | $24.99 US
Volume 2
978-1-68415-139-4 | $24.99 US
Volume 3
978-1-68415-208-7 | $24.99 US

Six-Gun Gorilla
Simon Spurrier, Jeff Stokely
978-1-60886-390-7 | $19.99 US

The Spire
Simon Spurrier, Jeff Stokely
978-1-60886-913-8 | $29.99 US

Weavers
Simon Spurrier, Dylan Burnett
978-1-60886-963-3 | $19.99 US

BOOM! STUDIOS™

AVAILABLE AT YOUR LOCAL COMICS SHOP AND BOOKSTORE
To find a comics shop in your area, visit www.comicshoplocator.com
WWW.**BOOM-STUDIOS**.COM

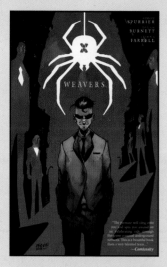

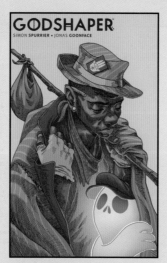

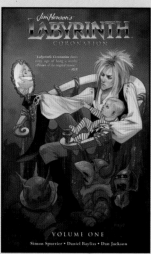

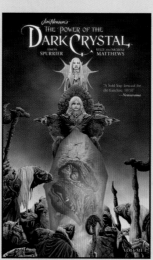

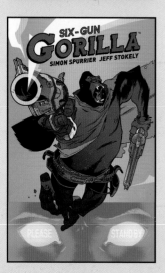

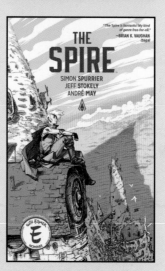

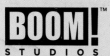